TOWNSHIP PLAYS

Township Plays

NO-GOOD FRIDAY

NONGOGO

THE COAT

SIZWE BANSI IS DEAD

THE ISLAND

Athol Fugard

Edited with an Introduction by
Dennis Walder

OXFORD
UNIVERSITY PRESS

OXFORD
UNIVERSITY PRESS

Great Clarendon Street, Oxford OX2 6DP

Oxford University Press is a department of the University of Oxford.
It furthers the University's objective of excellence in research, scholarship,
and education by publishing worldwide in

Oxford New York

Auckland Cape Town Dar es Salaam Hong Kong Karachi Kuala Lumpur
Madrid Melbourne Mexico City Nairobi New Delhi Shanghai
Taipei Toronto

With offices in

Argentina Austria Brazil Chile Czech Republic France Greece
Guatemala Hungary Italy Japan South Korea Poland Portugal
Singapore Switzerland Thailand Turkey Ukraine Vietnam

Oxford is a registered trade mark of Oxford University Press
in the UK and in certain other countries

Township Plays first published as an Oxford University Press paperback 1993
Reissued 2000

British Library Cataloguing in Publication Data

Data available

ISBN 978-0-19-282925-2

36

Printed and bound in Great Britain by
Clays Ltd, Elcograf S.p.A.

PREFACE

During that most decisive period in every writer's life, those early formative years when he discovers his voice and style and stakes out his territory for the first time, I was challenged by an encounter with two black townships. Like all white South Africans, I had obviously known since my childhood that they were there, but apart from a few scrappy images there was no real sense of what life in them was about. They were a closed and forbidden world, and conveniently remote from the bland white suburbia of my youth. The first of the two townships that challenged me out of my white complacency was the now famous Sophiatown, which the Apartheid government had targeted for total demolition because it was situated too close for comfort to white Johannesburg, and which had become, as a result, a hotbed of political activity.

The year was 1958, and my wife Sheila and I had turned our backs on secure well-paid jobs and a comfortable lifestyle in Cape Town, and driven up to Johannesburg to launch our careers as writers. A friend with strong anti-government political connections took us out one night on a drive to Sophiatown, where he was monitoring political resistance to the forced removals that were being carried out by the government. That visit was electrifying. We found ourselves in a world of vibrant, defiant life, made all the more so by the poverty in which most of its inhabitants lived. And, possibly even more important from my point of view, it was also Johannesburg's black bohemia. It was in its tiny smoke-filled tin shanties that we made some of the most decisive friendships of our career—Bloke Modisane, Can Themba, Lewis Nkosi, Nat Nakasa, Casey Motsisi, and a host of musicians like Kiepie Moketsi and Mackay Davashe. These friendships were the context for our formation of a drama group, Actors' Studio, for which I wrote and staged my apprenticeship and first full-length plays *No-Good Friday* and *Nongogo*. The second township, New Brighton, on the outskirts of Port Elizabeth, came five years later, after I had written the first of my plays to achieve real success, both critical and financial. That play was *Blood Knot*. I was back in Port Elizabeth writing a new one, *Hello and Goodbye*, when there was a knock on the door and into our lives trooped five men and women from the township. They had read about my success with *Blood Knot* and had come to ask me to help them to start a drama group. With some reluctance, because I resented anything that would interfere with my concentration on the new play, I agreed and Serpent Players was born.

The next ten years, climaxing in the creation and production of *Sizwe Banzi is Dead* and *The Island*, were of major importance, not just in my own work but in the whole South African theatre scene, in giving legitimacy for the first time to black actors and plays about township life. Those ten years also coincided with intense police activity and our group was targeted as highly suspect. Rehearsals were broken up by police raids, and periodically one of our number would disappear only to turn up later in a kangaroo court on trumped-up charges, which, in turn, would lead to imprisonment on Robben Island. Apart from our productions of established texts such as *Antigone*, *Woyzek*, *The Chalk Circle*, and *Coriolanus*, to name a few of our most successful productions, we also experimented with 'play-making'. *The Coat* is an early example of this work, and *Sizwe Banzi* and *The Island* the most well-known. After the group finally broke up, I never again returned to working in a collaborative context.

ATHOL FUGARD

October 1999

CONTENTS

INTRODUCTION

I

There are few, if any, living playwrights who can approach the commitment to theatre shown by Athol Fugard, South Africa's most well known and highly regarded dramatist. His commitment, to a practice involving writing, directing, and acting, and to a form with the potential to bear witness to the lives of others, has enabled Fugard to make a unique contribution to the cultural life of his country and, arguably, the rest of the world. This contribution emerges most powerfully today in what can be seen as the struggle to speak out on behalf of those silenced or ignored by their society; most notably in the five plays collected together here for the first time. These plays offer a compelling insight into the role of theatre in a situation of oppression. They were all produced for the first time in South Africa between 1958 and 1973, a period in which the racist division of society was being ever more ruthlessly entrenched. They are called the township plays because of their common inspiration in the everyday life of urban black people during that terrible period; and because they were produced in increasingly close collaboration with their black amateur casts—there is only one white role, and that is a small one, in the first play.

Set out in the order of their first production, the plays fall naturally into two groups, representing two distinct phases in Fugard's involvement with township life: the 'Sophiatown' plays, *No-Good Friday* (1958) and *Nongogo* (1959), first performed in the Bantu Men's Social Centre, Johannesburg, by members of the 'African Theatre Workshop' he and his wife organized with talented black amateurs befriended in the vast, multiracial ghetto; and the 'New Brighton' plays, including *The Coat* (1967), created and performed by the Serpent Players of New Brighton, Port Elizabeth, followed by *Sizwe Bansi is Dead* (1972) and its companion piece *The Island* (1973), both first performed by their co-creators and the most famous Serpent Players, John Kani and Winston Ntshona, in the Space Theatre, Cape Town. The Sophiatown phase lasted two years (1957–9), and was a limited exercise in collaborative theatre production, brought to an end as much by the enforced removal of that city-within-a-city as by the departure or exile abroad of its main participants. The New Brighton phase extended over a decade (1963–73). It involved, to begin with, a group of amateurs from the township outside the city, working on classic Western drama from *Antigone* to *The Caucasian Chalk Circle* under Fugard's informed and expert eye; succeeded by experimental playmaking drawn from their own lives (in *The Coat*) as political pressures increased under the post-Sharpeville clampdown; and, finally, the joint creation by Fugard, Kani, and Ntshona of drama of an unprecedented intensity and impact, in *Sizwe Bansi* and *The Island*.

Fugard's name is commonly attached to all five township plays, although the original title-pages of the last two described them as 'devised by' their co-creators, who also share the rights and royalties. Fugard would be the first to admit that there is an important sense in which the township plays belong less to himself than to the black performers whose lives they draw on, and who first helped create them, in rough or makeshift, often appalling conditions. His other work, from *The Blood Knot* to *'Master Harold' and the Boys* (available in a companion volume) is more obviously his own in theme and approach, even when he has cast black actors from the townships in their first production. He has always had 'an obsessional concern with the actor and his performance'; he has always regarded the completed text as 'only a half-way stage to my ultimate objective—the living performance and its particular definition of space and silence'.[1] Hence his determination to have a controlling hand in the opening run of his plays (in which he has often also acted himself), and to cast actors he has worked with during their creation. Hence, too, the difficulty of precisely weighing the proportionate contributions of writer, performer, and director;

---

[1] Athol Fugard, Introduction, *Statements: Three Plays* (OUP, London, 1974).

even more so when we consider the township plays, for which legal and racial barriers had to be secretly bypassed or overcome.

The uncertain, fractured identity of the township plays can be seen as a reflection of the uncertain and fractured identity of South Africa, a country now poised between a semi-colonial past and a newly emergent, decolonized future. In the present moment of painful, increasingly violent transition, one of the more hopeful signs is the sound of many voices speaking out. When the township plays were being produced this seemed increasingly unlikely; and perhaps the most important thing they demonstrate is the struggle to speak, in order to survive; although at a cost. Part of that cost has been resentment, as everyone engaged in their original production has acknowledged. But how could it be otherwise? The near-total hegemony of the white minority created by apartheid has meant that white liberals and other dissidents such as Fugard participate in the structures of domination which they attack; although a distinction must be made between their various forms of protest, and the willing submission to the system of most whites over the years. When whites direct, control, and enjoy even the alternative cultural practices which originate among black people, however, compromise and resentment is inevitable.

On the other hand, it would be a mistake to think of these plays as the only channel of communication or expression for black people even during the period of their production. The importance of the plays collected here is that they reveal one varying, uniquely fruitful and influential instance of creative interaction between urban black modes of expression and 'outside' or Western cultural modes; an interaction which took place despite the divisive pressures of the apartheid state. The recent changes in that state have brought a new awareness of the past as well as the present, leading amongst other things to a realization that indigenous cultural practices, including drama, go back a very long way. That theatre in South Africa has a history at all has come as a surprise to many. It is a history including activities ranging from rural rites and ceremonies, to urban song and dance, as well as Western-influenced written drama. More than half a century ago, the black playwright Herbert Dhlomo observed that Western and African drama stemmed from the same urge to re-create, through action, imitation, rhythm, and gesture, the sacred and secular stories of the community; although these different traditions had of course developed differently. According to Dhlomo, what was needed in South Africa was a bringing together of these distinct traditions.[2] Fugard's township plays represent the first really outstandingly successful example of such interaction.

Dhlomo himself wrote some twenty-four plays along broadly Western lines, none very successful or lasting, apart perhaps from *The Girl Who Killed To Save* (1935), about a nineteenth-century Xhosa prophetess, and the first published play in English by a black South African. More successful, at least in the townships of the time, were Esau Mtwetwa's Lucky Stars, who performed standard scenes on traditional subjects, enlivened by improvised dialogue, song, and dance[3]—key elements in later township drama. Dhlomo, however, helped found the Bantu Dramatic Society, based at the Bantu Men's Social Centre in Johannesburg, an influential black cultural venue, funded by liberal whites. By a revealing irony, one of the earliest plays performed there, with Dhlomo in a leading role, was Goldsmith's *She Stoops to Conquer*.

This helps remind us that mainstream theatre in South Africa has been influenced primarily by Western, predominantly British models, and has been on the whole a very conservative enterprise, often conducted by touring companies and focusing upon 'light entertainment' (farces, musicals, thrillers), with the occasional piece by Shakespeare, Shaw, or Beckett—not to mention Goldsmith—to leaven the fare. This overseas tradition continues, despite a drastic reduction of material from abroad

---

[2] Quoted Ursula Barnett, *A Vision of Order: A Study of Black South African Literature in English (1914–1980)* (Sinclair Browne, London, 1983), 228. See also Tim Couzens, *The New African: A Study of the Life and Work of H. I. E. Dhlomo* (Ravan Press, Johannesburg, 1985).

[3] See David Coplan, *In Township Tonight! South Africa's Black City Music and Theatre* (Longman, London, 1985), 125–6.

since the international playwrights' boycott instigated by Fugard (who later changed his mind) in 1963, and the British Equity boycott of 1966—both of which have stimulated the production of more indigenous, if often equally conservative work. The simultaneous setting up in the early 1960s of subsidized local Performing Arts Councils, and a Publications Control Board with draconian censorship powers, merely reinforced this trend, which continues yet, despite the recent relaxation of censorship and boycotts.

All the more astonishing, then, that as long ago as 1958 a young and inexperienced white playwright should have proclaimed that the 'most stimulating and promising field for a young playwright in South Africa' lay in the life of the black townships; where there were untrained performers capable of 'achieving an authenticity and vitality never seen before on the South African stage'[4]—views greeted with considerable scepticism at the time and later. Yet, as the extraordinary impact at home and abroad of the township plays and their black casts has shown, Fugard was right. Their impact varied: according to the abilities and experience of those involved, the nature and extent of their collaborative creation, and its shifting relationship with the changing history of the country. In the two Sophiatown plays, something of the brash but vital inner-city mix of jazz and booze, humour, poverty, and religion, which characterized the multi-tribal, pre-apartheid townships can be felt even within these early plays' somewhat limited, naturalistic scope. And as a series of successful revivals since 1974 have proved, they continue to exert a certain power. But by then the narrower and more sterile experience of the new 'model' apartheid township New Brighton, set up on the outskirts of the industrial complex for which its labour was required, and inhabited by a single tribe, provided the setting for the freer, more urgent and creative kind of theatre represented by *Sizwe Bansi* and *The Island*.

---

[4] 'Athol Plans an African Theatre', *Rand Daily Mail*, Johannesburg (17 Sept. 1958).

For Fugard, this development was in part the result of the influence of the European avant-garde, especially of the Polish director Grotowski, whose *Towards a Poor Theatre* (1969) encouraged a radically actor-centred theatre; for John Kani and Winston Ntshona, it had more to do with the surviving influence of indigenous African traditions of storytelling and response. The resulting synthesis challenged familiar theatre conventions, at the same time as it challenged the entangling ideologies of race and class in South Africa. The achievement of the New Brighton plays can easily lead to an underestimation of the earlier work, written by an apprentice playwright engaged in his first encounters with the townships. The Sophiatown plays nevertheless reflect the aspirations, violence, and vitality of urban black people, offering a window into the world of the correspondence student, the shebeen queen, the tsotsi (township hood), and the rural migrant for predominantly white, liberal audiences. They also helped legitimate everyday urban black experience as a subject, for blacks as well as whites.

It is now easier to perceive in the early plays the seeds of the later: for instance, in certain static, almost operatic moments, when the action pauses and a character 'speaks' his or her past experiences or future aspirations. Thus Tobias, the migrant worker adrift in the city, tells his wife at home about his arrival in the city of gold, his yearning for the countryside, and the job he hopes to get, in a letter dictated to Guy the saxophonist (*No-Good Friday*); or there is Queeny, the former prostitute who recalls her secret degradation as 'a woman for two and six' around the mine dumps at night, for Johnny, whose brief hopes for a better life she briefly shares (*Nongogo*). Such moments become almost intolerably moving as they become more profoundly integrated within the later plays. In *Sizwe Bansi*, actually structured as an overlapping series of monologic reminiscences, the play opens with an immense monologue in which Styles tells us about his past life at the Ford motor plant and the dream of independence which has led to his photographic studio, a 'strong-room of dreams' for his people; this is followed by the arrival of Sizwe Bansi, who reveals in turn, through a letter addressed to his wife in the rural 'homeland', how his dream of work in the city led him to take on the identity of a dead man. In *The Island*, the two political prisoners articulate a meaning for their suffering through another kind of dream, Sophocles' *Antigone*; thereby reactivating the ancient Greek tragedy so as to present a new and topical image. As Winston addresses the invisible prison audience and us at the end, he tears off his disguise, discarding the tragic role of a Greek princess accepting her doom, to become a black South African man going to his 'living death', unrepentant.

At this truly shattering theatrical moment, we are brought to understand what the township plays stand for: as John Kani says, they 'give back to the people their voices'.[5] The white liberal playwright has been taken by his creative collaboration with black performers to provide a medium for the voices of the marginalized, the obscure and humiliated, all those who now demand their right to recognition, to an admission of their place in the world.

II

Athol Fugard's personal history and career is a vital part of the history of the production of the township plays, although it is equally important to know about the background of his co-creators, especially Zakes Mokae, John Kani, and Winston Ntshona. Like a writer he resembles as well as admires, Albert Camus, Fugard belongs by birth and upbringing to the under-privileged sector of the dominant, white settler minority of his country; the source of the most virulent and persistent anti-black feelings. But, again like Camus, he has long since turned against this group's apparent interests, expressing instead a commitment to Western, liberal humanist views; views which have recently come to be sharply criticized for their Eurocentric and idealist assumptions. This explains the defensiveness of his

[5] Personal interview with John Kani, National Theatre, London, 11 Sept. 1990.

explicitly political utterances—'a classic example of the guilt-ridden impotent white liberal' he calls himself[6]—at the same time as it suggests how far beyond his own position the challenge of his township encounters has taken his work.

Fugard was born on 11 June 1932, on a farm near Middelburg, Cape Province, a small town in the sheep-farming Karroo region of South Africa. His parents ran a 'cash store' there, without success; in white South African terms, this meant poverty. His father Harold, a crippled former jazz pianist, was of nineteenth-century British immigrant stock; his mother, Elizabeth Magdalena, née Potgieter, came from one of the earlier, pioneering Dutch settlements. Fugard thinks of himself as of 'mixed descent' in white South African terms, inheriting both the Afrikaans, narrowly Calvinist but independent attitudes of his mother's background and the more liberal Christian views of the English-speaking community. In fact, his mother was the more tolerant, as well as the stronger parent. He was brought up and educated in English, although in practice he is thoroughly bilingual; and he chose to write in English—or, more accurately, in South African English, incorporating a rich mix of indigenous variations, dialects, and languages. In 1935 the Fugard family moved to Port Elizabeth, where they lived at first in a boarding-house run by Mrs Fugard.

Port Elizabeth has been the dramatist's home ever since, despite spells in such larger centres as Cape Town and Johannesburg, or abroad, and the purchase of a house in a small Karroo village and later one in America. He insists that, whatever the cost in personal terms (no longer as important as during the time of the production of these plays), he is unable to function as a writer outside his country. He has 'acquired the code' there, that 'degree of familiarity which is necessary for me . . . I must know the textures I'm going to deal with.'[7] Port Elizabeth, including New Brighton, is the setting of his best

---

[6] 'White Man on a Tightrope' (interview with Colin Smith), *Observer*, London (Jan. 1974); a remark repeated on numerous occasions since.
[7] Personal interview with Athol Fugard, Port Elizabeth, 3 Jan. 1982.

work, although of course the prisoners in *The Island* have been removed from the area. Situated on the Eastern Cape coast, Port Elizabeth (founded by the 1820 British settlers) is known mainly for its winds, motor-car factories, and snake park. It is one of the four main urban concentrations of South Africa (the others are Johannesburg, Cape Town, and Durban).

The majority of the population of close on a million were, until the recent repeal of the Group Areas Act, legally obliged to live in townships like New Brighton, set up near the factories which rely on their labour and which are run by major international companies such as Ford, Goodyear, and Volkswagen. The township inhabitants are mainly Xhosa-speaking Africans, but also include Asian minorities and a substantial number of 'Coloureds' (persons of mixed race), who have a township of their own. Whites generally have had little contact with blacks, apart from the army of domestic and other labourers who still service their needs; and less awareness of their aspirations, although that is now changing. Until the arrival of (heavily pro-government) television in the mid-1970s, 'culture' meant, on the white side, cinema and occasional overseas theatrical productions; on the black, popular township entertainments including music, dance, and song in church or community halls, such as St Stephen's in New Brighton. Almost everybody is keen on sport, and 'liberals' have been conspicuously absent, while blacks have had to make do with illegal or extra-parliamentary opposition. Many have died in township disturbances, or, like Steve Biko, in police custody.

Fugard attended the local 'technical college', where he had his first experience of amateur dramatics. He read omnivorously, and had begun writing before a scholarship took him to the University of Cape Town. Here his interest in European thought and belief was deepened, under the influence of a Cape Afrikaner philosophy professor, Martin Versveld, a Catholic existentialist. Fugard left without completing his studies, to hitch-hike up Africa before signing on as a deck-hand with a British tramp steamer—his first experience of working on equal terms with people of other races. Within a year he was back home, freelancing for the Port Elizabeth *Evening Post*, which published material by him on local subjects such as night schools for Africans. The inspiration to become directly involved in drama came when he met Sheila Meiring, at the time an actress in Cape Town. They married in 1956, and formed a theatre workshop called Circle Players, for which Sheila (later a poet and novelist in her own right) did the writing, until her husband began to contribute work, including two one-act plays, *Klaas and the Devil* (1956) and *The Cell* (1957). The latter was about a black woman who goes mad because of the death of her newborn child in prison.

It was not until 1958 that this concern for the local, and in particular the experiences of black people, began to bear fruit. A journalist friend (Benjamin Pogrund of the *Rand Daily Mail*) who shared Fugard's interest in the black experience urged him to come to Sophiatown—'approaching the sentence of death imposed by Nationalist apartheid, but still raucously alive and like nothing else in South Africa . . . your writing needs it', he said.[8] Unlike other townships, Sophiatown had grown over some fifty years as a freehold part of the 'white' city, with a racially mixed population, although, as Pogrund pointed out, it had already been re-zoned as white, and enforced removals begun. 'White' liquor was not then legally available to Africans, and so whites sold vast amounts to black bootleggers who resold it to shebeen 'queens', who in turn required protection outside the law, obtained from black mobsters like the notorious 'Boy' Faraday (Queeny in *Nongogo* relies on her former pimp, Sam, and the thuggish Blackie). Running a shebeen or a gang represented a kind of achievement; magnified by the extent to which it involved bypassing white controls.

The only job the hopeful playwright could find at first was as clerk in a 'Native Commissioner's Court', where pass-law offenders were tried, and jailed every few minutes. If he thought he knew his racist society was evil before, 'seeing the machinery

---

[8] 'Nights When *Tsotsi* was Born', *Rand Daily Mail*, Johannesburg (11 Feb. 1980).

in operation' taught Fugard 'how it works and in fact what it does to people'. Few white South Africans have seen or are fully aware of what happened in such places. 'I think my basic pessimism was born there, watching that procession of faces and being unable to relate to them.'[9] Yet, at the same time, the Fugards began an African Theatre Workshop based on their relationships with people in Sophiatown. The most remarkable performer among the extraordinarily talented people they met was Zakes Mokae, who struck Fugard at first as ideally suitable for 'the role of a thug', which he played in *No-Good Friday*. Fugard felt a growing sense of Mokae's creative talent, which led him to write the role of Blackie, Queenie's crippled and violent hanger-on in *Nongogo*, especially for him, 'and this was the start of one of the really rich working relationships of my life'.[10] It was also the first of his vital collaborative experiences.

Fugard and Mokae met in 1958 through the non-racial artists' equity association, the Union of South African Artists—or Union Artists, as it became when it acquired Dorkay House, the factory warehouse where township talent was presented before mainly white audiences in Johannesburg during the late 1950s. Mokae had never had an acting lesson (not surprising in a country without drama schools for blacks), but he had played some minor film roles. Johannesburg-born and bred, he attended St Peter's Anglican school in Rosettenville, where he came to know the superintendent, Father Trevor Huddleston. Huddleston, whose *Naught For Your Comfort* (1956) revealed conditions in Sophiatown to the world, and on whom Father Higgins in *No-Good Friday* is modelled, had formed a jazz band to which Mokae, an accomplished tenor saxophonist, belonged as a founder member. The success of a farewell concert for the much-loved missionary, held in the Bantu Men's Social Centre in 1954, had stimulated the growing interest among white entrepreneurs in township culture, and shortly after the appear-

---

[9] 'Keeping an Appointment with the Future' (interview with Mary Benson), *Theatre Quarterly*, viii (Winter 1977–8), 78.

[10] Ibid. 78.

ance of Fugard's first township plays, Union Artists (under the leadership of the theatrical promoter Ian Bernhardt) went on to present the enormously successful township opera *King Kong* (1959), scored by Todd Matshikiza and with Miriam Makeba in a leading role. *Kong*'s success at home and abroad led to a series of glossily packaged South African musicals and plays, produced by whites but with black actors, singers, dancers, and musicians, and with the blessing of the authorities, from *uMabatha* (a Zulu *Macbeth*) to *Ipi Tombi* (incorrect Zulu for 'Where Are the Girls?'). Unlike township plays such as *The Island*, whose appearance in London coincided with *Ipi Tombi* while drawing a fraction of its audience, these works have little to say about township life. Fugard's work was part of a larger movement of white entrepreneurs exploiting black performers, but the result was far from the packaged presentation of acceptable images of black South African life, which still appear in the West End or on Broadway, although coming to be displaced by musicals of more radical intent, if not effect, such as Mbongeni Ngema's *Sarafina!* (1987).

However, the receipts of *King Kong* at least enabled Union Artists to begin an African Music and Drama Association, which sponsored the Rehearsal Room, a private, experimental theatre space in Dorkay House, where Fugard and Mokae first performed *The Blood Knot* on 3 September 1961. The play was conceived by Fugard as a two-hander for Mokae and himself. Before its appearance, the small local success of the Sophiatown plays had enabled him—with the help of a visiting Belgian director who collaborated on *Nongogo*, Tone Brulin—to obtain his first work in professional theatre, as stage manager with the all-white National Theatre Organization. At the NTO's experimental *Kamertoneel* theatre in Pretoria, Fugard had a 'crash course' in modern Western drama, which led him to Europe for further experience; although by the end of 1960, with no work in prospect, the Fugards had returned to Port Elizabeth. The playwright had acted briefly with a 'New Africa Group' who appeared at a Brussels Avant-Garde Theatre Festival in a race drama set in the Karroo; he was revising a novel about township life (later published as *Tsotsi*, 1980); and he had begun his notes on *The Blood Knot*, which he was to complete at home.

A key adviser on the production of *The Blood Knot* was Barney Simon, a year younger than Fugard, and from a similarly near-poor-white background in Johannesburg. Simon, in advertising after working briefly with Joan Littlewood in London, shared Fugard's passion for small-scale, workshop productions as a way of reflecting the texture of everyday South African life. He has proved the only significant local influence, apart from performers, acknowledged by Fugard. Simon went on to create his own space for later township talent (like Mbongeni Ngema and Gcina Mhlophe) at the multiracial Market Theatre, which he opened with Mannie Manim in Johannesburg in 1976, after a lengthy struggle to obtain funding. The Market has provided the venue for Fugard's more recent work, including *My Children! My Africa!* (1989) and *Playland* (1992)—both of which featured John Kani, now an Associate Director—as well as revivals of the township plays.

The Blood Knot above all explored the South African issue of race, using it to define relations of power and dependence; although with a subtlety, humour, and resonance which ensured both immediate and lasting success. Two months after its Rehearsal Room opening, and cut from its original four to two-and-a-half hours, it reopened under professional management, and a tour was set up. It was the first play for a racially mixed cast, but Fugard and Mokae had to live and travel separately— a combination of challenge and compromise typical of the circumstances of Fugardian drama, the essentials of which *The Blood Knot* defined with exceptional clarity: involving a small cast of marginalized characters in a close (often blood) relationship embodying the tensions, fears, and hopes of their society; first performed by actors more or less involved in their creation; in a makeshift, 'fringe' or at least alternative, non-establishment venue. Plot was minimal, tending to revelation rather than development; dialogue and setting spare and suggestive. Questions of identity, and the nature of consciousness, merged with a concern for the oppressed or discarded.

During the following years Fugard wrote three more plays along the same lines: *Hello and Goodbye* (1965), about white siblings in a poor area of Port Elizabeth; *People are Living There* (1968), about poor-white lodgers in a Johannesburg boarding-house; and *Boesman and Lena* (1969), which he directed with himself and Yvonne Bryceland as the wretched 'coloured' couple whose long walk on the outskirts of Port Elizabeth, in search of a place to live, becomes a quest for identity. In Bryceland, Fugard found another remarkably creative performer, whose work was perhaps most poignantly seen in *Statements after an Arrest under the Immorality Act* (1972), a play which incor-porated much of her own material, and which has until now uncomfortably accompanied *Sizwe Bansi* and *The Island* in print as Fugard's so-called *Statements* plays (OUP, 1974). It is a much more personal, inward exploration of the destructive effect of South Africa's race laws.

Fugard's passport was taken away in 1967, 'for reasons of state safety and security', the day after *The Blood Knot* appeared on British television; in 1971, after a public petition helped secure its return, he accepted an invitation to direct *Boesman and Lena* at the Royal Court's Theatre Upstairs, with Bryceland as Lena and Zakes Mokae as Boesman. The production was a triumph, and the Court subsequently offered vital encourage-ment for the first British season of *Sizwe Bansi* and *The Island*, which made both those plays and their performers, Kani and Ntshona, famous abroad. Kani and Ntshona went on to an American tour, succeeded by film and other theatre work, while the rest of the New Brighton township group, having survived police harassment and the imprisonment of some of their members, languished. The effect of all this had by now driven Fugard towards the almost entirely private emphasis of the film *The Guest at Steenkampskraal* (about the Afrikaans poet and naturalist, Eugène Marais), and his play *Dimetos* (both 1975). This inward turn, in part a result of the pressure of events in the country after the Soweto rising of 1976, dominated the almost visionary *Road to Mecca* (1984) and the 'personal parable', *A Place with the Pigs* (1987). Yet, by the time of *My*

Children! My Africa! and *Playland*, Fugard's interest in exploring the white consciousness has been replaced to a degree by a newly direct engagement with the present; although without taking him away from the privacy of his writing-desk.

III

It was this privacy which was interrupted when, after Fugard's return home from the London production of *The Blood Knot* in 1963, and while he was completing *People are Living There*, there appeared on his doorstep Norman Ntshinga from New Brighton. Ntshinga came on behalf of a group of friends in the township, where the last (140th) visiting production of *The Blood Knot* was still remembered and, especially, the role of Mokae in the Fugards' Sophiatown workshop. Ntshinga brought a request, 'the old, old request', Fugard confided to his notebook at the time; 'actually it is hunger. A desperate hunger for meaningful activity—to do something that would make the hell of their daily existence meaningful.' Ntshinga's visit made him realize with a shock that with the success of *The Blood Knot* and travel abroad he had lost touch with the reality of his country; he felt 'bitterly guilty' and thought his work tainted with 'self-indulgence'.[11] But he did not leave it at that, and within two months the New Brighton group—a clerk, two teachers, a bus driver, and women domestics—held their first reading under Fugard's direction, of what was to become a popular township version of Machiavelli's *Mandragola*, *The Cure*. Half-way through, the Special Branch broke in, took everyone's names, read the play and Fugard's notes, and then left. This was to become a familiar experience for the Serpent Players.

This name was the result of the group being offered a place to perform through the playwright's contacts at Rhodes University in Grahamstown, which had taken over the old Port Elizabeth

---

[11] *Athol Fugard: Notebooks 1960–1977*, ed. Mary Benson (Faber, London, 1983), 81: entry for May 1963.

museum and snake pit. Intrigued by the idea of performing in the pit, with the audience peering down into its oval, open space, they called themselves the Serpent Players. Thus began a unique and influential experiment in theatre, which ran along-side Fugard's other work for nearly a decade. Improvisation was the key to the Serpent Players' practice; their aim at first simply to enlighten and entertain. In Mike Ngxokolo's words, to 'put across certain truths to my people'.[12] Within two years, they had gone on to produce cheaply mounted township versions of *Woyzeck*, *The Caucasian Chalk Circle*, *The Cure*, and *Antigone*, in venues such as St Stephen's Hall, without adequate lighting, seating, props, or backstage facilities. Discussion-readings and rehearsals were held where possible after work: in a 'Coloured' kindergarten, or Fugard's home garage, to avoid restrictions upon interracial activity. Such conditions harked back to the Sophiatown days. But this was not Johannesburg; and it was after the Sharpeville massacre (1960), an event succeeded by country-wide bannings, mass arrests, and detentions. The Players, their relatives and friends were watched by informers and police from the start. In December 1964, days before the opening of their Brecht play, Azdak (Welcome Duru) was arrested. Fugard took over the part, and the performance proceeded. But within months three more members were arrested, including Norman Ntshinga, who was about to play Haemon in *Antigone*.

The New Brighton group did not collapse. Instead, a new phase of playmaking, without texts or identifiable authors, began. Brecht's *Messingkauf Dialogues* provided particular inspiration. But it was the events of the time, as they impinged upon the Players, which had most effect. When Fugard attended Ntshinga's trial (Ntshinga was accused of belonging to the banned ANC), he took the actor's wife, the blues-singer Mabel Magada, along. She was recognized by an elderly man from New Brighton who had just been sentenced. The man took off

[12] 'Mike Ngxokolo', undated manuscript page; with others by Serpent Players (some dated Mar.–May 1965), 1338/25–30 in the Fugard Collection, National English Literary Museum, Grahamstown, South Africa.

his coat, his only possession, and gave it to her, saying, 'Go to my home. Give this to my wife. Tell her to use it.' This became the Players' first attempt to create a play directly out of their own experiences, a year-long process made visible in *The Coat*, 'An Acting Exercise from the Serpent Players of New Brighton', as it was presented to its first audience, a white Port Elizabeth 'theatre appreciation group' who had asked to see a sample of their work. The whites were expecting a comedy, Wole Soyinka's *Brother Jero*, but, since the Native Commissioner would only permit performance in a 'white area' on humiliating conditions (such as forbidding the black performers to use the toilets, and obliging them to return to the township after the show), the Players (after some bitter debate) decided to do a reading of *The Coat* instead, using pseudonyms from earlier roles to avoid trouble with the police, and a Brechtian actor-presenter who encouraged the white audience to think about, not merely sympathize with, what they were witnessing.

Fugard's aim was to 'shatter white complacency and its conspiracy of silence', although he realized the risk for them all; but the group went ahead as an act of 'solidarity', a testimony to their work together over the years.[13] For Fugard the evolution of the 'exercise' began with the image of the coat:

It was just there, magnetic, dominating the imagination, provoking other images. It had what I think of as a dynamo of its own, generating all the time. And opposed to this puzzling, rich complexity, was the lucidity with which we worked on it. We said to ourselves (the seven of us left who were sitting around), we said, 'The message that went back with the coat was, "Use it!" What does that mean? How can she use it?' . . . the results may look the same as any other one act play, on paper, but the way in which it came about was a revelation. . . .

We wanted first to see the moment when the coat was handed over, and we staged just that one scene. We just wanted to see the coat leave Mabel's hands and end up in the other woman's hands. And we wanted to see something from Mabel, when she stayed on with the other woman. [So we asked] 'what do you do with the coat now you've got it?' And [Nomhle Nkonyeni, the actress playing] the old woman

13 *Fugard: Notebooks*, 142–3: Nov. 1966.

says, 'Well, I'm in my house. I've now heard about my husband. I'm not going to see him for five, six years. I've got his coat in my hand. I'll hang it up, first of all, and go on working. And I'll think about the coat.' She was a good actress and in the course of all this a thing happened there. It took a few exercises to, to fatten it, you know what I mean? The first time she tried it there was a very strong act but a very crudely defined line.

I jotted down several of her attempts, and at the end we compared notes and I said, 'Now, this is how it came out.' And the actors said, 'Yes, that's right. And remember that other thing she said which was rather good? She spoke about the street.' 'That's right', I said, and I made a little note and handed this to her and said, 'Take it away. Come back same time, same place, next week. Think about it. See if you can fatten it, fill it out a bit.'

She did, and next week we provoked her and she re-enacted the scene for us. Then we provoked her again by questions and a little bit of discussion ... And that's how it grew.

At one stage we were trying to corner her. We said to Humphrey [Njikelane], 'Right. Come on, now. We need the man at the rent office, you know, where she's going to appeal. Will you take that on?' So the two of them discussed it for a minute to get the rough geography [of the encounter], and we said 'O.K. Put that on. Just try it.' And again, I acted as scribe, made my little notes, and at the end said, 'Right, this is how it came out ...'[14]

Fugard's function as 'scribe' and *provocateur* is clear. He also kept an eye on the overall structure. The collaborative procedure was vindicated by the end result, which left the Players' audience of 150 frozen 'in horror and fascination'.

From then on, the Players alternated 'classic' European productions with other improvisations on township issues, such as *Friday's Bread on Monday*, *The Last Bus*, and *Sell-Out*, which appeared in unofficial venues, although without the impact of *The Coat*. Meanwhile, two new members began to show promise: John Kani, who replaced the arrested Ntshinga in *Antigone* in 1965 and who was 'Haemon' for *The Coat* two years later; and

[14] 'Interview with Athol Fugard about "The Coat"' (with Don MacLennan, Feb. 1969), *Athol Fugard The Coat/Don MacLennan The Third Degree* (Balkema, Cape Town, 1971), 3–4.

Winston Ntshona, an old friend of Kani's from Newell High School in New Brighton, whom he introduced to the group in 1967. Both men had already been bitten by the 'theatre bug' at Newell, where they took part in a school production of Witness Thamsanga's popular Xhosa play *Buzani ku Bawo* ('Ask Father'), directed by their history master, Sipho Mndela. But no further theatrical opportunity had emerged before Kani came across the Serpent Players through a friend and member of the group, Fats Bokhilane.

John Bonisile Kani was born on 30 August 1943 in a two-roomed house in Port Elizabeth. The son of a policeman, he was brought up in 'ordinary poverty' with five brothers and four sisters. Winston Zola Ntshona was born on 6 October 1941 in King William's Town in the Ciskei region of the Eastern Cape. He lived with an uncle in a Johannesburg township for four years, while his mother, two brothers, and a younger sister lived in a single room near Port Elizabeth, before they all moved into one of the larger, New Brighton township houses. After he left school in New Brighton, Ntshona became a factory janitor for eight years. He was a laboratory assistant when Kani brought him to the Players. Kani, too, began as a janitor (at the Ford car plant), thereafter going on the engine assembly line for years (before being fired in 1971)—an experience embodied in the opening of *Sizwe Bansi*. He then became a welfare assistant with the Bantu Administration in New Brighton. Like the other Serpent Players, both Kani and Ntshona are Xhosa and come from a part of the country with a long history of struggle and resistance to white rule.

The effect of the arrival of Kani and Ntshona upon the depleted Players and their director Fugard was soon apparent; but it was not until 1972 that the two men performed together in a major production, Camus' *The Just*, retitled *The Terrorists*, at the Space Theatre in Cape Town, which Fugard had inspired Yvonne Bryceland's husband Brian Astbury to set up. The production led to a remarkable decision. In a country which did not officially recognize black actors or their theatre, Kani and Ntshona decided to give up their jobs and become full-time performers. This meant they had to be classified in their passbooks as Fugard's domestic servants. Within months of the decision, their joint commitment issued in the workshop productions *Sizwe Bansi* and *The Island*. According to John Kani, Fugard and the two actors had been looking for a 'two-hander' to do, preferably drawn from everyday urban black experience; and, after toying with Soyinka's radio play *The Detainee*, finally found their 'mandate' in a photograph of a smiling black man who, they agreed, would only smile like that if his passbook was in order. Thus began the experiments which led to *Sizwe Bansi is Dead*, in which the central character, played by Ntshona, takes on the identity of a dead man so as to live and work in Port Elizabeth without harassment—although not for ever. 'A black man stay out of trouble? Impossible', as he tells his friend 'Buntu' (Kani). 'Our skin is trouble.'

Acting as a means of survival for black people was central to the brilliant combination of monologue, mime, improvisation, and remembered gesture which ensured immediate local recognition for the play and its co-creators, and an invitation from the Royal Court before a written script had been put together. And while the three waited for permission to leave for London, they decided to apply the same workshop techniques to material accumulated (in Fugard's case, over many years) from friends and former colleagues about life on Robben Island—including a two-man version of *Antigone* arranged by Ntshinga and another imprisoned Player, Sipho 'Sharkey' Mguqulwa, on the basis of their memory of the play they were to have done when arrested. (Kani's elder brother, too, had spent five years in the maximum security prison for belonging to the ANC.) To begin with, there had once again been no more than an image, but one with a peculiar resonance which the three soon realized would give them their subject. Fugard simply took a large blanket and spread it outside his house on the ground, asking Kani and Ntshona as an exercise to explore its space, to stand in the centre, to walk around the edge. Then he folded the blanket again and again, until there was just room for the actors to stand. Then he asked them, 'What do you think this means?' They realized it was a cell, and knew instantly where the exercise was leading them: 'To take the island and say something about it. We joined our hands, closed the garage door and after two weeks, we were on stage in Cape Town.'[15] The play was called *Die Hodoshe Span*, 'The Hodoshe work-team', after an infamous Robben Island warder nicknamed 'Hodoshe' (Xhosa for 'carrion-fly')—a usefully obscure title for an unscripted play, since it was illegal to make public information about prison conditions.

The first appearance of *Sizwe Banzi* (original spelling, Xhosa for 'big nation', mistakenly altered later) before a multiracial audience was prevented by the police, but Astbury's Space reopened the next night as a massively enlarged 'club', effectively defying the authorities and creating a stir which reached the ears of Oscar Lewenstein at the Royal Court. *Die Hodoshe Span*, with two characters called Bonisile and Zola speaking a lot of Afrikaans and Xhosa, played to limited audiences for a brief private run, before it emerged as *The Island* in Britain, with John and Winston using their own names and predominantly English dialogue, to follow *Sizwe Bansi* at the Royal Court Upstairs as a 'South African Season', with playbills outlining details of the apartheid laws the season challenged. The season was packed out, critics full of praise, and a tour set up. But there were also complaints that the plays 'contained propaganda aimed at discrediting the South African Embassy in London, the Government, and White South Africans in general'.[16] And when, four years later, Kani and Ntshona performed *Sizwe Bansi* in the Transkei 'homeland' just before 'independence', they were imprisoned briefly before an international outcry secured their release. Eleven years later, playing a revival of *The Island* in Cape Town, Kani and Ntshona declared that every performance was an 'endorsement of the local and international call for the immediate release' of Nelson Mandela 'and all political prisoners and detainees'.[17]

[15] Personal interview with John Kani, National Theatre, London, 1990.
[16] 'Plays not anti-SA—Fugard', *Eastern Province Herald*, Port Elizabeth (5 Feb. 1974).
[17] 'An Island of Dreams', *Weekend Argus*, Cape Town (2 Nov. 1985).

Needless to say, neither the South African Embassy, the Government, nor 'White South Africans in general' are mentioned in these plays; neither is Mandela; although *Sizwe Bansi* did (and still does) contain derogatory remarks about the Bantustans. The point is, the plays do 'contain propaganda', in the sense that they offer explicit statements about the injustice of apartheid laws; as well as the opportunity, through their improvisational structure, for comment by performers on current issues. But their lasting popularity as well as their influence—most drama from South Africa today bears their mark—demonstrates how they also transcend the limitations of immediacy, or agitprop. This element of relative autonomy is the result of Fugard's recognition after *The Coat* that, despite the 'more immediate and direct relationship with our audience' made possible by the Serpent Players' improvisations, such work was ultimately 'two-dimensional'. 'Facts, and somehow we never managed to get beyond facts even though they were important facts, are flat and lacking in the density and ambiguity of truly dramatic images.' Alternative methods of 'releasing the creative potential of the actor' came with his Grotowskian excursion into a new, extreme form of theatrical language in 1970–1 when, after the 'orthodox experience I had been retailing for so many years since *The Blood Knot* . . . the *writing* of a play . . . *setting* that play in terms of local specifics . . . actors *assuming* false identities', he turned his back on these 'securities' by superimposing the image of a young white radical hanged in 1964 for a bomb outrage upon that of the ancient Greek tragedy of Orestes. The ten-week 'rehearsal' with three white actors (including Yvonne Bryceland) produced 'an experience which lasted for sixty minutes, had about 300 words, a lot of action—strange, almost somnambulistic action—and silence'.[18]

The main significance of the apparently unscriptable *Orestes* now lies in what it enabled Fugard to do with Kani and Ntshona—their lives, histories, experiences, the very shape of their bodies—yet without ever jettisoning his own role

[18] Introduction, *Statements*, 1974.

as a writer, his own obsessional complex of images, or his responsibility for the final dramatic structure of the result; which, because it then became scriptable, became repeatable, even by performers unfamiliar with the realities of the black township experience the plays were mediating.

IV

The texts of *Sizwe Bansi is Dead* and *The Island* reprinted here therefore represent in a more than usual sense 'versions' of a performance, Fugard's chosen record of a definitive version of the plays produced by being able to 'write *directly* into' the stage's 'space and silence via the actor'. When the writer-director and his two actors thought the response to their 'initial mandate' (the image or complex of images which set them off) was 'of value and significance in terms of our intentions, we then applied ourselves to disciplining and structuring it so that the gesture, word, or event was capable of controlled repetition'.[19] That repetition is controlled by a text which, none the less, is 'open', signalling at certain moments the potential for alternative rendition, in action as well as word. The simplest example is provided by the newspaper improvisation which opens *Sizwe Bansi*; more complex demands are made by the range of language varieties present in the plays.

The characters in many of Fugard's plays would normally speak Afrikaans, which he 'translates' into his own Eastern Cape English idiom. But the characters in these township plays speak a mixture of English, Afrikaans, and African (mainly but not exclusively Xhosa) languages, as appropriate and reflecting the polyglot nature of their world—a range which covers several African varieties of English, developed at mission schools (the migrant worker), or in emulation of black American culture (the jazz musician, the bootlegger, the city slicker), or a patois derived from all of these, the so-called *tsotsitaal* ('gangsterspeak'), in which the dominant constituents vary according to origins

[19] Ibid.

and region, even within a specific township. All the township plays have been produced using black actors who add or substitute their own languages or varieties of South African English for what appears in the printed texts. *No-Good Friday* and *Nongogo* are almost entirely 'translations' into standard South African English of African English and *tsotsitaal*—the latter indicated, for instance, by the gangster Harry's demand for '*Vyf* bob, five shillings. *Betaal, jong!*' Tobias's letter to his wife is an attempt to render Sotho into English, using a cadenced, figurative discourse: 'But for this letter I need words and a word is only a wind . . .'. In the three New Brighton plays, however, speech comes nearer to the urban African variety of English in South Africa, including African and Afrikaans expressions, while remaining a 'translation' of what such characters would actually say in the given situation. This is indicated most obviously by Aniko's appeal in *The Coat* to the Headman to speak to the white Superintendent on her behalf, because 'I can't speak his language': we are to understand that she is addressing him in Xhosa at that point. For this edition, I have added a glossary of South African words and phrases for those unfamiliar with them—which includes non-township dwelling South Africans, too. The Notes are intended as an aid to the historical placing of the plays, which go back to a period many would now prefer to forget or ignore; a dangerous symptom at any time, but especially in the present, when easy assumptions of the arrival of a 'post-apartheid' dispensation only lengthens the process of real change.

It is obviously important to check (as I have) the detail of dialogue for errors and inconsistencies of expression, spelling, and punctuation against the available earlier extant manuscript or typescript versions—now lodged with the National English Literary Museum in Grahamstown;[20] but it becomes equally if not more important to check the detail of the increasingly

[20] Whose kind assistance in obtaining copies of all the relevant materials I would like here to acknowledge.

lengthy stage directions, which 'score' the physical, gestural subtexts vital for this kind of theatre. It remains for producers to decide when and how to vary their interpretation of moments such as Robert/Sizwe's sublimely comic 'snap', when he holds his fancy Xhosa pipe in one hand, his city man's cigarette in the other: some have had Styles jam the cigarette into his client's hand without noticing he already has his pipe out (as indicated by this text); others have had the beaming innocent slowly take his pipe out as Styles returns to his camera after making the rural illiterate take a cigarette in his hand.

Numerous minor errors have crept into all the available printed versions of these texts, including, for example, mistaken references to time (important in all Fugard's plays) in Scene Four of *No-Good Friday*, and some muddle about who addresses whom in *The Coat*. The varying use of capital initial letters in these as in other Fugard texts may seem a small matter; but when the word involved is 'Whites', or 'Headman', it is a delicate task to ensure that the degree of emphasis is intended, or whether an anachronistic usage or simple carelessness has produced the choice of the upper-case—which has obvious political overtones in such examples. I have attended to the immediate context of the play as the first indication of a solution to such puzzles, where there are no, or conflicting, external (typescript or manuscript) alternatives. Fugard himself corrects or revises his texts for performances he directs, but does not consistently check every detail of the published versions—not only because of his primary concern for image, gesture, and the rhythm of performance (although this should not be taken to mean he does not care about words), but also because he is no longer as interested as later readers and producers might be in earlier, collaborative work. Earlier editors have allowed errors to stand or creep in, which remain in the available printed versions. Understandably, it is his current work which always absorbs this playwright's attention.

The editorial task involved in ensuring the survival in print of as accurate and consistent a text as possible is fully deserved by plays such as these, in which playwright and performers, isolated by race and position within their fractured, semi-colonial society, have been led by their joint commitment to the potential of theatre, to become actors in the transformation of their country.

DENNIS WALDER

London 1992

NO-GOOD FRIDAY

CHARACTERS

REBECCA, *a young woman living with Willie*
GUY, *a young jazz musician and friend of Willie's*
WATSON, *a township politician*
WILLIE, *a man in his thirties*
FATHER HIGGINS, *a white priest*
TOBIAS, *a 'blanket-boy' or rural migrant on his first visit to the city*
PINKIE ⎫
⎬ *backyard characters*
PETER ⎭
MOSES, *an old blind man*
SHARK, *a township gangster*
HARRY, *one of his thugs*
A SECOND THUG

All the characters apart from Father Higgins are Africans. The play is set in Sophiatown, a township where Africans employed in Johannesburg have their homes.

Scene 1—a backyard on a Friday late afternoon; Scene 2—the same, about two hours later; Scene 3—Willie's room the following Sunday night; Scene 4—the same, Friday night five days later; Scene 5—the backyard, a few minutes later.

NO-GOOD FRIDAY was first performed in the Bantu Men's Social Centre, Johannesburg, on 30 August 1958, by 'Theatre Workshop' with the following cast:

REBECCA	Gladys Sibisi
GUY	Cornelius Mabaso
WATSON	Preddie Ramphele
WILLIE	Stephen Moloi
FATHER HIGGINS	'Hal Lannigan' (Athol Fugard)
TOBIAS	Ken Gampu
PINKIE	Daniel Poho
MOSES	Mike Mokone
SHARK	Bloke Modisane
HARRY	Zakes Mokae
SECOND THUG	Peterson Kanduloa

The production was directed by Athol Fugard, with his wife Sheila Meiring (stage manager) and Aaron Witkin (set). For a single performance before an all-white audience on 17 September 1958 in the segregated Brooke Theatre, the cast had to be all-black, and Lewis Nkosi played the role of Father Higgins. Cornelius Mabaso directed a 'Township Tour' in Mofolo Hall, Soweto, on 23 April 1970 with Stephen Moloi and Ken Gampu.

NO-GOOD FRIDAY had its first performance outside South Africa at the Crucible Studio, Sheffield, England, on 6 November 1974, with Temba Theatre Company, including Alton Kumalo as Willie, Jimi Rand as Guy, Merdue Jordine as Rebecca, and Lloyd Anderson as Shark. Director: Peter James.

SCENE ONE

A backyard in Sophiatown,* late Friday afternoon. Clustered about it are a few rusty corrugated-iron shacks. Rebecca, *a young woman in her early twenties, is taking down washing from a line strung between a fence and one of the houses. A few other women drift in and out of doors preparing for the return of their men.* Watson *is seated on the stage.* Guy, *a young musician carrying a saxophone case, enters.*

GUY. Hi, Reb.

REBECCA. You're back early.

GUY. Doesn't feel like that. Feels like I've walked clean through to the soles of my feet.

REBECCA. No luck?

GUY. Luck! You've sure got to have that to get a break in Goli. And I don't get the breaks. *Ja,* what I need is luck, lots of it, like old Sam. Remember him?

REBECCA. He stayed with Lizzie.

GUY. That's him. Old bearded chap. We shared the same room for a time. Old Sam bought his luck ... small bottles of trash from one of those herbalist quacks in Newclare.* Every Friday night he'd trek out there with his pay packet and bring back the latest lucky charm. I argued like hell with him about that stuff. They picked him up just before they started selling the stuff to keep the police away. Poor old Sam. Wish I could believe in it like him.

REBECCA. At the price they charge you've just got to believe.

GUY. Anyway, I couldn't buy it even if I did. I haven't even got enough for a secondhand pair of shoes, and one more session like today and I'll need them.

REBECCA. Patience, Guy, patience. You got the talent.

GUY. Patience! I knocked on the door of every recording shop in town. If I'd known how many chaps were playing the sax I would have stuck to a penny whistle. When my break comes, I won't have enough wind left to blow a false note.

REBECCA. Did you try the place Willie mentioned?

GUY. You mean the hotel? That's the nearest I got to a job. They didn't need any musicians ... 'But we've got an opening for a kitchen boy' ... 'Opening', mind you! I should have told him, his opening was my back door.

Another bloke gives me a pat on the back after I've blown three bars and says, ever so nicely: 'You boys is just born musicians ... born musicians I tell you. You got it in your soul.' So I says: 'But a job, Mister?' And he says: 'Nothing doing. Too many of you boys being born.' You know something, Reb? I should have settled down to book learning. That way you always eat. Like Willie. Now there's a smart Johnny.

REBECCA. Willie's all right.

GUY. All right! He's more than just right, he can't go wrong.

REBECCA. He's just like any other fellow.

GUY. I didn't mean it that way. I know Willie can go wrong, if he does some stupid thing. What I mean is, it's up to himself. But like me now ... I know I play well, everyone says so, even some of the top boys. But how does that help me? I still get buggered around. And the way I see it Willie won't make no mistakes. What's this latest thing he's up to?

REBECCA. You mean the course?

GUY. Yes, that's it.

REBECCA. First year B.A. . . . Correspondent.

GUY. There, you see. Now who but Willie would think of that. [*Pause.*] Now ... actually ... where does that get him?

REBECCA. If he passes, to his second year.

GUY. Well, what do you know! [*Pause.*] And then?

REBECCA. The third year.

GUY. Doesn't it end sometime?

REBECCA. If he passes that, he gets his degree. Bachelor of Arts.

GUY. He's a smart one, that Willie. Now tell me, Reb, what does Willie do with his bachelor when he gets him?

REBECCA. [*Laughs.*] A better job ... more pay.

GUY. Just like I thought. If there's a catch in it, Willie will find it. You're proud of him, aren't you?

REBECCA. He gave me a better word the other day. I said how we was all proud of him. He corrected me. The word was 'admire'.

GUY. Admire! Proud! What's the difference?

REBECCA. Well, there is a difference. I looked it up in that book of his with all the words. You're proud of something you had a hand in, but you admire someone that went it all alone, Guy. Not even his poor old canary in her rusty cage helped him. Sometimes I wonder if it was best that way.

GUY. You mean you don't think he's doing all right?

REBECCA. No, course not. But it's made him . . . independent. A big word, isn't it? But he says it's his ideal and he's getting there. Willie could snap his fingers at anyone . . . walk out any time. He just doesn't need anyone. Not you . . . not even me.

GUY. When you put it that way it does add up. But then remember, Reb, you can't always add up on paper what a man needs, like your instalments on the stove each month. I'm no book bug, but I know that.

REBECCA. Too bad that advice isn't in any of the books he reads.

GUY. He's no fool, Reb. He won't make that mistake.

REBECCA. Let's hope you're right.

GUY. Course I am. Why the two of you's been together for . . .

REBECCA. Four years.

GUY. Four years. That's a long time.

[Pause.]

REBECCA. You thinking something, Guy?

GUY. Such as?

REBECCA. Like four years, and he hasn't married her yet.

GUY. He's just waiting for his course to finish.

REBECCA. Maybe he is. Anyway, we don't talk much about marrying no more.

GUY. You got nothing to worry about. You and Willie are fine. Just fine.

[*Rebecca exits into the house. Watson is addressed by Guy.*]

GUY. *Ja*, Watson, how's the politics?

WATSON. We're fighting, we're fighting.

GUY. You been fighting for our rights today, Watson?

WATSON. Sort of. Been thinking about my speech for tonight.

GUY. Another meeting?

WATSON. Important one. We've got delegates coming from all the other branches.

GUY. Hey, sounds good. What you going to say?

WATSON. Not sure yet. Round about lunchtime, I had an idea. A stirring call for action! 'The time for sitting still and submitting to every latest injustice is past. We gotta do something about it.' But then I remembered that this was a meeting of the Organizing Committees and they might not like that. Just now, I had another idea. 'We must weld ourselves into a sharp spearhead for the liberatory movement.' That'll have to do.

GUY. You been sitting here the whole day thinking that?

WATSON. The meeting's going to last all night, isn't it?

GUY. Watson, I want to ask you something.

WATSON. Sure, go ahead.

GUY. How do you earn a living?

WATSON. Living? What you mean living?

GUY. You don't get up every morning at six like Willie and old Moses. You don't walk the streets looking for a job like me.

WATSON. I make sacrifices for the cause.

GUY. That must be tough. Telling *us* guys not to work for three pounds a week.

WATSON. You too must make sacrifices for the cause, otherwise the heavy boot of oppression will for ever be on our backs! Hey, that's good. [*He makes a note.*]

GUY. You know something else, Watson, I've never seen you a single day in the streets when there's a riot.

WATSON. We can't all be leaders. Some must lead, some must follow.

[*Mrs Watson calls from offstage in a shrewish voice.*] Coming dear. [*He exits.*]

   [*Rebecca appears at the door shaking a tablecloth.*]

GUY. Say! Do you want to hear something?

REBECCA. Any time.

GUY. I got so fed up this morning I took out the old blowpipe and blew . . . and what do you know! A wonderful sound comes out. Kind of sad . . . And this being Friday and every other sucker coming home with a pay packet except me, I've decided to call it 'Friday Night Blues'.

   [*Guy plays 'Friday Night Blues'.* Willie *enters the backyard; he stops and listens to the music.*]

WILLIE. Say, that's all right.

GUY. Friday Night Blues. Inspired by an empty pocket.

WILLIE. No luck?

GUY. Nope. They've picked up all the gold on Eloff Street. No nuggets left for Guy.

WILLIE. Remember what I said. When you're down to the last notch in your belt come along with me. I can always find you something at the office.

GUY. That sounds like a pension scheme. Hold on, man! I haven't even been given a chance yet.

WILLIE. Okay, so your old age is insured.

GUY. That's a comforting thought when you're twenty-two.

REBECCA. Supper will be ready in twenty minutes.

WILLIE. No hurry.

REBECCA. Aren't you hungry?

WILLIE. I'll eat when I see it.

REBECCA. Anything go wrong at work?

WILLIE. Everything is fine, just fine.

REBECCA. I wish you'd tell me, Willie.

WILLIE. Tell you what?

REBECCA. Whatever's bothering you.

WILLIE. Nothing's bothering me. Let's just say I'm a tired man, okay?

REBECCA. Okay. [*She goes into the house.*]

9

WILLIE [*shouting to her*]. Can you scrape three plates from the pot?

REBECCA [*from inside*]. Who's the extra?

WILLIE. Crazy musician. We'll make him sing for his supper.

GUY. Three cheers for the African Feeding Scheme.*

WILLIE. You dedicate Friday Night Blues to me, boy.

GUY. It's sad music.

WILLIE. I get sad sometimes.

GUY. Sure, we all do. But this is real sad . . . Sort of . . . you know . . . you got the words.

WILLIE. Melancholy, loneliness, despair. They all add up to the same thing. [*Pause.*] The bus queue was a mile long tonight. That's a lot of people. A mile of sweating shouting bastards, all happy because there was a little bit of gold in their pockets. I've never been so lonely in all my life. It's my song, Guy.

GUY. If you want it, okay. 'To Willie.'

[*He plays 'Friday Night Blues' a second time. In the course of it* Father Higgins *enters, followed by* Tobias, *a newcomer to Johannesburg.*]

HIGGINS. Evening, Willie . . . Guy! We've missed you at the Jazz Club meetings.

GUY. I've been meaning to look in, Father. Just that I've been trying to get started as a professional and that takes time. All of it.

HIGGINS. How far have you got?

GUY. I've reached the first stage. I'm blowing the sax on an empty stomach.

HIGGINS. You'll be all right, Guy. In fact I want to see you about something. Come up to the church on Sunday afternoon and we'll talk about it. How's Willie?

WILLIE. Surprised. It's not often we see you here, Father.

HIGGINS. You should be grateful, it means there is no trouble. You laugh, but it's true. Every time I leave a house here in Sophiatown, I can see the neighbours putting their heads together to discuss the troubles of the family I've just left.

WILLIE. Sophiatown is a fertile acre for troubles, Father.

HIGGINS. Every garden has its weeds, even the white ones.

WILLIE. Yes, I've seen them. I was walking down a street the other day with neat white houses on each side and a well-trained dog snarling at me behind every gate. Those gardens were neat all right, the grass so green I couldn't believe my eyes. And in one of them is a dear old lady with a fork looking for a weed which she finds dying among the flowers, so she digs it out and everything is just fine and blooming nice again. Do you want to plant a daffodil in this yard?

HIGGINS. That's up to you. But I'll tell you what I do want. A little help for a friend. This is Tobias, Tobias Masala. He has just arrived here from the Eastern Transvaal. [*Willie stares at the newcomer with little warmth.*] A simple man, Willie, like so many of our people.

I was wondering if you could help. He'll do anything provided there is enough in it for him to live and maybe save a little each month.

WILLIE. Why do they do it!

HIGGINS. Do what?

WILLIE. That! Why do they come here, like *that*!

HIGGINS. He only wants to live, Willie. You know better than I do the stories they bring with them of sick women and hungry children.

WILLIE. When it rains over here we have to walk up to our ankles through muck to get into our shacks. There is another patch of muck we have to slosh through every day, the tears and sympathy for our innocent brothers.

HIGGINS. His life is a supreme gift. He must cherish it. He asks for nothing but a chance to do that.

WILLIE. It's muck, I tell you. This is Goli, not a quiet reserve. He wasn't made for this. They flounder, go wrong, and I don't like seeing it.

HIGGINS. Then what was he made for?

WILLIE. His quiet reserve.

HIGGINS. That's what they say about all of us.

WILLIE. I'm no simple Kaffir!

HIGGINS. I'm sorry. I didn't want it to end like this. Come, Tobias, we must go somewhere else.

[*They start to leave.*]

GUY. Come on, Willie, give old Blanket-boy a break.

WILLIE. Don't you understand, Guy, the breaks usually break them.

GUY. He's going to be broken a lot quicker if he's picked up. Have a heart, man! What about that lift job you told me about?

[*Tobias moves up to Willie.*]

TOBIAS. I'm not frightened of work.

GUY. There, you see, old Blanket-boy's got guts.

TOBIAS. At Machadodorp, I work eleven hours when harvest comes.

WILLIE. Why didn't you stay there?

TOBIAS. It's not my district so they say I must go back to my home. But there is no work there and the soil is bad.

GUY. Can you work a lift?

TOBIAS. Lift? Yes, I have to lift heavy grain bags on to the lorry.

GUY [*laughing*]. You're all right, Blanket-boy. What do you say, Willie?

WILLIE. I'm making no promises.

HIGGINS. Thanks.

WILLIE. No promises, understand. If he sinks, he sinks.

HIGGINS. Stay here, Tobias. They will try to help you. Good night. [*Exits.*]

TOBIAS. What is it I must lift?

GUY. A building full of white people. Us blacks use the stairs.

TOBIAS. I don't understand.

GUY. That's not important. We're meant to be dumb. What's more important is a little lesson in grammar. Now, what did you call the white induna on the farm where you worked?

TOBIAS. Mr Higgerty.

GUY. No, Toby. Over here it is 'Baas'. Do you understand? Just: yes baas, no baas, please baas, thank you baas ... even when he kicks you on the backside.

Now take off your hat and grin, come on, cock your head, that's it ... and say what I just told you.

TOBIAS. Yes baas, no baas, please baas, thank you baas, even when you kick me on the backside.

WILLIE. [*jumping forward and striking the hat out of his hands*]. Stop it, damn you!

CURTAIN

SCENE TWO

The backyard about two hours later. It is now dark. The houses are nothing more than shadows, the yellow squares of windows throwing a dim light on the activity in the yard. Attention is focused on a small group of men: Guy, Pinkie, and Peter are playing cards. Watching them is Tobias, and seated a little to one side, warming his hands over an open brazier, is old Moses, a blind man. Guy shuffles a pack of cards.

PINKIE. It's likc I said. I'm serving them tea . . . Every eleven o'clock I do it . . . I take it round from the kitchen.

GUY. Pick up your cards.

PETER. Pass.

GUY. Pass.

PINKIE. Now this chap . . .

GUY. What are you doing?

PINKIE. I was telling you, serving the tea. I'm the tea boy in the office.

GUY. The game, Pinkie, the game. Peter passes, I pass. What do you do?

PINKIE. I'll take two. [*He throws out two cards and Guy deals him another two.*]

GUY. Three aces.

PETER. I'm out.

PINKIE. Same here. [*They all throw in their cards. Guy picks them up and shuffles the pack.*]

Now this chap . . . van Rensburg . . . he says he gave me the coupons for his tea, but I haven't got them! And I tell him, I tell him nicely. He starts swearing at me . . . What he doesn't call me!

[*Guy starts dealing.*]

Every door opens, everybody sticks out their head to see who's started the riot and there I am with the tea tray and this chap shouting at me. What would you have done, Guy?

GUY. Pick up your cards.

PINKIE. But he didn't give me a coupon.

14

GUY. I'll take two.

PETER. Three.

PINKIE. Then the big boss ... Mr Cornell ... he calls me in.

GUY. What are you doing?

PINKIE. Pass. This van Rensburg chap goes in first and has his say. Then I go in. But do I get a chance? You listening, Guy?

GUY. Sure ... Two pairs.

PETER. Full house.

GUY. What you got?

PINKIE. One pair.

[*Cards are thrown in again. Guy shuffles.*]

PINKIE. So you see, I'm not even given a chance to tell my side of the story. Short and sweet: Cornell says I must apologize by twelve tomorrow morning or I'm sacked. Not even fired, mind you, but sacked! Now what do I do?

GUY. Pick up your cards.

PINKIE. To hell with the cards. I'm asking you for advice and you haven't heard a word I've said.

GUY. I've heard everything you said.

PINKIE. Then what would you do?

GUY. How much do you like your job?

PINKIE. But I tell you he never gave me the coupons for the tea.

GUY. You go and tell that to Watson. He's been sitting here the whole day looking for something to say tonight. Go ask him to raise it in parliament.

PINKIE. You think that's funny?

GUY. You playing or aren't you?

PINKIE. How can I play when I got my problem. Look, Guy, do I or don't I apologize to Mr van Rensburg? That's my problem, see. They want me to apologize for something I never done.

GUY. Okay. If it hurts you so much, don't apologize. Now are you playing or aren't you?

PINKIE. But then I lose my job.

GUY. Let's try black lady.

[*Peter nods his agreement. Guy deals for two.*]

PINKIE. What would you do, Peter?

PETER. It's like Guy said. Find what hurts you most: apologizing or losing your job. Then you got your answer.

PINKIE. That sounds nice and easy, doesn't it! Well I don't want to lose my job and I don't want to apologize.

GUY. Sounds like you got to choose one or the other.

PINKIE. But which one, Guy? Which one? What would you do?

GUY. Look, Pinkie . . .

PINKIE. I know . . . But just suppose it was you . . . just suppose. What would you do?

GUY. Well. I suppose it depends.

PINKIE. On what?

GUY. On how you are right now. You sober?

PINKIE. You bet. Smell.

GUY. Well, you're sober, you're calm, you got control of yourself. Now think. It's a good job. It's good pay. It's Friday night. You're going to have yourself a good time. Right?

PINKIE. Right.

GUY. So what! This van Rensburg's not in Sophiatown. You only see him for five minutes every morning and five minutes every afternoon. Why worry about him! Apologize and keep your job.

PINKIE. That makes sense. Guy, you've helped me. That pay packet was welcome, you know, what with Shark coming round. I wouldn't like to be here without five bob when he comes. Of course. It's a job like you said, it's regular pay! That old van Rensburg, we know he was wrong, don't we? So I say: 'I'm sorry, Mr van Rensburg' and I laugh at him in the kitchen. You're right, Guy!

[*Pinkie makes a move to exit.*]

GUY. Where are you going?

PINKIE. Rosie's. Just a quick one before Shark comes. I'm going to town tonight . . . with something special! Boy, what a woman.

GUY. Go easy on the quickies, Pinkie. Shark doesn't like to be kept waiting.

[*Guy and Peter continue a few hands of black lady. The door of Willie's house opens and he appears in his shirt sleeves.*]

GUY. Reached the end of the alphabet?

WILLIE. Couldn't get started. I begin with the A and the only word I can think of is ass. So I pass it up and go on to B and I get the adjective ... bloody. Bloody ass! That's what I think of a B.A.

GUY. So? We're all bums in our own way. But stick to your books and you'll be a big one.

WILLIE. What a future! Everybody wants a backside to kick in this country.

GUY [*throwing in his cards*]. I've had enough.

[*To Willie.*] Forget the books tonight if they make you feel so bad.

WILLIE. Forgetting is the problem.

GUY. I always just thought of it as a bad habit.

WILLIE. It is, the way most people do it. What I was getting at was being able to forget just what you wanted to. Learn to do that, Guy, and you'll be the most contented man in the world. You got accounts? ... Forget them! They summons you? ... Forget it! They jail you? ... Forget there's any better place to be.

GUY. I don't know about that.

WILLIE. Take me. Sometimes I forget to put my pen in my pocket before I go to work. Now how does that help me? But there are some things you can't forget. They won't allow it. They'd call that bad memory, high treason.

GUY. I don't see that, Willie.

WILLIE. The moment you forget you were black, they'd say you were red.

MOSES. Willie's right.

GUY. What's this? Another brain specialist?

MOSES. About forgetting. Willie's right.

17

GUY. Come on, Moses! You been blind so long you just can't remember nothing no more.

MOSES. Who says? Who says just because my eyes are dark I can't see nothing? I see things, man. I see things all day long.

GUY. What do you see?

MOSES. My home, my wife, my kiddies. I seen them, man, I tell you I seen them. Only it's not like you seen things, because with me they don't change. Like my boy. You know my little boy? All today when I sat in the sun on the pavement, I seen him, *ja*, I seen him, only I seen him like he was ten years ago. Now he must be a man.

TOBIAS. How long you been here?

MOSES. A long time.

TOBIAS. When you going home?

MOSES. Home? My boy's coming to fetch me.

TOBIAS. When?

MOSES. He's coming.

WILLIE [*to Guy*]. What's the time?

GUY. Another half an hour to go.

WILLIE [*looking at everybody sitting and waiting*]. He's sure got us trained, hasn't he?

GUY. As Shark would put it: I've put a lot of money and time into training you boys. God help the chap that forgets.

WILLIE. I reckon he's about the only one God would want to help.

GUY. If he'd forgotten about Shark the only help God could give would be a free pass into heaven. You'd be finished with the good old earth if you ever forgot eight o'clock on Friday night.

WILLIE. You think we're scared, Guy?

GUY. Sensible. Pay up and you'll at least have the seven days to next Friday.

[*Pinkie reappears. A few drinks have made him slightly more aggressive than when we last saw him.*]

PINKIE. Hey, Guy, how the hell can I apologize!

GUY. You back?

PINKIE. Listen, man, I forgot that argument of yours that convinced me I should apologize. Come on, Guy. How did it go?

GUY. It started with you being sober. You still sober, Pinkie?

PINKIE. I'm not that drunk. I just had a few tots.

GUY. Okay. So now you don't apologize.

PINKIE. I tell you I'm not that drunk. It's a good job. Four pounds a week. For a bachelor man that's good dough. And he says I got to apologize... That Cornell... he says I got to apologize. Ain't I got rights?

GUY. Go ask Watson.

PINKIE. Come on, Guy. On the level. What would you do? But remember he didn't give you a coupon for a cup of tea. He swore at you for bugger-all.

GUY. Oh shut up! I also got squeals. I been looking for a job for three weeks. Just let each of us keep his squeals to himself.

PINKIE. Well, when you get a job, I hope they tell you to apologize for something you never did. For something you never did.

GUY. My consolation is that by then you'll either be fired or you'll still be working, and I can go to you for advice.

PINKIE. As if I'll give it. You wait. Because it's a problem, you understand, a problem.

[*At this point Pinkie notices Tobias who has been listening carefully to everything said.*] You been listening carefully, I seen you. You're not like these bums.

TOBIAS. I been listening.

PINKIE. Yes, I seen you. Now what would you do? Wait! Before you speak. He never gave you the coupon for the tea. He never did. Because in every office they give you the coupon for the tea and you put them next to the saucer with the biscuits, and *then* you give them the tea. But there was no coupon there! He never gave it to you. So you see he swore at you for bugger-all and they're asking you to apologize for something you never did. Now tell me, what would you do?

TOBIAS. I... [*Pauses, not knowing what to say.*]

PINKIE [*encouraging him*]. *Ja*, come on.

TOBIAS. I don't know.

PINKIE. You don't know. You don't know. Let me go ask Rosie.

GUY [*slapping Pinkie on the back as he passes*]. Cheer up, Pinkie. Go ask old van Rensburg for his advice. That man takes too much.

[*Pinkie exits.*]

WILLIE. I don't blame him.

TOBIAS [*to Guy*]. You help me with my letter now.

GUY. Is it gonna be long or short?

TOBIAS. Just to my wife, to let her know I have arrive safely at Johannesburg.

GUY. Okay, but let's be quick. Shark doesn't like to be kept waiting and I'm on his list. You help me with the spelling, Willie.

WILLIE. Sure.

TOBIAS. Who is this man Shark?

GUY. Insurance. He insures your pay packet. Every Friday night five bob and you get home safely.

[*Guy and Tobias exit. Rebecca, who has appeared on stage a few minutes earlier, moves up to Willie.*]

REBECCA. Couldn't you get started at all?

WILLIE. Start what?

REBECCA. With the books.

WILLIE. Maybe later. You heard Guy, we're well trained in this yard. Life starts after eight o'clock.

REBECCA. He always comes on time.

WILLIE. Yes, I suppose we could call that one of his virtues.

[*Guy's head appears at the window. He calls out 'Maxulu'. Willie spells it out.*]

REBECCA. It's true what Guy said.

WILLIE. What did he say?

REBECCA. If you stick to your books you'll go places.

WILLIE. That's a sharp observation.

REBECCA. Why do you get sore every time someone just mentions it?

WILLIE. I'm sick of hearing it.

[*Guy's head appears.*]

GUY. I've got a big one, Willie. 'Circumstances'.

WILLIE [*spelling*]. C-I-R-C-U-M-S-T-A-N-C-E-S. [*To Rebecca.*] Sick of hearing it. Can you understand that?

REBECCA. No.

WILLIE. I'm sick of being bright when I know it means nothing. I'm sick of going places when I know there is no place to go.

REBECCA. That wasn't what you used to say. When you first got the papers for the course you said it would mean a lot. Extra pay, a better position.

WILLIE [*impatiently*]. Oh...

REBECCA. Well, didn't you?

WILLIE. Yes, I said that, two years ago.

REBECCA. Well, isn't it true?

WILLIE. Yes, it's true.

REBECCA. Then why complain?

WILLIE. Complain? I'm not complaining. And if I was, what's wrong with it, when everybody expects me to parcel up my life in the application form for a correspondence course?

[*Guy's head appears at the window. This time the word is 'frustrated'. Willie spells it out.*]

It's just possible that a man can get to thinking about other things than extra pay and a better position.

REBECCA. Such as?

WILLIE. Such as himself. What's he doing? Where does he fit in?

[*Rebecca turns away and walks dejectedly back to the house.*]

I'm sorry, Reb. There's nothing I can do about it. When a man gets to thinking like that he doesn't stop until he finds what he's looking for. Like I told Guy: it's one of those things you can't forget. If I could, life would be simple again. But you've got to know where you're going. I'm doubting what I used to believe in. The shine has worn off. Life feels like an old pair of shoes that everyone is trying to force me into, with me knowing I couldn't walk a block in them.

[*Guy's head appears at the window.*]

GUY. Last one. 'Yours faithfully'. One word or two words?

WILLIE. Two words.

REBECCA. Does a man always find the thing he looks for?

WILLIE. If he doesn't he might as well be dead.

REBECCA. I'm going to tidy up. Shall I leave your books out?

WILLIE. Yes, I'll try again.

[*Rebecca exits. Guy and Tobias enter.*]

GUY. How's this for a letter? Toby provided the ideas and I gave the English. Go on, read it to him, Toby. Show Willie he isn't the only bum around here with a bit of learning.

TOBIAS [*reading*]. 'Dear Maxulu, I have arrive at Jo'burg. You do not know it. You cannot see it in your mind. They have buildings here like ten mission churches on top of one another, so high you cannot see the cross on the top. They make mountains by digging the gold and they tell me they dig the gold under the ground like moles. You do not know it, Maxulu, it is not like anything you know. I have not seen one cow, one goat, or even one chicken, but the motor cars are more in one street than the cows of the chief, and the people more than the biggest impi.

'Here also I find Sophiatown where I stay with Mr Guy Modise. I meet his friend, Mr Willie Seopelo, who will get me a job in one of the tall buildings, taking the whiteman to the top. They call it a lift. But I don't lift, I just press a knob and then the box takes us all to the top.

'If everything goes right I will send some money this month. Call in at the Post Office and buy another blanket. The red ones. If circumstances permit, I will get home on leave in a year. Wait for me. Get Mr Mabuza to write to me about you, the children, and the cow. Also get him to read this letter to you. Yours faithfully, your husband. Tobias Masala.'

It's a good letter.

WILLIE. Yeah, it's fine.

TOBIAS [*pointing at Guy*]. He's clever. He writes. But there are things I do not say. If she was here, she would feel it in me tonight when we lie together, and she would know. But for this letter I need words and a word is only a wind. If I must find a wind for this that I cannot speak, it would be long and soft like that which chases the shadows in the grass in summer when we wait for rain. Do you know? The grass is long, the oxen fat, the sun heavy. I remember. I took the oxen into the hills when I was small and I heard that wind and all I could say was, God is lonely. It spoke the thing for which I have no words. The words, Maxulu, the words. You must know when you read, that I have not got the words.

WILLIE [*getting up quickly and moving to Guy*]. Did you tell him old Moses has been writing those letters home for ten years?

GUY. Have a heart. Old Moses is fifty. No one finds work at that age. What's the point in discouraging him?

WILLIE. I wasn't thinking of discouragement. Just the truth.

GUY. The truth is Toby is not old, and you're going to help him get a job, and Toby will go back in a year.

WILLIE. A year in this place is like a stray bitch, it drops a litter of ten like itself before it moves on.

GUY. What are you trying to do, Willie?

WILLIE. Stop him dreaming.

GUY. Suppose he is? What's wrong with that? Don't you dream?

WILLIE. I woke up a long time ago.

GUY. I don't get it, Willie. You used to be the one sucker who always had time for a sad story. Any bum could come here and knock on your door and Willie would help.

WILLIE. Have you been talking to Rebecca?

GUY. How does she come into it?

WILLIE. She also found a better past, a better Willie that used to be.

GUY. Okay, let's drop it. When you start getting suspicious about me talking to you like I always talk to you, it's time to shut up.

[*Pinkie, this time quite drunk, appears on stage.*]

PINKIE. He's a bastard. That's what he is! A bloody Dutch

bastard. Him and the boss, Mr Cornell. I bet his mother was also a van Rensburg. Well if they think I'm going to apologize they got another guess coming. Because I got rights. They'll protect me.

GUY. Who?

PINKIE. They.

GUY. Who is they?

PINKIE. Them.

GUY. So you found your solution to the problem.

PINKIE. Solution? It's rights! And I got them. And I don't apologize because I didn't do nothing. I mean anything. I didn't do something! Anyway, he swore at me for bugger-all and I don't apologize.

[*At this point, Watson, smartly dressed and carrying a briefcase, appears on his way to a meeting.*]

GUY. Hey Pinkie, there goes Watson. Go and ask him to help you.

PINKIE. Watson, a word with you, my friend. Watson, I know you can help me because you fight for our rights.

WATSON. Try my best, but I'm in a bit of a hurry, old man.

PINKIE. Wait, Watson, wait. The question is to apologize or not to apologize.

WATSON. *Ja*, it's a problem all right. I'll think about it.

PINKIE. No, Watson, no! Whatever you do don't think about it. Because it's life and death to me.

WATSON. Well, you see I'm in a bit of a hurry. There's a meeting over at Freedom Square and I got to address the delegates.

[*Pinkie and Watson who have moved across the stage now find themselves suddenly confronted by Shark and two of his thugs. Watson tips his hat and disappears. Pinkie drops back frightened to the other men who have all stood up and are clustered together.*]

SHARK. Well, isn't anyone glad to see me?

HARRY. Lot of dumb bastards. Come on, *betaal jong!*

SHARK. Don't be so vulgar, Harry. You're always thinking about money.

24

HARRY. That's what we come for.

SHARK. Yes, that is true. It is Friday night. All you boys got paid?

HARRY. They wouldn't be here if they wasn't.

WILLIE. Here's your five shillings, Shark. Take it and go.

SHARK. Don't rush me, Willie. You're as vulgar about money as Harry.

I want to report to you chaps. After all you are entitled to something for your subscription. That is, other than the protection we give you. Now you boys have been paying very well and very regular. I reckon this about the best yard in Sophiatown. Isn't that so, Harry?

HARRY. The very best. We've had no trouble from these bums.

SHARK. And for that reason you've had no trouble from us. You travel home safely with your pay packets every Friday night. My boys are all along the way keeping an eye on you chaps. Nobody, but nobody, elbows their way into your hard-earned cash. You know something, I reckon you boys got yourselves a bargain. Now some of my customers haven't been as appreciative as you boys. Yes, in fact I've had quite a bit of trouble. Especially down in Gold Street. Heard about Charlie? Poor Charlie. Tell them about Charlie, Harry.

HARRY. He didn't get off the train tonight.

SHARK. That is, not until they found him. Then they carried him off. Looks like foul play. The police are investigating. But hell, what can they do? I mean, those trains are so crowded. It's a shame. They should give you boys a better service, really they should. Okay, Harry, collect.

[*Harry and the other thug move forward collecting from the men. The second thug has a bit of trouble with Tobias who doesn't know what's going on. Harry moves over.*]

HARRY. What are you waiting for?

TOBIAS. I'm waiting for nothing.

HARRY. Then give it.

TOBIAS. Give what?

HARRY. *Vyf* bob, five shillings. *Betaal, jong!*

25

GUY. Lay off him. He's just come here.

SHARK. What's the trouble, Harry?

HARRY. Another Charlie, here among the good boys.

GUY. Hang on, Shark, this bloke's a stranger.

SHARK. A new arrival! They're always a bit of a risk.

WILLIE. He knows nothing about what's going on. Leave him alone.

SHARK. That's stupid advice coming from you, Willie. I mean you got some brains. Aren't you a B.A., boy? A man works hard to get a little business organized, you know, regular customers, and then along comes the stranger who doesn't want to buy. It's a bad example. Who knows, you might be the first one to follow his example.

WILLIE. You've got a monopoly. We all buy what you sell.

SHARK. Even the stranger. [*To Tobias.*] Will you buy what I sell?

TOBIAS. What do you sell?

SHARK. What do I sell? Protection! This is a bad place.

TOBIAS. [*Bursts into laughter.*] Protection! I'm not a baby.

[*The atmosphere is suddenly tense. The other men realize Tobias is in trouble.*]

SHARK. What's your name?

TOBIAS. Tobias. Tobias Masala.

SHARK. Tobias? No, that's no good. We'll call you 'stoopid'! [*There is a pause and then Shark's voice is almost at a scream.*] Stupid! Because that's what you are. A dumb bloody ox. Okay, Harry.

[*Harry and the other thug move like lightning. A knife flashes, it is quick and sudden. Tobias is left lying on the ground. Shark turns and looks at the men, then spits on the body and leaves. Willie moves forward and bends down to the dead Tobias. He withdraws instantly, rubbing the palms of his hands on his trousers.*]

CURTAIN

SCENE THREE

Willie's room. It is Sunday night. He is sitting at a table with a number of books open in front of him, but he is not giving them any attention. Behind him Rebecca *is cleaning up after the evening meal.*

REBECCA. Oh yes, and something else. Betty and Solly is engaged. They want to get married in November. I met them on the street. He asked about you. Wants to know when you going to visit him. Says I must tell you to leave the books alone one evening and to go over. He's changed his job, you know. In a lawyer's office now, getting much better pay. That's how they can get married. I'll be seeing her tomorrow. Shall I tell her we'll be over sometime this week? Willie!

WILLIE. Sorry. What's that you were saying?

REBECCA. Am I disturbing you?

WILLIE. No, I wasn't reading.

REBECCA. You wasn't listening either.

WILLIE. Just tired, I guess.

REBECCA. Been at it all afternoon.

WILLIE. At what?

REBECCA. Books, silly. You been learning all afternoon.

WILLIE. Yes . . . yes, that's it. I been learning all afternoon.

REBECCA. Then give it a rest now. What you been doing? History?

WILLIE. You don't have to talk about it as if you were interested.

REBECCA. But I am.

WILLIE. All right. You are.

REBECCA. Why always so suspicious? Every time I try to understand you shut up, like you didn't want to share anything.

WILLIE. I share the money. [*Pause.*] I'm sorry. I didn't mean to say it.

REBECCA. You just got so many chances of saying a thing like that.

27

WILLIE. I didn't mean it.

REBECCA. Then why did you say it?

WILLIE. I don't know.

REBECCA. Maybe it's because you want to use up all your chances.

WILLIE. What are you getting at?

REBECCA. That although I don't read as much as you I can understand simple language, so if you want to say 'get out' say it and I'll go.

WILLIE. What does that mean?

REBECCA. We aren't married.

WILLIE. So?

REBECCA. So there's nothing to stop you from saying it. But remember when you say it, that I'm not in here for the money.

WILLIE. I don't want to say it, Reb.

REBECCA. Then stop acting like you wanted to. I can't help it if it looks that way to me, Willie. I haven't changed, I'm the same Rebecca. But you aren't like you used to be. We don't talk about things any more.

WILLIE. Like getting married.

REBECCA. Yes, that's one of them. Why don't we, Willie? I mean talk, even just talk?

WILLIE. Maybe because you don't talk about that sort of thing in a voice as rusty as old junk in a backyard.

REBECCA. Can't we change that?

WILLIE. Change what? My voice? Must I only start cooing like a turtle-dove in the blue gum to have everything back cosy and warm again?

REBECCA. What's wrong with having life cosy and warm?

WILLIE. Nothing, absolutely nothing if you're still up there in the blue gum. But something has shaken it and I've fallen out of the nest. It's not cosy and warm down here and I don't see how I can kid myself that it is.

REBECCA. Okay, Willie. You've said that so many different ways I can't count them no more. But please, just for once, try and tell me what's shaken you down.

WILLIE. 'A slow soft wind of loneliness.' That doesn't mean much to you, does it?

REBECCA. Not a thing. You couldn't have been very settled in your nest if a slow soft wind kicks you out.

WILLIE. I was a fool to have said it. I should have known you wouldn't understand.

REBECCA. Understand? When all you give me is something about a wind that doesn't mean a thing to me. Try it simple, Willie. Have you grown sick of me? Just say 'yes' and I'll understand.

WILLIE. I'm sick of my whole life. Everything! Every single thing that I've done or believed in looks stupid. Is that clear enough for you?

[A knock on the door. Guy's voice calls 'Anybody home?']

REBECCA [pulling herself together]. Coming, Guy. [She opens the door.]

GUY [entering]. Willie at home? There you are. Where were you this afternoon? I knocked twice and got no answer.

[Pause.]

REBECCA. [to Willie] I thought you stayed home this afternoon.

GUY. Hey? Have I said anything I shouldn't?

WILLIE. It's okay, Guy. [There is another pause. Willie can feel Rebecca's eyes on him.] I went for a walk.

REBECCA. Guy says he knocked twice.

GUY [quick to make amends]. Yes, but they was very close together. I knocked on the door, went over to Moses to ask if he'd seen Willie, then I came straight back and knocked a second time, thinking maybe Willie was sleeping. Honest, Reb.

WILLIE. I went for a walk.

GUY [breaking the uneasy silence]. Tell you what I wanted to see you about. The big show they're putting on for the mission... know about it? Top-line talent. Well, one of the boys... plays the sax... has fallen ill and I take his place. I get paid! [Guy looks excitedly from Willie to Rebecca. The excitement in his eyes fades at their poor response.] I just thought you might like to know.

WILLIE. It's a good break.

GUY [*recovering*]. You think so? You really think so?

WILLIE. Of course ... it's a big show. You'll be heard by the right people.

GUY. That's what I thought. But I haven't told you the best yet. I play a solo and you know what its going to be? 'Friday Night Blues'! How's that? I'm going to keep it just like I told you. 'Inspired by an empty pocket.' You'll be along, won't you, to hear I mean? Being a soloist, I get my two seats, and I want you and Reb to have them. And I'll see they're front row. Nothing but the best.

REBECCA. Thanks, Guy.

GUY. I couldn't have done a thing without you and Willie.

REBECCA. Had any supper?

GUY. See what I mean?

REBECCA. There's coffee, bread and jam.

GUY. I was so excited, I've forgotten to eat.

REBECCA. Now's as good a time as any.

GUY. Let me buy something. I still got a few bob. Shark didn't take it all ...[*His sentence trails off into silence.*]

WILLIE. That's all right. I think we have all nearly forgotten by now.

GUY. I reckon so. A fellow gets all excited about something that happened to him ... and you forget about other things. [*Pause.*] They buried him this afternoon.

WILLIE. Did they?

GUY. Why you always so tough about old Blanket-boy, Willie?

WILLIE. Do you think a few tears can help him now?

GUY. Toby was all right, Willie. There's a lot of those chaps about. They don't mean nothing wrong. It's like Father Higgins said, he just wanted to work.

WILLIE. And it all turned out like I told Father Higgins ... They come to the city and go wrong.

GUY. But Toby didn't go wrong.

WILLIE. What's right about being six feet underground!

GUY. I see what you mean. Yes, there's nothing right about

that. I thought you meant wrong . . . like Shark . . . You know. Toby didn't have enough savvy to peddle dagga. He was a good chap. When we was writing that letter in my room on Friday night he told me about himself. What he was going to do with his cash when he got home.

WILLIE. Let's leave that for somebody who wants to write a sad story about a black skin.

GUY [*placating*]. Sure . . . sure.

[*There is a knock at the door. Rebecca opens it. Father Higgins stands there holding a bundle.*]

HIGGINS. Hello, Rebecca. Is Willie home?

REBECCA. Yes, come in.

HIGGINS [*entering*]. Hello, Willie, Guy.

GUY. I'm sorry I didn't get to the funeral this afternoon, Father, but I was jumping around getting organized for the concert.

HIGGINS. I understand. Actually it went off all right, didn't it, Willie?

GUY. Willie!

REBECCA. Willie?

HIGGINS. Yes, Willie was there. Just the two of us and the diggers.

WILLIE. What do you want, Father?

HIGGINS. Am I disturbing you?

WILLIE. Yes.

HIGGINS. It's about Tobias. There will have to be a letter home to his people and this death certificate.

GUY. There is also a few of his things in my room. Shall I get them for you, Father?

HIGGINS. Please. I'll make up a parcel and send it all back.

GUY. Won't be a minute. [*Exit.*]

REBECCA. Sit down, Father. Can I give you some coffee?

HIGGINS. Don't go to any trouble.

REBECCA. No trouble. It's ready.

HIGGINS. How are you keeping?

REBECCA. So so.

31

HIGGINS. So so? Why are Sundays always so miserable in Sophiatown?

WILLIE. Nothing to do except sit around and think. And what we got to think about ain't so good either.

HIGGINS. The Lord's Day.

WILLIE. You aren't shouting Hallelujah any louder than us.

HIGGINS. How can I, Willie? You were at the graveside with me.

WILLIE. What was it you wanted to see me about?

HIGGINS. A letter home to Tobias's family. I only knew him from the few minutes he spent with me when he came for help. I was thinking that someone over here, maybe you, got to know him a little better and . . .

WILLIE. And you want me to write the letter.

HIGGINS. Yes. I meant to speak to you about it this afternoon.

WILLIE. I can't very well say no.

HIGGINS. I don't want to force you. Don't force yourself.

WILLIE. I'll write it. Let's leave it at that.

HIGGINS. [*Takes up the bundle of clothing he brought in with him. He feels around in it and finds the letter Guy wrote for Tobias.*] I suppose the address will be the same as on this. Do you think this letter should go with it?

WILLIE. No.

HIGGINS. It was his last letter home.

WILLIE. It's better they don't get it.

HIGGINS. Why?

WILLIE. Because it's full of dreams. Because it tells them what a wonderful place Johannesburg is and asks them to wait for him. If that letter goes I don't write.

HIGGINS. I leave it to you.

[*Guy appears. He has a few of Tobias's belongings with him.*]

GUY. This was all there was.

HIGGINS. I'll parcel it up with the rest. Not very much, is it?

GUY. There's a little money here. [*He counts.*] Five shillings.

[*Willie and Guy exchange a look. Higgins sees it.*]

HIGGINS. Five shillings. I've heard about that.

WILLIE. So have we.

HIGGINS. Yes . . . you must know a lot.

WILLIE. Over here you only know as much as is good for you.

HIGGINS. Even someone like yourself?

WILLIE. Why should I be different from the rest?

HIGGINS. I just thought you might be.

WILLIE. Say it straight.

HIGGINS. All right. Tobias was an innocent man. A simple and a good man. He came to me on Friday looking for a chance to work and live. He asked for nothing more. This afternoon, two days later, I buried him. You know what it was like. You stood at the graveside with me. A fistful of flowers and a wooden cross. I've buried others like that, Willie. It wasn't my first time even if it might have been yours. I know life is 'cheap' here; I've heard that sort of talk until I'm sick of it. But something inside me finds five shillings just a little too cheap. I was hoping you might have felt the same.

WILLIE. Nobody over here thinks five shillings expensive!

HIGGINS. Then why does it keep on happening? There are going to be others like Tobias. They'll walk in full of hope and be carried out in a coffin.

GUY. So?

HIGGINS. It doesn't have to be like that if only someone will do something about it.

GUY. Such as?

HIGGINS. Someone must have seen what happened out there on Friday night. Go along to the police and give a sworn statement. Get others to do the same. If only we can get as far as an official charge . . .

GUY. Whew! You're not asking for courage . . . you're asking for suicide. This character we're up against, he doesn't go to church. Maybe you don't know him like we do.

HIGGINS. Ask for police protection.

GUY. Don't you understand? He's got shares in the police

station. If I go along like you said, they'd let me talk for fifteen minutes. Sure, they'd listen to all I said. But when I was finished: 'Where's your pass?' Now I haven't got a permit to stay in Sophiatown, so I'd be in for fourteen days. And when I come out . . . ? If you think Toby was cheap at five bob I wouldn't be able to sell myself for a sixpence. He'd be waiting and he'd get me. You can forget about the police. They protect a fellow like Shark. You see they're only interested in our passes. But a Kaffir laying a charge against a criminal . . . that would be a joke. We are all criminals. Look, Father, don't be hard on us. You know what I've just said better than any other white.

HIGGINS. Sure. I'll leave this letter with you, Willie. Thanks for the coffee, Rebecca. Good night.

GUY. Say, Father, is it still all right for the show?

HIGGINS. Of course, Guy. Practice hard.

[*He leaves with the bundle of Tobias's clothing. There is a pause after his exit. Guy and Rebecca look at Willie.*]

REBECCA. Why didn't you tell us you went to the funeral?

WILLIE. Why should I? Everybody has just about forgotten what happened on Friday night.

GUY. But not you.

WILLIE. Give me time, give me time.

GUY. It's your advice, Willie. If you can forget, life will be easier. Remember saying that, on Friday night?

WILLIE. I remember.

GUY. Those were true words. I mean . . . if you can't forget you might . . .

WILLIE. What?

GUY. I don't know. That's why I say, try hard, Willie. Try real hard.

WILLIE. I said give me time, didn't I?

GUY. Sure.

WILLIE. What's eating you, Guy? Speak up.

GUY. You don't look as if it's going too easy.

34

WILLIE. Should it be easy? What are we saying? Easy! We make a proud job of living, don't we? Let's make it easy. Let's make the whole thing easy. Easy come, easy go.

GUY. That's the way it is.

WILLIE. I know the way it is! Only it's not quite so easy to take at times.

GUY. Life's hard enough for a bloke to want to soften it up a little.

WILLIE. The only way we can soften life is by softening ourselves.

GUY. Like how?

WILLIE. Like forgetting a silly bastard was killed out there and we stood around because that way life was easy.

GUY. Hey, Willie! Look ... look at me. You know me, Guy, the bum you always help. You owe me nothing, Willie, so what I say is on the level, see. Willie. Forget it. Go back to your books, grab yourself a hunk of living, get married ... Do anything you like, but forget Friday night.

WILLIE. We make a proud job of living.

GUY. Do you want to end up dead?

WILLIE. How else does a man hope to end up?

GUY. Okay, you're quick on the words. But how about next Friday? ... next Friday ... like Tobias out there in the yard.

WILLIE. Will you forget that just as easily?

REBECCA. Willie! What are you saying! You want to chase the whole world away from you? Guy speaks to you like a friend and what does he get? A kick in the backside.

WILLIE. I'm sorry, Guy.

GUY. Skip it. Father Higgins made us all jumpy talking like that about doing something.

WILLIE. Guess so. That and the funeral. It's still close, you know, this afternoon. And now this letter he's asked me to write back to the woman. Let me get this off my chest and I'll feel better. The whole business is hanging round my neck. Yes, that's it. Let me get this off and I'll feel better.

GUY. Of course. You'll write a good letter. Nobody could ask for more.

[*Willie sits at the table and takes up a pen and starts writing.*]

WILLIE. 'Dear Mrs Masala . . .' [*The words dry up. He tears off the paper and tries again.*] 'Dear Mrs Masala . . . Dear Mrs Masala' [*Again the words dry up. Willie looks up and sees Guy and Rebecca watching him.*]

CURTAIN

SCENE FOUR

The setting is the same as the last scene. It is Friday night, five days later. The time is about seven o'clock in the evening. Rebecca is alone in the room, and is hurriedly packing a suitcase. She is obviously upset and having a hard time controlling her emotions. There is a knock at the door. She starts, looks around quickly for some place to hide the suitcase. The knock comes a second time and she calls out . . .

REBECCA. Who's there?

GUY. [*from outside*]. Only me. Open up.

[*Rebecca opens the door and Guy comes in. He is breathless and looks quickly round the room.*]

GUY. Where is he?

REBECCA. I don't know.

GUY. What's he doing, Reb? Tell me. What does Willie think he's doing?

REBECCA. I don't know.

GUY. He's asking for trouble like I've never seen any man ask for it and that's for sure. That's for damned sure. They're talking about it on every street corner. Willie Seopelo . . . Willie Seopelo . . . If Shark hasn't heard about it by now he must be stone deaf. Aren't you worried?

REBECCA. Worried?

GUY. Yes, worried. You know he went to the police station.

REBECCA. Did he?

GUY. Cut it out, Reb, this is no joke. The police station! To report Shark! And they laughed at him just like I said they would, and now everybody in Sophiatown knows he went. And that includes Shark. Willie's making it dangerous just to be a friend of his. Listen, Reb, do you realize what this means?

REBECCA. Well what do you want me to do?

GUY. Look worried, get scared. Because it's Willie.

REBECCA. It's always Willie.

GUY. Well this time it's for sure. Didn't you try to stop him?

REBECCA. Have you ever tried arguing with Willie? . . . When

37

you don't even know half the words for the things you want to say?

GUY. Then why's he doing it, Reb? There must be a reason. [*Pause.*] Didn't you ask him?

REBECCA. I did. He said he wanted to be able to sleep at night.

GUY. That's all?

REBECCA. That's all he said.

GUY. Is he coming back here?

REBECCA. I suppose so.

GUY. Suppose? Look, what's going on here? Don't you know what Willie does any more?

REBECCA. He doesn't tell me and I stopped asking.

GUY. What's happening to the world!

REBECCA. You been away too long, Guy. You got a lot to catch up on.

GUY. Only five days . . . I had to do my practising for tonight in town. It's only five *days!* Things can't change as much as this in five days. Anyway I came as soon as I heard about it. Pinkie came round and told me about it this afternoon. But why, Reb, what's got into him?

REBECCA. Stop asking me like that.

GUY. Then who must I ask?

REBECCA. I don't know, but don't ask me because I don't know and I don't care.

GUY. Don't care!

REBECCA. That's what I said. I don't care.

GUY. Hey, easy Reb, easy. You don't mean that.

REBECCA. Why shouldn't I mean it? I'll say it again: I don't care. I mean every word of it.

GUY. That means you not going to put a bunch of flowers on Willie's grave on Sunday. Yes! On his grave. Because if you think it's going to be any other way you're wrong. He hasn't got a snowball's chance in hell against Shark. And if you don't care about it, all right. [*Pause*] What you doing, Reb? What's this?

38

REBECCA. A suitcase and I'm packing it.

GUY. You're getting out?

REBECCA. Can you give me a good reason for staying?

GUY. Yes. Willie. Look Reb, let me explain very clearly: if we don't do something he's finished. Everybody's waiting to see what happens. Shark knows that. He knows that if he doesn't put Willie down hard, he might as well pack up and try his hand at a dagga racket. So he's going to put Willie down hard. We've got to stop that.

REBECCA. How are you going to stop it?

GUY. I'll speak to Willie.

REBECCA. What are you going to say that I haven't already said? Tell me, Guy, what are you going to find in your friendship that I couldn't find in my love?

GUY. It can't be as bad as that.

REBECCA. Tell me what you're going to say to him.

GUY. It can't be like you said, Reb.

REBECCA. Why can't it?

GUY. Because Willie is sensible. He listens to reason.

REBECCA. You can't reason with a mad man. You think I'm talking wild now, carried away by my emotions as Willie always said. Well this time it isn't true. I've been carried away nowhere. For five days I've lived in here with Willie and watched him change until I don't recognize him anymore. I've sat here and watched Willie's big brain get hold of him and destroy him. He sat here day and night for five days with one idea until it nearly drove me mad as well . . . until it drove him to the police station.

GUY. What was this idea, Reb?

REBECCA. Tobias!

GUY. Toby. I should have known.

REBECCA. But don't think he told me. Not Willie. Not any more. I could be the doormat he wipes his feet on for all the notice he takes of me.

[*She dips her hand into a wastepaper basket and pulls out a handful of crumpled papers.*]

39

Do you see this? It's the letter Father Higgins asked him to write to Tobias's wife. Well that's all he does . . . and he can't even do it. Look at this. Do you see? Our address and then 'Dear Mrs Masala.' He never gets any further.

GUY. But Willie was so damned good at letters.

REBECCA. This one he can't write. He's been sitting with this letter ever since last Sunday.

GUY. So he couldn't forget. But why? Have you tried speaking to Willie, Reb? I mean really tried?

REBECCA. Oh, Guy! What you think I been doing here these five days? What? Do you think I just been sitting here watching . . . making coffee when he wanted it . . . cooking his food? I knowed with something inside me that this was our last chance, and if you think I've wasted it I'd call God down to give witness. If He even heard half my prayers He would have a lot to say. I've tried everything—everything a woman can try I've tried in here. I've tried just being with him, just being here so that if he wanted something he could ask. I've tried it on that bed at night . . . offered him the comfort only a woman can offer a man. I would have let him take me like a dog takes a bitch in the street if I thought it would be comfort. Because I know that if I could have given Willie that, in any way, there would still be hope. [*Pause.*] I haven't been able to comfort, help or do anything a woman should for her man.

GUY. And now you're clearing out?

REBECCA. Clearing out or being kicked out. I don't know which it is. I only know that I'm going, that I should have been gone a long time ago. I've overstayed my time.

GUY. There is no time to you and Willie.

REBECCA. Hearing you speak like that makes me realize what Willie must have thought of the things I said. You sound stupid, Guy. It's over and you're still trying to kid yourself it isn't, like I been doing. And all the time Willie knew it was over. Only he was too much of a gentleman to kick me out. He waited for me to realize it was time to go.

GUY. Before you go, Reb . . . Remember you still love him.

REBECCA. Love him! I feel like I been to bed with one man and woke up to find a stranger beside me. I might have loved the man I went to sleep with, but the man I found this morning fills me with shame. And it's so deep, Guy, I just want to run away from what causes it.

GUY. He needs you, Reb.

REBECCA. He hasn't said it.

GUY. He's blind! He doesn't know what he's up against.

REBECCA. Well, if he doesn't it's no use. Can't you see that, Guy? Willie is a man and because of that you can't force a thing down his throat like a mother with a child that won't take medicine. He's a man, Guy, so he lives his own life and if he doesn't want anything, he doesn't want it and this is how it is with me. It's over. You walked in at the end. Life isn't like a gramophone record where you can go back to the beginning.

GUY. Where you going?

REBECCA. Back to my mother.

GUY. That's going to be tough, Reb.

REBECCA. Only place to go. Anyway it's easier than staying here.

[*The door opens and Willie enters.*]

WILLIE. I thought you were practising in town.

GUY. I came as soon as I heard.

WILLIE. About me going to the police?

GUY. Yes. Well, what are you waiting for?

WILLIE. What do you mean?

GUY. You're not going to sit there and wait for him, are you?

WILLIE. You mean Shark.

GUY. Who else is going to visit you?

WILLIE. If he comes . . .

GUY. If he comes! What do you think he's going to do? Run away? You think you've scared him? He's going to be around here as certain as today's Friday, and it won't be a social call.

WILLIE. Do you want me to run away?

GUY. Yes. They're not nice words but that about describes it.

WILLIE. I'm sick of running away.

GUY. You've never run away from anything before, Willie.

WILLIE. I've been running away my whole life.

REBECCA. Willie . . .

WILLIE. Don't try and tell me that's not true because it is.

REBECCA. Listen to me . . .

WILLIE. No! For once there is something I'm going to work out for myself. The way I want it, the way I feel it should be worked out, without advice or kind encouragement from anyone.

GUY. And we must sit around and watch you make a balls-up of everything?

WILLIE. If you can't take it, get out.

GUY. You coming, Reb?

WILLIE. Guy! Guy, please. Turn off the pressure, man. You're pushing me. I've been pushed so much I can't take it any more.

GUY. Who's pushing you?

WILLIE. Everybody.

GUY. Don't let it bother you no more. I've stopped as from right now.

WILLIE. Look, Guy. *I've* got to live my life, not you.

GUY. Why do you think I asked you to clear out? Because I want you to live it, not throw it away.

WILLIE. I'm not throwing it away.

GUY. Okay, okay. Now you tell me what you think Shark is going to do when he comes around here looking for you. Pat you on the back, shake your hand? Sure, they might do that before they put the knife into you like with Tobias. Willie . . . You remember last Sunday, here in this room? Last Sunday, I said that the man who thought of trying to report Shark to the police wouldn't be worth a sixpence. You remember me saying that? You remember me saying that even if he did get as far as the police station it still wouldn't mean a thing because the police wouldn't be interested? You remember all that, Willie? . . . You know it, don't you?

WILLIE. Yes.

GUY. You know all that but you went along to the police. Now forget the big words, Willie . . . I want you to tell me in short ones that I can understand why you went.

WILLIE. I went for myself. For myself. Not to get Shark. Before I even start reckoning with him I've got myself to think about, the part I played in Tobias's death. The emotion inside me is shame, not anger, shame. You see, Guy, I'm involved as surely as I stood there and watched him go down.

GUY. You had nothing to do with it. None of us did.

WILLIE. Didn't we?

GUY. No.

WILLIE. Then why can't I forget? Why? Why can't I write that letter?

GUY. You was always so good at letters.

WILLIE. Good at letters! How do you speak kindly of a man's death when the only truth about it is its stupidity? How do you tell a woman that her man died for bugger-all and that his death means bugger-all? Where's the comfort, Guy? Where? Go squeeze Tobias's blood out of the mud in the yard before you ask me to find it. Comfort, Guy, not a cliché. Not a stupid 'I'm sorry' or 'He was a good man' but a sweetness as clean as his mother's pain when she dropped him into the world. Tobias is dead, and all I can say is that there is a little more muck in our backyard.

GUY. And I thought you didn't like him.

WILLIE. Of course I didn't. I hated him. I hated him because I feared him. These 'simple men' with their innocence and dreams. How can we dream? When I was a child I used to lay awake at night in the room where my mother and us kids used to sleep. I used to lay awake and think. I'd say to myself, 'You're black.' But hell it was so dark I couldn't see my own hand. I couldn't see my blackness, and I'd get to thinking that maybe the colour wasn't so important after all . . . and because I'd think that, I could dream a little. But there was always the next morning with its light and the truth. And the next morning used to come so regularly and make the dream so stupid that I gave up dreaming. Tobias reminded me of too much, Guy. He was going to make some money and live happily ever after. The cosy little dream ... like this! Willie and Rebecca lived happily ever after! That's how the fairy stories end and it's stupid because out there is life and it's not ending happily.

REBECCA. Don't worry about that no more. You got your unhappy ending.

GUY. Hold it, Reb. Look, Willie, there's nothing wrong with a man trying to make a decent life for himself.

WILLIE. Yes there is, if he uses it as a fire exit every time life gets a little hot.

GUY. So what must everybody do? Chuck up all they got and live in rags?

WILLIE. I'm not talking about everybody. I'm talking about myself. You can do a good thing for a wrong reason ...

REBECCA. Shut up! I know it all. Every word he's going to say ... I've heard it all before.

GUY. She's pulling out, Willie.

WILLIE. Leaving?

GUY. That's it. Reb is leaving, Willie. Say something!

REBECCA. So at last I found it, Willie.

WILLIE. What?

REBECCA. I found the thing that leaves you without words. We've been in here four years ... I don't think there was anything I done in those four years for which you didn't have something to say. Is there really nothing, Willie? Not even 'I don't want you to go'? What about 'Goodbye'?

[*Rebecca leaves.*]

GUY. You let her go like that? You let Reb walk out like she just come to sweep the floor? She's at the steps, Willie ... Run, man ... run! Willie, I'm asking you!

WILLIE. I can't.

GUY. Did I see it end . . . here, in front of me? Did I see Reb leave, and you standing there saying nothing, doing nothing?

[*The door bursts open, Pinkie rushes in.*]

PINKIE. Willie! . . . Shark's outside. He's asking for you.

CURTAIN

SCENE FIVE

The backyard of Scenes One and Two. The various characters, Watson, Moses, *et al. are standing around tensely, their attention focused on* Shark *and his two thugs. The door of* Willie's *room opens and he comes out, followed by* Guy *and* Pinkie.

SHARK. Hi, Willie. How's life treating you, boy?

WILLIE. What do you want?

SHARK. What do I want? Did you hear that, Harry?

HARRY. *Ja.* He asked what you want.

SHARK. What do I want?

HARRY. Five bob.

SHARK. There you go again. Always thinking about money. You're crude, Harry, real crude. I wanted to chat with you, Willie. A quiet talk just between you and me. This place is crowded, let's go into your room. Harry will see to the business. Okay, Willie? I just want to talk, boy.

WILLIE. Say it here if you're man enough. You don't go into my house.

SHARK. Why not?

WILLIE. It's clean.

PINKIE. . . . Ah . . . ah . . . Here's my five shillings, Shark.

SHARK. Go away, little man. Okay, I'll say it here. I was going to spare you the embarrassment, but I'll say it. You done me dirty, Willie. You done me all wrong. You went along to the police like any cheap blabbermouth to cause me trouble. Did you hear that, all of you? To the police . . . the bastards who lock us up for not carrying our passes. That's who Willie went to see. You got to watch him. Because if you don't, he'll report you as well. Yes, he will. You, Watson . . . he'll report you to the Special Branch. He's ambitious, this boy . . . He'll do it. Now Willie, I reckon it's my public duty to tell you, to warn you that it's got to stop. Do you understand? S-T-O-P. I'm telling you, because these men pay me to protect them, and that's what I intend doing. It's your type that takes advantage

46

of them. Like that little man over there . . . he's just a little man. What can he do about a type like you? Or Watson. Good old Watson, who fights for our rights and fights so damned well, he hasn't realized how dangerous you are, a government spy . . . right under his nose. Now . . . I'm prepared to give you a chance . . .

WILLIE. Like Tobias.

PINKIE. Take it easy, Willie.

SHARK. What about him?

WILLIE. The 'chance' you gave him.

SHARK. He was getting rough with Harry. It was self-defence. [*To Harry.*] Wasn't it, boy?

WILLIE. It was murder.

SHARK. I could sue you for that. For making incriminating statements against me. I got witnesses. Haven't I, boys? [*Addressing the others.*] I came here . . . I just wanted to talk to Willie, but you all heard the way he's been carrying on against me. He's asking for trouble. [*To Willie.*] You're lucky you got me to protect you against yourself.

WILLIE. I might have been.

SHARK. Might?

WILLIE. Past tense. The protection is finished. I don't buy any more.

SHARK. You're not going to pay?

WILLIE. That's what I said.

PINKIE. No, Willie.

SHARK. On my way down here I heard talk like that. Ain't you feeling well, boy? You do look sort of pale. Strange that, huh . . . how pale a black skin can get when the man inside it is shit-scared of dying.

WILLIE. I don't scare that easily.

SHARK. Look boy, you went to the police station. Now that was a silly thing to do. But I can square that up. After all, you might have thought it your duty and I got no objection to a man doing his duty, even though I would have liked you to

47

come and see me about it first. Anyway I can forget your little jaunt to the police station ... even though I know what you tried to tell them. Yes, I know, Willie. I know everything! But I am willing to forget that. I can square it up with the boys. But I can't forget this talk about not paying. That's insulting. It's revolution! Haven't you bums had enough already?

WILLIE. Are you finished?

SHARK. Look, Willie ... are you trying to scare me? With what? What you got that can scare me? These bums? Is that it? You going to organize a vigilance committee?

WILLIE. They got nothing to do with this.

SHARK. They'd better not if they know what's good for them.

WILLIE. Is that the lot?

SHARK. The lot! I haven't even started with you yet. And when I do you'll wish you'd stuck to the sample I gave you last Friday night. Listen, Willie, let's talk this over sensible-like. What's worrying you? Old Stoopid? Is that it? Okay. Here's a pound. One pound of the money I've sweated for. Send it to the woman in the kraal. Tell her it comes from a sympathizer. Now how's that?

WILLIE. Go stick that on the nail in your lavatory.

SHARK. If that's the way you want it, okay. Now listen to me. Two hours, Willie ... two hours. You be here with your five bob waiting in two hours' time, or clear out. Talk big then. Because I'll be coming around for you ... just for you.

HARRY. Why wait?

SHARK. No, this is business. Serious business ... and I want Willie to think about my proposition. [*He moves off with his thugs. Just before his exit he turns.*] Two hours, Willie!

[*Shark's exit leaves behind a dead silence.*]

PINKIE. Don't you think you'd better start packing, Willie?

WILLIE. Packing?

PINKIE. *Ja*, He's only given you two hours. Aren't you going, Willie?

GUY. How can you ask Willie such a stupid question, Pinkie?

48

Willie here is going to show us how to live . . . how to live really big . . . Aren't you, Willie? You are going to show what miserable bums we are and how a man really behaves . . . how a man really throws his life away. Ain't I right, Willie? But there's something I've left out. Why don't you say it?

WILLIE. Say what?

GUY. Why don't you ask who's going to keep you company in two hours' time?

PINKIE. Don't talk like that. It makes me nervous.

GUY [*still at Willie*]. Because that's what you're thinking, isn't it?

WILLIE. I'm not thinking anything.

GUY. You bet you aren't, because I've never seen anything so Goddamn stupid in all my life. And you are the clever one, remember, the Thinker!

WILLIE. Am I?

GUY. That's a good question. Maybe I should have said 'was'. Because you been sitting in there the whole week thinking and this is the result. Anyway you'd better start again, start thinking quick because you got a lot to think about . . . and only two hours to do it.

PINKIE. Hey Willie, you want to borrow five bob? I got paid today. I can manage it. You want it? Because you see, Willie, I got a good job. Four pounds a week, that's good dough for a bachelor man, huh? I don't want to lose the job, Willie . . . Maybe I should say I don't want the job to lose me.

WILLIE. This doesn't involve you, Pinkie, or anybody else.

PINKIE. I wasn't just thinking of myself.

WILLIE. No?

PINKIE. No . . . What I mean is . . . we had one killing in here that was all a bad mistake. Let's not have another. Death is kind of infectious, you know. It's like a disease . . . it spreads. Look at old Tobias . . . He went . . . and now you . . . maybe we follow.

WILLIE. Whatever happens you just carry on like nothing had happened. Like we all did last Saturday.

PINKIE. But you don't have to . . . He's given you a chance . . . a chance to live.

WILLIE. What does that make him? God Almighty?

WATSON. Look, maybe I can help. I don't want to get involved in something that doesn't concern me . . . I mean . . . I wasn't here when this . . . this . . .

WILLIE. He called it self-protection.

WATSON. *Ja* . . . when this self-protection happened. But I been a neighbour of all of you for a long time . . . and . . . What I'm trying to say is . . . ah . . . What can these chaps do against a man like Shark?

WILLIE. I told you before that's their problem and I'm not trying to solve it, for anybody.

WATSON. Now that's just where I think I can clear up the whole business. I'm prepared to put forward a resolution at the next Congress,* deploring the high incidence of crime and calling for an immediate . . .

PINKIE. Watson, why don't you go home? But he's right, Willie. What can we do about Shark?

WILLIE. Let's get one thing straight. I haven't been having nightmares about what we can do or what we can't. I been waking up at night sweating with shame because of what we did . . . Did! . . . Here in this yard when Tobias went down. Can you remember what we did? Nothing.

PINKIE. But what could we have done?

WILLIE. Do you know what you've just said? In the space of one minute you've asked me what *can* we do and what *could* we have done. Don't you know what to do at all? Is there nothing you can do except be booted around by life until it looks like your skin was black from the bruises and from nothing else? Guy's right about the thinking I did in there for a week. That's a lot of thinking, but there was a lot to think about. You know one of the ideas I've come out with? The world I live in is the way it is not in spite of me but because of me. You think we're just poor suffering come-to-Jesus-at-the-end-of-it-all black men and that the world's all wrong and against us so what the hell.

Well I'm not so sure of that any more. I'm not so sure because I think we helped to make it, the way it is.

WATSON. Are you denying the oppression?

PINKIE. We don't like things the way they are, Willie.

WILLIE. Nobody but a moron would like them. But there's a lot of it we make ourselves, and a lot we accept.

PINKIE. Such as?

WILLIE. Such as Tobias's death and a character called Shark. Our handiwork. We've been good customers. Every Friday night on the dot ... five shillings ... for a long time. So when a man like Tobias walks in he's out in the cold if he doesn't pay ... And being a man he wouldn't want to pay. There's nothing that says we must surrender to what we don't like. There's no excuse like saying the world's a big place and I'm just a small little man. My world is as big as I am. Just big enough for me to do something about it. If I can't believe that, there's no point in living. Anyway this doesn't concern any of you and the sooner you leave me alone to solve it my way the better. Well? What are you waiting for ... or do you want to see how he does it a second time?

[*They all exit except Willie and Guy.*]

WILLIE [*to Guy*]. You'll be late for the show.

GUY. I'm going ... but not like that. Are you going to wait for him, Willie? [*Pause.*] Willie ... the world was sweet ... the world was sweet ...

WILLIE. It's the way we made it.

GUY [*turning to Willie*]. Then we made it all wrong ... all wrong and rotten. When I think back to what it was like just a week ago ... just a week ... and now. I walked in here with my sax and I found Rebecca. Right there! Taking the washing down. You know who I'm talking about don't you, Willie, or have you forgotten her already?

WILLIE. I won't forget her, Guy.

GUY. Pity you didn't tell her that when she went. It might have saved her a couple of tears ... even just a couple. Because you do know what you said, don't you, Willie? You said nothing!

Christ, Reb . . . what happened? What has happened, Willie? No, don't you tell me, don't say a thing. I couldn't take any more from you. Yes, I came home and there she was taking the washing down and talking. She got a little sad about you . . . but she was here! Just a week ago. We even laughed about old Sam. It was here . . . I was here, and Reb, and you were coming home. And it was life . . . tough, hard, but it was life, and I wasn't sorry to be part of it. And then Tobias walked in.

WILLIE. If he hadn't, someone else would have and it wouldn't have made any difference.

GUY. Drop the big words and the clever reasons, Willie. Because it was him . . . him . . . Tobias. He walked in here and buggered up everything, buggered up life until I can't recognize it any more. I don't know it . . . I don't know myself . . . I don't know you. You know what Reb said to me this afternoon? She said it was like she went to sleep with one man and woke up to find a stranger beside her in the morning. She meant you. Why did you have to do it? Anything else . . . but why did you have to do that to her, to the two of you? You and Reb was one of the things a fellow could believe in. Whatever else happened, you two were there. They could kick me around, Moses could be on the bum but there was always Willie and Reb and they were going places. A good man and a good woman. Now? I can't call you a good man, Willie. I can't believe in what you have done.

WILLIE. Stop trying. There's nothing to believe in.

GUY. What about Willie Seopelo's one-man crusade against crime?

WILLIE. There's no crusade. Just something I had to do, and I'm trying to do it.

GUY. I'm wasting my time arguing with you.

WILLIE. Why must you argue?

GUY. What do you want me to do? Pat you on the back and say 'Good boy'?

WILLIE. What you think you been doing all these years? You,

Rebecca, everybody. Good boy, Willie, you passed another exam! Good boy, Willie, you got a rise! Don't you think I'm sick of it? Anyway, that's finished now.

GUY. Are you doing this just because you want to stop that?

WILLIE. No, but it ties up. It was part of everything. It's a long story.

GUY. Too long for two hours.

WILLIE. It's taken me my whole life to live it.

GUY. Your whole life . . . Willie, the future could be just as long. Why make it two hours?

WILLIE. Because those two hours . . . Well, I've found something I been looking for, for a long time. Peace, Guy, peace. Peace of mind . . . peace of heart. You know, the two old enemies . . . they're not fighting any more . . . This is the first time in a long time. But don't think I'm not scared . . . shit-scared as Shark would say. I'm scared, boy. But there are lots of things to think about and if I try hard enough I can forget . . .

GUY. Do you want to? Why? Look, Willie . . . what are you trying to do? . . . Hide away from what's coming, pretend it's just another Friday night! Shark's coming round . . . for you . . . in two hours' time. Are you going to wait? Answer, boy . . . Because if you can't, start running. [*Pause.*] Are you going to wait?

WILLIE. Yes.

GUY. You're scared, Willie . . . Run . . .

WILLIE. No.

GUY. Remember Tobias . . . they'll do it that way. For the last time, are you going to wait?

WILLIE. It's no use, Guy. I'm scared all right. But then that's human, isn't it? A man's got a right to be scared about a thing like that. Anyway, it's not too bad. I can swallow hard and keep it down and hope it will stay down.

GUY. It's not easy to walk out . . . you know . . . just walk out with you standing there.

WILLIE. You'll be late for the show, Guy. It's your big break.

GUY. Help me, Willie . . . It's hard.

WILLIE. Rebecca. Knock on her door tomorrow. She'll need you. And tonight, play sweet. It's my song. Play sweet, boy.

[*Guy exits and Willie is left alone for a few seconds before Moses, the blind man, enters.*]

MOSES. Is that you, Willie?

WILLIE. Yes.

MOSES. Pinkie's locked the room and gone to the show and I got nowhere to go. So I'll just sit here if it's okay with you, Willie. It won't make no difference . . . being blind I don't see nothing. He knows that . . . he knows I can't say nothing in court.

WILLIE. Moses, is it true what they say about blind men, can you hear better than those that see?

MOSES. Yes.

WILLIE. Moses . . .

MOSES. I know, Willie . . . I'll tell you when I hear them coming.

[*Willie moves back to the house. Guy's saxophone music is heard in the background.*]

CURTAIN

54

NONGOGO

CHARACTERS

JOHNNY, *a young salesman*
QUEENY, *a shebeen proprietress in her forties*
BLACKIE, *her hanger-on*
SAM, *a friend of Queeny's*
PATRICK, *one of Queeny's customers*

All the characters are African, and the setting is a shebeen in a Johannesburg township.

Act I—Queeny's shebeen late Friday afternoon; Act II, Scene 1—the same, next morning; Act II; Scene 2—that afternoon.

NONGOGO was first performed in the Bantu Men's Social Centre, Johannesburg, on 8 June 1959, then transferred to the Darragh Hall, 15–27 June 1959, where it was staged 'in the round', with the following cast:

JOHNNY	Solomon Rachilo
QUEENY	Thandi Kumalo
BLACKIE	Zakes Mokae
SAM	David Phetoe
PATRICK	Cornelius Mabaso

The production was directed by Athol Fugard, with Tone Brulin assisting.

NONGOGO had its first performance outside South Africa at the Crucible Studio, Sheffield, England, on 27 November 1974, with Temba Theatre Company, including Jimi Rand as Johnny, Ena Cabayo as Queeny, and Alton Kumalo as Sam, directed by Peter James. The first American production was at the Manhattan Theatre Club on 3 December 1978, directed by Oz Scott with Mary Alice as Queeny, Thomas Martell Brimm as Johnny. On 12 November 1981, the play was revived at The Laager, Market Theatre, Johannesburg, with the following cast:

JOHNNY	Ramolao Makhene
QUEENY	Thoko Ntshinga
BLACKIE	Andrew Mabizela
SAM	Patrick Ndlovu
PATRICK	Fats Dibeco

The director was Lucille Gillwald.

ACT ONE

Queeny's shebeen in one of the townships around Johannesburg.* The time is late Friday afternoon. The room is small, with two doors—one at the back leading onto the street, the other on stage-right leading into a kitchen, which is not seen. There is one window looking onto the street.

The furniture includes a divan at the back which is curtained off to suggest an alcove. There are also a table, chairs, a sideboard, and a dressing table. The furniture is expensive by township standards but nevertheless there is a suggestion of slovenliness about the room. The window curtains, for example, are nondescript, while those separating the divan from the rest of the room have a few rings missing and hang askew. There is no order or pattern to the ornaments and oddments in the room. Odd articles of female clothing are scattered about.

As the scene opens the room appears empty; the curtains surrounding the divan are drawn. Street noises are heard from outside. Then someone knocks at the door and gets no answer. The door, pushed lightly from outside, swings open and Johnny *comes in. He is a young man, neatly but quietly dressed. An open collar and loose tie suggest a hot day. He is carrying a suitcase. He looks around, sees nobody, and is just about to leave when something about the room attracts his attention. He comes back and looks at the table, runs a finger along it, and whistles approvingly. He is examining the sideboard when one of the curtains round the divan is drawn back roughly and* Queeny *sticks out her head. She is in her forties; a woman of powerful personality; what must have been tremendous beauty in her youth now shows the signs of age. She is a personification of the room: the very best but neglected.*

QUEENY [*rudely*]. What do you want?

JOHNNY. Sorry . . . The door was open and . . .

QUEENY. And you just walked in!

JOHNNY. Yes . . . But I did knock.

QUEENY. Okay. Now walk out just as quietly. I only start selling at seven.

JOHNNY [*bewildered*]. Selling?

57

QUEENY. You heard me. Seven. Either stay thirsty until then or find some other place . . . There's enough of them.

JOHNNY [*recognizing the room*]. I see. A shebeen.

QUEENY. I said seven o'clock.

JOHNNY. I don't want a drink.

QUEENY. Get out!

JOHNNY [*trying to calm her down*]. Look . . . Let me explain . . .

QUEENY [*going to the window and calling into the street*]. Blackie! Blackie!

JOHNNY. Who's Blackie?

QUEENY. You'll find out.

JOHNNY [*bending down to his suitcase*]. All I wanted . . .

[*He gets no further. The door opens and* Blackie *comes in. An ugly hunchback, about twenty-three, his arms hang loose at his sides like those of a large ape.*]

BLACKIE. What's the matter?

QUEENY [*points at Johnny and then turns her back*]. Him!

JOHNNY [*retreating before the menacing figure of Blackie who comes towards him*]. I didn't know this was a shebeen . . . and I don't drink . . . All I wanted to do is try and sell you a table cloth.

QUEENY [*astonished*]. A what?

JOHNNY. A table cloth. I sell table cloths.

QUEENY [*suspicious*]. Are you fooling?

BLACKIE [*threatening*]. Get out!

[*Johnny turns to Queeny imploringly. Blackie hesitates. Queeny pauses for a second, looks carefully at Johnny, then gestures to Blackie to leave.*]

BLACKIE [*pausing at the door and looking suspiciously at Johnny*]. I'll be outside. [*He exits.*]

JOHNNY. What was that?

QUEENY. A friend.

JOHNNY [*incredulous*]. A friend? . . . You mean a watchdog. Just like the whites. Only you don't have a notice on your door.

QUEENY. You shouldn't frighten people.

JOHNNY. Frighten?

QUEENY. Coming in here like you was up to no good.

JOHNNY [*shaking his head*]. Me? . . . Frightening people? . . . Up to no good? All I do is sell table cloths. Which reminds me . . . It's not a very big range, only red and blue, but the colours don't run.

QUEENY. What do I want with a table cloth?

JOHNNY. For your table. Look, that's good wood. [*He examines the table closely.*] . . . And here, see! Stains! I say, it's essential for a respectable shebeen with a good table like this to have one of my table cloths.

[*Queeny has been watching him carefully. She starts smiling and at the end of his little sales talk bursts into laughter. Her personality changes . . . the moody, aggressive person is gone.*]

JOHNNY [*responding immediately*]. You don't laugh very often, do you?

QUEENY [*stopping abruptly*]. Why do you say that?

JOHNNY. I never expected it.

QUEENY. [*The aggression returns.*] Why don't you go sell your table cloths?

JOHNNY [*wearily*]. *Ja*, I suppose I'd better. Where's the best part to try?

QUEENY. You mean has anybody got any money? [*Johnny nods.*] Nobody's got any money over here.

JOHNNY. Except you . . . and you got it all.

QUEENY. Look . . .

JOHNNY. It's true, isn't it?

QUEENY. Better watch your tongue if you want to stay out of trouble.

JOHNNY. I'm always getting that advice . . . and quite often the trouble. But I can't help it. It's what you see that starts you talking and I see just the same as other folks, don't I? [*Gesturing towards the room.*] But then maybe I don't . . . Like your laugh. Maybe other people never seen that.

QUEENY [*turning away*]. Maybe not. [*Pause.*] No, not many people have seen that.

JOHNNY. You should show it off. It's good. [*Queeny turns and looks at Johnny. It is a split second of embarrassment. Johnny picks up his suitcase.*] Anyways ...

QUEENY. Look, maybe I like the way you speak. Have a drink on the house.

JOHNNY. I don't drink.

QUEENY. Cup of coffee?

JOHNNY. Thanks ... but I'd better try selling or I won't be able to buy myself one tonight.

QUEENY. That's right ... I forgot. You sell table cloths. You know, maybe I do need one after all.

JOHNNY [*hopefully*]. You think so?

QUEENY. *Ja*, a blue one.

JOHNNY. No!

QUEENY. What do you mean, no?

JOHNNY. The red one.

QUEENY [*bewildered*]. The red one?

JOHNNY. Yes. It suits this room much better.

QUEENY. You think so?

JOHNNY [*enthusiastic*]. Of course. It's a good strong colour ... it matches you. These things go together, you know. [*Explaining.*] Look, if you were buying a scarf or something you'd match it, wouldn't you ... see that it goes with your best dress or something like that? [*Queeny nods in agreement.*] Well, same thing in the house, and this red is your colour.

QUEENY. All right, a red one. How much?

JOHNNY. Five bob.

QUEENY. There.

JOHNNY. My first sale today.

QUEENY. Maybe you'll sell four in the next street.

JOHNNY. Maybe. Anyway, thanks.

QUEENY. Okay ... Now don't go frightening people or you won't sell any. [*She is trying to delay his departure.*] Hey, look ... when you finish tonight come around and have that cup of coffee.

JOHNNY. Don't know if I can. I gotta catch the bus back to Alex.

QUEENY. Tomorrow?

JOHNNY. I won't be back after tonight. Looks like nobody wants table cloths except you. Anyway, thanks.

[*Johnny exits. Queeny looks blankly at the door that has closed in her face. She is alone. She is alone again. She sits down on the divan, takes out a cigarette, lights it, and puffs away thoughtfully for a few minutes. Then she gets up and goes across to the mirror and examines her face carefully, running a finger over a few lines. She stubs out her cigarette in disgust and returns to the divan, only to light another and surrender herself to the boredom which Johnny's entrance and exit have now highlighted. The door opens and Blackie comes in. He stands there, looking at her, waiting for a word. He gets none. He hobbles a little closer.*]

BLACKIE. He's gone. [*Queeny nods her head.*] I saw him go down the street. [*Pause.*] I followed him a little way to make sure he wasn't coming back.

QUEENY [*sharply*]. I told you to leave him alone!

BLACKIE [*hurt*]. You said nothing.

QUEENY [*irritable*]. Well I'm telling you now.

BLACKIE [*sees the red table cloth and picks it up*]. Why'd you buy this?

QUEENY [*jumps up and takes it away from him*]. Because I wanted it, that's why.

BLACKIE [*trying to please*]. I can get you better.

QUEENY. I wanted this one. It matches the room.

BLACKIE. He said that.

QUEENY [*angry*]. You been listening at the door again!

BLACKIE. You was speaking loudly.

QUEENY. Your mind is like your body. [*He starts whimpering like a dog.*] Shut up. Anyway, if he said it or I said it makes no difference. It does sort of fit in with everything.

BLACKIE. I'll bring you a better one tonight. I got a job at Houghton. I'll bring you the best cloths they got in the house.

QUEENY. All you'll ever bring me is trouble. They'll catch you one day.

BLACKIE. I'll bring you something nice.

QUEENY. If I want anything I can buy it. There are people that do that, you know; who earn what they get and buy what they want. Not like me and you . . . or Sam over there. This fellow [*points to the table cloth*] . . . he's living honest.

BLACKIE [*gloomily*]. He'll die poor.

QUEENY. You think that worries him?

BLACKIE. Why do you like him?

QUEENY [*sharply*]. Who said anything about liking? A man comes in here selling table cloths and I buy one. Is that so strange? [*Blackie looks at her.*] Anyway he's not like everything else. He made me laugh. Have you ever made me laugh?

BLACKIE. I'll bring you something good tonight.

QUEENY [*ignoring him*]. I like talking to him. [*She is holding the cloth, thinking, prepared to put it onto the table.*]

BLACKIE. He said he's not coming back.

[*Queeny stops arranging the cloth. The truth of the words hits her, she pulls the cloth off and throws it into a corner. She goes back to the divan, takes another cigarette.*]

BLACKIE. I seen the house we doing tonight. The girl there is a friend. She let me in the other day. They got lots of things; a big clock like the church, that sings the time. You want that? Or pictures . . . just so big . . . ? I'll bring it to you. Just tell me what you want.

QUEENY [*with pity*]. It's not your fault, is it, Blackie?

BLACKIE. What do you mean?

QUEENY. That you're the way you are.

BLACKIE. I'm strong, in my arms.

QUEENY [*ignoring what he has said*]. And the same for me. I don't suppose it's my fault, or even Sam's. [*Pause.*] Then who . . . who the hell do you swear at and hate?

[*There is a knock at the door.*]

QUEENY. Who's there?

SAM [*from outside*]. Me.

QUEENY. It's open.

[Sam *comes in. He is about the same age as Queeny, but meticulously dressed where she is inclined to be slovenly. He is a large and self-assured man full of the sort of confidence that a little money breeds. We see him mopping his face with a white handkerchief. In his movements about the room he frequently stops in front of the mirror for inspection and small adjustments to his clothing.*]

SAM. They'll be thirsty tomorrow.

QUEENY. They're always thirsty.

SAM. *Ja*, but this weather and pay day will make a difference. You got enough?

QUEENY. No such thing as enough in the townships. If there was I'd be out of business.

SAM. But I mean for tomorrow. [*Queeny lifts her shoulders in an indifferent gesture.*] I got a case out in the car.

QUEENY. What's it?

SAM. Half and half . . . gin and brandy.

QUEENY. What's your profit, Sam?

SAM. Come on, I give it to you cheap. If it was somebody else they'd pay all right, but with you it's different.

QUEENY [*laughs bitterly*]. I been with you too long, Sam, to believe that. Still it's nice to hear you say it.

SAM. I like doing business with you, Queeny.

QUEENY. I don't like bargaining.

SAM. That's because you know you always get your bargain from me.

QUEENY. Okay, bring it in.

SAM [*turning to Blackie who has been sitting in a corner*]. Hey! Get it out of the car!

QUEENY [*coming to Blackie's defence*]. His name is Blackie, just like yours is Sam and mine is Queeny.

SAM. Get it out of the car, Blackie . . . please! [*The last word for Queeny's benefit. Blackie goes out.*] Satisfied?

QUEENY. Ask him. You were speaking to him.

SAM. How long are you going to keep him hanging around?

QUEENY. Why shouldn't I?

SAM. Why? Because he's going to get us into trouble one day, that's why. Every time I see him he's fighting. He'll kill somebody one day.

QUEENY. He won't if they leave him alone.

SAM. Leave him alone! . . . And him looking like God had the shakes when he made it.

QUEENY. Okay! Let's just say I need him.

SAM. You *need* him? That's a new one.

QUEENY. Sure . . . need him.

SAM. What for?

QUEENY. Protection.

SAM. And what about me?

QUEENY. What about you?

SAM. Don't I protect you?

QUEENY. Do you?

SAM. All those years when we was together. Did any man ever get rough with you or beat you up?

QUEENY. No, they never did that.

SAM. So?

QUEENY. So those years are past and better forgotten, and Blackie stays around because it's nice to have a man around.

SAM [*bursting into laughter*]. A man!

QUEENY [*quietly*]. He'll hear you one day, Sam.

SAM. You think I'm frightened?

[*Blackie comes in with the case of liquor from the car. He puts it down and Sam takes over packing away the bottles.*]

BLACKIE [*shuffling up to Queeny*]. I'm going.

QUEENY. Okay.

BLACKIE. It's a good job.

QUEENY. You said that already.

BLACKIE. Don't you want the clock?

QUEENY. If I did I would buy one.

BLACKIE. But I can get this for nothing.

QUEENY. You don't get anything for nothing in this world ... even if you steal it you don't get it for nothing.

BLACKIE. They won't catch me.

QUEENY [*contemptuously*]. They? Who are they? Anyway if they do catch you, tell them to go to hell with my regards.

[*Blackie does not understand. He waits uncertainly for Queeny to say something else ... something he will understand. When she doesn't, he leaves. Sam has finished packing away the liquor. He pours a drink and then joins Queeny.*]

SAM. Did I say enough? You know, you got enough there to start an off-sales. Don't you keep no record of the stuff you get in and what you sell? [*Queeny doesn't think the question worth replying to.*] You know, Queeny, it's all wrong. It goes right against my sense ...

QUEENY. ... of good business.

SAM. *Ja*, that's it. Like I told you ...

QUEENY. You told me once too often, Sam.

SAM. But that's because you won't listen. Now take me and my shop. It's all down in the books. If I want to know how much I'm making, I take up the books and there it is ... in black and white.

[*Sam has got quite excited about the subject of good business. Queeny is looking at him directly.*]

QUEENY. You like your shop, Sam.

SAM. I waited for it a long time, Queeny. You know that. Like you waited for this.

QUEENY. *Ja*, but it's different. You and your shop and me and this.

SAM. Nonsense. In the old days when we were ... you know what I mean ... I used to talk about the shop and you used to talk about having your own shebeen. It was just the same. And we both got what we wanted. I bet if you kept books you'd find you was making more than me.

QUEENY. That only means I'm making good money. It doesn't make anything else the same.

SAM. What else is important?

QUEENY. You haven't changed, Sam.

SAM. If you mean I still believe in this . . . [*rubbing his thumb and forefinger together to indicate money*] you're right. That's the only difference between the full belly I got now and an empty one, between these clothes and rags. And look at you. You got this. What did you have in the old days? This is what we worked for and this is what we got. So let's be happy.

QUEENY. Is it as easy as that?

SAM. What more do you want? Show me another woman around here with half of what you got.

QUEENY. What about the things they got that I haven't?

SAM. Such as?

QUEENY. A man.

SAM. [*bursts into rude laughter*]. Didn't you have enough . . . ? [*A deadly look from Queeny kills the laugh.*] Well you know what I mean. What's the matter with you? A man. You'll be saying a home next, with kids . . . and then you've had it. We got no complaints, Queeny. We live comfortable . . . no attachments . . . We're free . . .

QUEENY. Free!

SAM. Yes, free. Who is telling you what to do or where to go? Nobody.

QUEENY. I might even like that for a change.

SAM. A change?

QUEENY. Yes . . . a change from this. You think this is so very different from the old days? Well let me tell you it's not. You just seen the outside. You don't know what it's really like. I still sit around waiting for the night; I still spend the whole day painting my nails, only now it's not so nice any more 'cause my hands are getting fat . . . Fat and a little more money. But what else? Nothin'. Just wait for the night and the usual crowd so I can take their money off them and get a little more rich and a little more fat. You never thought of it like that, have you, Sam? But you wouldn't know. Even in the old days you didn't know.

SAM. I looked after the money. If it hadn't been for me where would you have been?

QUEENY. In the gutter most likely . . . but who cares? *Ja*, that's something else . . . who cares? Who cares a damn?

SAM. I would.

QUEENY. Sure! You'd shake your head for five minutes and then put somebody else in here 'cause you like your drinks nice and handy.

SAM. You believe that?

QUEENY. Am I wrong?

SAM. After all we been through together?

QUEENY. *You* been through? You don't know half of it. You still don't and you're not getting any wiser.

[*Now at the window.*] When I stand here during the day I can see you in the shop, talking like hell to somebody, getting all excited 'cause there's a chance of selling something. And inside here it's quiet and empty and everything is waiting for the night. When I look at you I think: he's forgotten. Maybe there wasn't so much for *him* to forget. I almost hate you when I think that, Sam, I almost hate you.

SAM. You got the blues bad, Queeny.

QUEENY. Blues? You think I'm going to wake up when tomorrow comes and think life's any better? Anyway, what's it like out there, are they still asking questions?

SAM. You know people: What's her real name? Where does she come from? But they're not getting any wiser.

[*Their conversation is interrupted by a knock on the door. Sam opens it and lets in* Patrick. *The newcomer is about the same age as Sam but has a false-friendly manner and is over-eager to please: the true 'little man'. He is shabbily dressed.*]

PATRICK. Hello, Sam . . . Queeny.

SAM. How's the wife?

PATRICK. [*The expansive smile fades.*] Okay . . . okay . . . It's started.

QUEENY. [*making no attempt to conceal her dislike of the man*]. Shouldn't you be with her?

67

SAM. Leave him alone. Don't you know what a man's like when his wife is having a baby?

QUEENY. If he's the man, the answer is going to be drunk.

SAM. It's a big thing for a man. Patrick just wants a tot to steady his nerves.

PATRICK. *Ja*, that's it. A tot to steady my nerves.

QUEENY. What you got to be nervous about?

SAM. It's his baby.

QUEENY. It's her fifth.

PATRICK [*coming forward hopefully*]. I got a bit of work today, Queeny. I can pay. [*He holds out a few coins in his hand.*]

[*Queeny turns away in disgust at the interpretation he has placed on her reluctance to sell. Patrick is left bewildered. Sam is not so slow. He dips into the outstretched hand and pushes Patrick down into a chair.*]

SAM. Sure you got money. The usual?

PATRICK. *Ja.*

[*Sam serves him with a drink and then comes over to Queeny.*]

SAM. What's the matter with you? He paid.

QUEENY. And his wife?

SAM. He said one drink.

QUEENY. One drink!

SAM. It's not your fault if he doesn't know when to stop.

QUEENY. I'm selling it.

SAM. So you don't sell it? He just goes three houses down and gets it there. You at least sell it to him straight from the bottle. You know how she dilutes. [*Pause.*] It's about time you started as well.

QUEENY. What?

SAM. Diluting. Everybody in this line knows it's legitimate business to dilute a little. These new taxes is making it impossible to give your customers a decent drink at a low price. So you don't want to use water ... methylated spirits! That's got a kick and I can get you as much as you want through the shop. Even I been forced to start. That cheap line of coffee ... any case when you're down to buying that, you expect it.

[*A few memories come back to Sam. He smiles and shakes his head.*]
Water in the liquor! Pea-flour in the coffee! Times have
changed.

QUEENY. People were doing that long before we started.

SAM. I mean us. Me and you. We sure got innocent. Because we
scorched this town. We made them feel they was in hell.

QUEENY. I wasn't so far from feeling that myself at times.

SAM. You don't play with fire without picking up a few blisters.
You know I read somewhere that when the world ends it's
going to be with fire. If that's true you must have been the
prophet of bad times.

QUEENY. Why me?

SAM. You made it hot for a lot of men.

QUEENY. I wasn't the only one.

SAM. I never met another woman that made men sweat like you
did. Anyway, they can always say they had their taste of hell
before dying.

QUEENY. What about me? Do you think it was my taste of
heaven?

SAM. I'm not saying you liked it.

QUEENY. I'm telling you I hated it.

SAM. We went through it together, Queeny. There's no need to
tell me.

QUEENY. I'm not so sure about that any more.

SAM. You're not trying to say I wasn't there with you?

QUEENY. You were there all right. But I haven't learnt how to
laugh it off and call it the good old days; or how to forget it.

PATRICK [*breaking into the conversation*]. Say ... how about
another tot before I go?

[*Sam gets up and fills Patrick's glass. In the ensuing conversation
Queeny goes back to her divan, lights a cigarette, sits down and broods.*]

SAM. What you going to call the kid, Patrick?

PATRICK. You know I been sitting here thinking about that.

SAM [*taking a tot for himself and sitting down*]. Well let's hear the
ideas. I never had no kids myself but I got good ideas.

PATRICK. Well I given it a lot of thought. I'm pretty fussy about names. Take mine now . . . you konw I'm named after one of the disciples?

SAM. Patrick?

PATRICK. *Ja*, the disciple of Ireland. That's what they told me up at the church 'cause they gave me the name.

SAM. I was wondering how you got such a good name.

PATRICK. Well now you know.

SAM. Hey! I got a good idea. Why not call it Patrick . . . after yourself?

PATRICK. And suppose it's a girl?

[*Sam laughs back quietly and flatteringly at the other man's wisdom.*]

SAM. You old . . .

PATRICK. You see you gotta think. Listen, give me another . . . it helps me think.

SAM [*passing the bottle*]. Of course.

QUEENY [*breaking into the conversation*]. You've had enough.

SAM. Look, the man's thinking! There's going to be something out there just now that's going to want a name and Patrick here is finding it. Aren't you?

PATRICK. Just like that.

SAM. So he can go home and walk right in and say hello . . . whatever its name is going to be . . . Isn't that so?

PATRICK. Just so.

SAM [*pouring another tot and taking Patrick's money*]. So we can't call it Patrick.

PATRICK. Nuh. But I think I got one . . . Augustine.

SAM. What's that?

PATRICK. Another disciple.

SAM. You can't have a whole family of disciples . . . and suppose it's a girl?

PATRICK. I'm prepared. Augustina!

SAM [*with a wry face and sceptically*]. Augustina? That's a mouthful.

PATRICK [*the look of triumph fading; uncertainly*]. You think so?

SAM. Of course. Go on, try it...go on...Try calling August...whatever it is, aloud. Go on.

PATRICK [*opening his mouth, then abandoning the attempt*]. *Ja*, maybe you're right.

SAM. You want something short and snappy... 'cause that's modern. You take the names of things today, like...Let me see...Jik. [*Repeats it.*]...Jik.

PATRICK [*incredulous*]. Jik?

SAM. *Ja*...that stuff that cleans...Or Coke...there's another one. I'm not suggesting you call the kid after a cold drink, but think along those lines. This Augustina stuff is out.

[*A knock at the door interrupts the discussion between the two men. Sam gets up and goes to the door, opens it and peers out. A few words are spoken, including a very loud 'What?' from Sam, who turns back to Queeny.*]

SAM. Will you please come and tell somebody that we don't serve coffee?

[*Queeny looks up, for a moment not realizing who is outside. When she does, she stands up, unbelievingly. All trace of boredom has vanished. Sam goes back to his chair and watches the next few minutes from that position. Queeny lets Johnny in.*]

JOHNNY. I missed my bus, so I thought I'd take that cup of coffee after all.

QUEENY. Sure...sure...sit down. I'll put the kettle on. [*Moves to the kitchen door, pauses.*] How did it go? [*She goes into the kitchen.*]

JOHNNY [*calling after her*]. You was right. I didn't sell any more.

SAM. What?

JOHNNY. Table cloths.

SAM. Table cloths!

JOHNNY. I sell table cloths. [*Seeing the table is uncovered, he looks for the one he sold Queeny.*] Where's the one I sold her? [*He finds it in a corner.*]

SAM [*surprise turning into veiled resentment and dislike; it is obvious that these two are not going to like each other*]. What do you think you are going to do with that?

JOHNNY [*ignoring the tone*]. Put it on the table. I sold it to her 'cause this table was getting marks from all the glasses.

SAM [*sarcastic*]. Now isn't that a pity?

JOHNNY. It is. It's a good table.

SAM [*turning back to Patrick, deliberately ignoring Johnny*]. Well, we're having a private conversation.

JOHNNY [*refusing to be ignored*]. Aren't you used to table cloths or something?

SAM [*nettled*]. Look, I don't know who you are, where you come from or what you do ...

JOHNNY. Name's Johnny, I come from Alex and I sell table cloths. And you?

SAM. A friend ... a very good friend.

JOHNNY. In that case I don't see how you can mind me putting this on the table.

[*There is a dangerous little moment that could easily become nasty, but for Queeny's entrance into the room. Seeing Johnny with the red table cloth in his hand she comes up apologetically.*]

QUEENY. Oh yes, the table cloth ... I hadn't put it on 'cause I wanted to clean the table proper first. But I'll do it now. [*She takes a rag, forces the men to lift their glasses, wipes the table off and then puts the cloth down.*]

JOHNNY. Looks good, doesn't it?

SAM. Looks like any other table cloth to me ... and not such a good line at that.

JOHNNY. I never said it cost much ... I don't charge much.

QUEENY. Who says that's important? It matches in with everything else like you said.

SAM. Sounds like you two had a long talk about table cloths.

[*Queeny doesn't answer, but the look she gives him is warning enough. He shuts up, pours himself another tot. Patrick also gets a drink. Queeny turns her attention to Johnny. There is a small embarrassed pause.*]

QUEENY. Sit down while you're waiting for the coffee. It won't be long ... [*Johnny sits.*] Or maybe you're in a hurry to get home?

JOHNNY. Should I be?

QUEENY. Folks waiting for you . . . wife maybe?

JOHNNY. I got nobody.

QUEENY. You look the sort.

JOHNNY. What sort is that?

QUEENY. Wife and kids . . . maybe a home.

JOHNNY. Why do you say that?

QUEENY. You just do. I seen them before . . . people trying to do something with their lives.

JOHNNY. Aren't you?

QUEENY [*laughing*]. You say the damndest things.

JOHNNY. Well . . .

QUEENY. Let's say, I'm hanging on to what I got.

JOHNNY. Maybe making it a bit bigger as well.

QUEENY [*laughing quietly*]. *Ja.* That's not much, is it?

JOHNNY. Depends. I knew a fellow once . . . had a horse and an old cart . . . people used to laugh at him 'cause he didn't make much and what he had he always spent on the horse and the cart. Sometimes he went without supper just so the horse could eat! Everyone thought he was mad but he carried on like they wasn't there. One day I asked him: Joe, why don't you sell that horse and buy yourself some good clothes and eat well for a month. He looked at me: What do I do after the month? Get a job, I said, like everybody else. He shook his head: Johnny, you're asking me to sell my freedom for a good meal and clothes. I thought a lot about what he said. That horse meant nobody could call him 'boy', or say do this or that. He was his own boss. Maybe it's like that with you.

QUEENY [*thoughtfully*]. I got a little money. That's all I'm hanging on to.

JOHNNY. That's a big word.

QUEENY. What?

JOHNNY. Money. It could mean security, three meals a day, a roof over your head and independence . . . like Joe.

QUEENY. And you?

73

JOHNNY. Me?

QUEENY. *Ja*, you. What you doing?

JOHNNY. Same as Joe.

QUEENY. Horse and cart.

JOHNNY. No, my own boss.

QUEENY. How long you been like that?

JOHNNY. Off and on. I'd hoped these table cloths would be my real break. If I'd made some money I was going to try something good.

QUEENY. What was that?

JOHNNY. What's the use. [*Gesturing towards the suitcase.*] They haven't sold. I'll be looking for a job on Monday.

QUEENY. You're not going to like that.

JOHNNY. Would you? Get a couple of quid a month so somebody can kick you around and feel like a white man. Old Joe was right.

SAM. [*He has been listening to the conversation, now breaks in.*] What's old Joe going to do when the horse dies? Make biltong? [*Laughter.*]

QUEENY [*annoyed*]. Can't you keep your mouth shut, Sam?

SAM. I'm just interested in old Joe. No harm in asking.

JOHNNY. Joe died before the horse.

SAM. Too bad, too bad . . . Would have been nice to know what he would have done. It's also bad about old Joe dying, of course. But that's not exactly progress, is it? Dying with only a horse and cart, and maybe just dying before the horse 'cause that was also getting old.

QUEENY. What you trying to do, Sam?

SAM. Just joining in a conversation, Queeny. Of course if it was private . . .

QUEENY. Maybe it is.

SAM. Okay. I'll be back when it's not so crowded. [*Sam goes out.*]

QUEENY. Don't pay no attention to him.

JOHNNY. Me pay attention to him? It was the other way around. Is he your partner?

QUEENY. Just a friend. He's got the shop across the street. Comes in here for his drinks.

JOHNNY. And that chap I saw this afternoon? The hunchback.

QUEENY. You mean Blackie.

JOHNNY. That's the name.

QUEENY. Also a friend. [*Johnny just nods his head.*] You're thinking I got strange friends.

JOHNNY. Maybe. I don't know much about shebeens.

QUEENY. Blackie's not the same as Sam. He's ugly, all right . . . but then he was born that way. He didn't choose it. If he was straight I think he would have been a good man. But being crooked like that nobody has given him a chance.

JOHNNY. He's got a good friend.

QUEENY. Me? I don't know. A lot of kids was teasing him one day, I watched it through the window. What got me was the big people standing around doing nothing . . . Some of them was smiling, they thought it funny. I went out and swore the whole lot of them into hell. I just wanted them to stop, that's all. But Blackie hung around. For two days he just sat outside there on the pavement watching me come and go. Every time I looked out of the window he was sitting there. So I called him in and gave him some food . . . he's been hanging around ever since.

I'll get that coffee.

[*Queeny goes into her kitchen. Patrick, disturbed by the sudden silence, looks up from his glass and sees Johnny. Patrick is drunk.*]

PATRICK. Edward.

JOHNNY. What?

PATRICK. And if it's a girl . . . Edwina.

JOHNNY. Who's that?

PATRICK. My kid.

JOHNNY. You got a kid?

PATRICK [*an edge of despair and cynicism to his words*]. Have I got a kid! [*Lifting his glass.*] This is my fifth . . . Kid, I mean. This is my fifth kid and it should be here by now. I been sitting here trying to find a decent name for it 'cause that's all I'm ever likely to give it. That's not much, huh?

JOHNNY. Why don't you go back to your wife?

PATRICK. You think I'm drunk. Maybe I am. But I only meant to have one. You see this is my fifth ... Child, I mean, it's my fifth child. When you already got four and another comes along ... I dunno ... it's sort of too much. You sort of sit here and wish it wasn't coming and that is a hell of a start for it, isn't it? I only wanted one drink but when I got to thinking like that, I had another to try and stop myself. And now I'm saying I wish it wasn't coming. You got kids?

JOHNNY. No.

PATRICK. Don't.

JOHNNY. Why?

PATRICK. It's hell. In every way it's hell. You know they should make it that we blacks can't have babies ... 'cause hell they made it so we can't give them no chances when they come. They just about made it so we can't live. But with babies it's hell! They cry, you don't get no sleep, they need things ... and they suck the old woman dry. God, she's a wreck. And she was a woman. I mean I wouldn't have married her if she wasn't. You see what I mean, don't you?

[*Patrick accidentally spills his drink over Johnny.*] How did that happen?

JOHNNY. It's okay.

PATRICK. Hell ... I'm sorry ...

JOHNNY. Forget it.

[*Queeny comes in with coffee.*]

QUEENY. What happened?

JOHNNY. Just an accident.

QUEENY. Him?

JOHNNY. Forget it.

QUEENY [*to Patrick*]. You messy little bastard.

PATRICK. We was just having a chat and I ...

QUEENY. And as usual you didn't know when to stop.

JOHNNY. Forget it, Queeny. It's an old jacket.

QUEENY. First you mess up your own life and then you want to make a mess of everybody else's.

PATRICK. I paid you.

QUEENY. Get the hell out of here.

PATRICK. Okay.

QUEENY. Get out.

JOHNNY. Easy, Queeny, it was just an accident.

QUEENY. Keep out of this, Johnny.

JOHNNY. I don't see why I must. He spilt it over me.

QUEENY. Are you standing up for him?

JOHNNY. I'm standing up for nobody.

QUEENY. Then keep out of it. [*To Patrick.*] I said get out.

JOHNNY. Have a heart, Queeny.

QUEENY. With trash like him?

JOHNNY. His money was all right wasn't it?

[*Sam comes in.*]

SAM. One of your kids outside, Patrick. Says the baby's arrived. They want you over at your place.

[*Patrick stands up unsteadily. Sam, having poured himself a drink, turns his attention to Patrick.*]

SAM. What you going to call it?

[*Patrick has a glass in one hand, the other in his pocket. He takes out the latter and looks at it. It holds the last of the money he brought in with him . . . a sixpence.*]

PATRICK. Sixpence.

SAM. Sixpence! Hey, that's good.

[*Patrick lifts his glass to his lips. He doesn't drink. Sam's laugh releases his pent-up bitterness. He smashes the glass to the floor and moves to the door.*]

QUEENY. Wait!

[*Patrick stops, turns. Queeny is sorting out the money on the table.*]

Here is every penny you spent here tonight. [*She throws a handful of coins at Patrick's feet. He bends down and picks them up.*] Take it and get out . . . and don't come back!

[*Patrick exits.*]

SAM [*who has watched Queeny's last actions with disbelief*]. What's this? Hand-out time at the mission?

[*Queeny doesn't answer.*]

You going mad or something? He didn't give you back the drinks he bought.

QUEENY [*to Johnny*]. You satisfied?

JOHNNY. Why ask me?

QUEENY. You made me do it.

JOHNNY. I didn't say anything.

QUEENY. Okay, you didn't say anything, but you made me do it. I could see it written all over your face, the 'good' looking at the 'bad'. I lived with that look too long not to know it.

JOHNNY. Shall I go?

QUEENY. No! Please . . . I don't know what's got into me.

SAM. And neither do I. If that's how you're going to carry on we might as well . . .

QUEENY. It was my money, Sam, and this is my place. It's got nothing to do with you.

[*These words stop Sam. It is the first time Queeny has ever thrown his words back in his face. He drops back to a chair against the wall and watches developments.*]

QUEENY. [*to Johnny*]. I been getting sick of it lately. It's not much of a life is it?

JOHNNY. You know.

QUEENY. [*She fetches a broom and sweeps up the pieces of broken glass.*] Well, it's not. I'm telling you it's not. It doesn't mean anything when you get your money from bums like him . . . Not if that's the only way you've ever got money . . . selling something that he's ashamed of or . . . you're ashamed of. I know what he felt like when he smashed that glass. 'If only it was my life lying in pieces on the floor.' Just sweep them away and start all over again. But you're stuck with it . . . him, me . . . Blackie . . . There's somebody else who wouldn't mind taking it apart and putting it together again, with a few improvements. But where do you start? You think I'm mad?

78

JOHNNY. Just never heard a woman talk like that before.

QUEENY. And it sounds crazy.

JOHNNY. It sounds like sense.

QUEENY. *Ja?*

JOHNNY. I know what you mean. I also felt like that.

QUEENY. You?

JOHNNY. I'm no different.

QUEENY. You're not like Patrick.

JOHNNY. I'm younger, that's all. When he was my age...

QUEENY. No, Johnny, when you're his age you'll be different. It's like I said, you're trying to do something with your life. Me? I'm in business because I got some money and there's plenty of bums like Patrick. But what else could I do?

JOHNNY. Sell table cloths.

QUEENY. You're laughing at yourself.

JOHNNY. It's a joke, isn't it? I'm the man who's doing something with his life and the first thing I try... nothing doing. My own boss but I'll be looking for a job on Monday.

QUEENY. No use talking like that. So the first thing you tried didn't work? You just got to try something else.

JOHNNY. Such as?

QUEENY. Medicines! There's something everybody buys. Try selling that.

JOHNNY. It wouldn't be the same. It's not just a question of selling something. I... never mind.

QUEENY. Go on.

JOHNNY. It's another funny story.

QUEENY. I didn't laugh at the last one.

JOHNNY. Well, you see, I just don't want to sell. I'm not a salesman. In fact it's hard for me to sell... you saw that yourself this morning. I want to start my own business.

QUEENY. Doing what?

JOHNNY. I worked with a white chap who was an interior decorator. You know what that is? [*Queeny shakes her head.*] It's got to do with the way you fix up your house. The interior decorator gives you ideas about what you must buy, and how you must match things. Like this table cloth . . . Remember me saying the red one? . . . that it's your colour . . . well that's interior decorating on a sort of small scale. I mean I would only operate on a small scale 'cause our people just don't have the money to do it in a big way. I was actually going to concentrate on one line, materials . . . You know, curtains, bedspreads, cushion covers . . . that sort of thing.

QUEENY. Sounds like you'd need a bit of money to get started.

JOHNNY. No. I thought of a great idea. The big factories that make materials sell a lot of bits and pieces cheap . . . sometimes there's something small wrong with it or maybe it's just a piece left over. But they let it go cheap. I was going to buy a lot of that and sell it with my ideas. You see I got a feeling for matching things . . . the white chap told me. I'd come to a house and give the woman ideas. Like . . . take this room. You see that window? Yellow curtains! What that window needs is yellow curtains. This is a dark room and that colour would liven things up. It would go with your table cloth. And next month when I come around again you take something with yellow and red for your bed . . . and cushions with red in them. Can you see the difference?

QUEENY. [genuinely pleased]. You got good ideas, Johnny.

JOHNNY. You see, it's important, Queeny . . . trying to make life better. I'm not saying my idea is going to change the world, but maybe it will give us a bit more guts, and make waking up tomorrow a little bit easier. You said you were getting sick of life the way it is . . . so why don't you start changing things? You could start with this room.

QUEENY. What's wrong with it?

JOHNNY. Nothing . . . if you got no complaints. But you sounded like you had plenty. So you put up those yellow curtains . . . a vase with some flowers on this table . . . a little mat at the door so that nobody starts tramping mud into the room.

QUEENY. I think I'd like that.

JOHNNY. Of course you would. And you'd start getting proud . . . and *then* let anybody try leaving marks on your table, or on your cloth, or messing up your floor.

QUEENY. I'm your first customer, Johnny. When do you start?

JOHNNY. When? Looks like never. The table cloths. Remember the table cloths? I sold one today ... to you. They were supposed to be my start. If I'd sold them I would have had ten quid ...

QUEENY. Ten pounds? Is that enough?

JOHNNY. I tell you I checked. I went down to the factory and saw what I could have bought with ten quid. There was more than I could have carried away. But they haven't sold.

QUEENY. You're not going to let that stop you?

JOHNNY. They didn't sell. There's nothing I can do about that.

QUEENY. Get your money somewhere else.

JOHNNY. Where?

QUEENY. [*after a pause*]. Me.

JOHNNY. You?

QUEENY. Why not?

JOHNNY. Why? ... Why? Because it's just silly, that's why.

QUEENY. Why is it silly?

JOHNNY. Look, don't you be silly as well.

QUEENY. Well, tell me why you can't borrow ten quid from me.

JOHNNY. Because it's ten quid.

QUEENY. I take that much in here on a bad night.

JOHNNY. Because you never saw me before today.

QUEENY. I trust you.

JOHNNY. Because you don't know if the idea is worth anything at all.

QUEENY. We'll never answer that one without first trying.

JOHNNY. Look, Queeny, just drop it. I didn't come in here for that.

QUEENY. I'm not saying you did. You didn't ask me. I offered.

JOHNNY. No.

QUEENY. Johnny ... suppose I want to. Suppose I really want to.

JOHNNY. But why? You're making better money here than I will ever get from selling rags.

81

QUEENY. You saw how. Did you like what you saw? Answer me.

JOHNNY. [*Pause.*] No.

QUEENY. And you talked a lot about changing things. Give me a chance.

JOHNNY. But if it doesn't work . . . I can't pay you back.

QUEENY. Ten pounds isn't going to break me, Johnny. In any case I want to be your partner . . . I want to be part of it. You got the idea, I give the money. That's fair isn't it?

[*Johnny is beginning to waver.*]

JOHNNY. It might work.

QUEENY. Of course it would. When I heard your ideas I thought they was good. I would have bought. Other women will be the same.

JOHNNY. I've worked it out at fifty per cent profit.

QUEENY. That's good legitimate business.

JOHNNY. And there's big possibilities . . . I mean for expansion.

QUEENY. *Ja?*

JOHNNY. Sure. To begin with, I'd sell the material myself, going from door to door. But if it catches on and the profit is like I said . . . well, we'd build up a big stock and that could mean a shop.

QUEENY. With them coming to us.

JOHNNY. You've got the idea.

QUEENY. A shop . . . with counters, and all the stuff behind . . . And a name! We got to have a name for the shop.

JOHNNY. We'd find one.

[*At this point the street door opens quietly and Blackie comes in. He is holding a clock. During the ensuing scene he tries with small furtive gestures to catch Queeny's attention. It is obviously her clock, but in the excitement of her talk with Johnny she does not see him.*]

QUEENY. We'd open it up at nine in the morning. That's the time any decent shop opens, and we'd be busy with all the customers coming and going and at five o'clock we'd close up, count up our money and think about tomorrow. You know something?

JOHNNY. What?

QUEENY. We'd be respectable.

JOHNNY. There's nothing to be ashamed of.

QUEENY. Johnny, it's the best thing I've ever heard of. When do we start?

JOHNNY. Well ... look Queeny, don't you want to think about it for a day or so ... ?

[*Her answer is to go to the sideboard, take out her money box, count out ten notes and put them on the table in front of Johnny.*]

QUEENY. There. I thought about it and that's my answer.

JOHNNY. Right now?

QUEENY. Take advice from somebody who knows ... don't waste time or chances. Now. Tomorrow's pay day around here. Get your material in the morning and sell in the afternoon. That's when the women get back with their men's pay. [*Johnny still hesitates.*] Take it! If we don't start now maybe we will never.

JOHNNY. I can be down at the factory first thing and then come here when I got the material.

QUEENY. I'll be waiting.

JOHNNY. I can't believe it.

QUEENY. Do you think I can? Nothing like this has happened to me before.

JOHNNY. I'm going. [*Takes his suitcase.*] I'll leave these cloths and try and sell them as well, but the suitcase I need for the material.

QUEENY. Buy big, Johnny.

JOHNNY. You leave that to me [*He is at the door.*] Thanks, Queeny.

QUEENY. Till tomorrow.

[*Johnny exits. She watches the door close behind him, her face shining and happy.*]

QUEENY. Sam ...

SAM. You gone mad or something?

QUEENY. [*ignoring the remark*]. Sam, you got yellow material?

SAM. Look, I don't know what was in that coffee, but sober up, will you! You just let ten quid walk out of your life without even a farewell tear.

QUEENY. It will be back. Now how about that yellow material?

SAM. Look, Queeny, I'm being serious. That was ten quid we worked for.

QUEENY. I worked for.

SAM. Okay! So I just don't like seeing a friend lose it. You think you going to see it or that rag-bag man again?

QUEENY. Tomorrow.

SAM. Queeny! I've also tried that racket.

QUEENY. That was you. This is Johnny.

SAM. Will you wake up!!

QUEENY. I have! And for the first time in my life. I've woken up to something that looks like it might be fun and nice and clean. And don't shout at me, Sam. Material . . . yellow material. You got some?

SAM. Okay, if you don't mind making a fool of yourself and losing ten quid . . .

QUEENY. Yellow material!!!

SAM. [*irritably*]. Sure I got yellow material. I got everything.

QUEENY. I want some. Enough for curtains.

SAM. I'll send it over in the morning.

QUEENY. I want it now.

SAM. Now . . . ?

QUEENY. Yes, now! Fetch it. I'll use as much as I want and give you back the rest. Well, what are you waiting for?

[*Sam leaves. Queeny has in the meantime managed to get down the curtains. Blackie, alone with her at last, comes forward. She bumps into him.*]

QUEENY. Blackie! What have you got there?

[*Blackie says nothing, just holds up the clock.*]

I told you I didn't want it. Go give it to Sam to sell.

[*Blackie is still holding the clock outstretched as Queeny returns to her work at the curtains. She is humming softly. The clock in Blackie's hand begins to chime.*]

CURTAIN

ACT TWO

Scene 1

Queeny's shebeen the next morning. It is empty. The room has changed ... yellow curtains, table cloth, and a vase of flowers. After a few seconds Blackie, still carrying his clock, comes in through the street door.

QUEENY. [*from the kitchen*]. That you, Johnny?

[*Queeny enters from the other room. Her excitement dies when she sees that it is only Blackie.*]

BLACKIE. Nobody else got one what sings like the church. Listen!

[*He moves the hands of the clock and it begins to chime.*]

QUEENY. Which way did you come?

BLACKIE. Along the street.

QUEENY. Did you see the chap who was here last night?

BLACKIE. Him?

QUEENY. Yes, him. Did you see him?

BLACKIE. No. Sam said he wasn't going to come.

QUEENY. Sam says everything.

BLACKIE. Sam says ...

QUEENY. I'm sick of hearing what Sam says. What's the time? [*Blackie lifts up the clock for her to see.*] That thing's crazy. Why do you carry it around if it don't tell the time?

BLACKIE. But you don't listen. [*He moves the hands again.*]

QUEENY. [*impatiently*]. I've heard it once and it doesn't change it's tune.

BLACKIE. Why you shouting at me? I done nothing.

QUEENY. [*collecting herself*]. I'm jumpy this morning.

BLACKIE. You remember what I said! I do anything for you if you don't shout or laugh at me.

QUEENY. Okay, Blackie! [*Pause during which she looks around the room desperately.*] Let's do something. These curtains ... ja ... maybe there's still time for that. Give me a hand.

[*With Blackie's assistance she gets down the old curtain around the divan. She proceeds to sew on extra rings.*]

QUEENY. Why you staring at me like that?

BLACKIE. You doing that for him.

QUEENY. What's so strange about sewing a few rings onto a curtain?

BLACKIE. You never done it before.

QUEENY. So I'm doing it now.

BLACKIE. You never done no sewing or fixing up like this before.

QUEENY. You said that already. Don't always repeat yourself. It's a bad habit you got. My hearing's all right.

BLACKIE. This chap...is he going to make you like other women?

QUEENY. What do you mean? I am a woman.

[Sam *enters from the street.*]

QUEENY. What's the time, Sam?

SAM. [*chuckling*]. So you're getting worried.

QUEENY. The time, Sam.

SAM [*speaking very deliberately*]. He's half an hour late already...according to my reckoning. And I've been generous. I had him out of bed at eight...which you must admit is not too early for a man starting off on a new business venture...I gave him half an hour from Alex to town...might have missed the first bus...half an hour choosing his goods and half an hour coming out here and another half just in case he stopped over somewhere. That makes ten...which it was half an hour ago. Of course there could, as they say, be a weak link in the chain. And according to my acquaintance with human nature the weak link in this case is the first one. That getting out of bed at eight part. Do you really think he's going to swap a crisp ten quid for a heap of rags? If you do you're not the same woman that cleaned up this town with me. Ten quid on rags! Like I told you, it's an old racket.

More likely than not he's lying nice and comfortable in bed right now, thinking about spending that money. Don't forget it's not every day that you can pick up ten quid like that. [*Clicking his fingers.*] However, old Sam never deserts a friend. When you get around to waking up, send this yellow stuff back and I'll sell it for you . . . make it a fancy line and double the price. That way we should get your loss down to about nine quid.

QUEENY. If you so much as touch those curtains you'll never come in here again.

SAM. I was only trying to do you a favour. Of course they don't look too bad now you come to think of it. Maybe he did have a few good ideas after all. Pity he wasn't straight.

QUEENY. What I said about touching those curtains goes for your mouth as well . . . Say something else like that . . .

SAM. When are you going to wake up, Queeny?

QUEENY. I woke up last night, Sam, and don't ask too many questions, otherwise I'm going to tell you what some things look like now that I got my eyes open.

SAM. Okay, I'll shut up. [*Picks a flower for his buttonhole.*] Anyway, what is ten quid on pay day? Maybe I'm being a little tight.

QUEENY. With my money.

SAM. You're my friend. I just don't want you to turn around and say I let you down. I never done it in the old days.

QUEENY. The only reason you never let me down is because we were already at the bottom. Anyway I don't want no more talk about the old days . . . not to me or anybody else.

SAM. I get you [*turning to go*]. [*He pauses at the door.*] But don't forget them.

QUEENY. Why?

SAM. So you don't expect what you didn't buy. None of our customers thought they was getting a wife for our price. You paid ten quid last night for a small kick and nothing else.

BLACKIE [*shuffling forward to Queeny; it is obvious that she is upset*]. You want me to go to Alex and get your money? I'll find him and bring it back. Okay?

QUEENY. Get out.

BLACKIE. Tonight I'll . . .

QUEENY. Just leave me alone.

[*Blackie takes up his clock and goes. A few seconds later the door, which was left slightly ajar, swings open and Johnny comes in carrying his suitcase.*]

QUEENY [*not looking around*]. I told you to get out!

JOHNNY. It wasn't me you told.

QUEENY. Johnny!

JOHNNY. That's your man, plus the finest selection of material any township has ever seen.

QUEENY. Johnny!

JOHNNY. You been crying or something?

QUEENY. I thought you wasn't coming.

JOHNNY. And you cried? Well you can stop 'cause I'm here and just take a look at this.

[*He opens his suitcase. A flood of coloured material spills out onto the floor. For Queeny it is a moment of release which starts with a gasp of surprise.*]

And you wanted to know if ten pounds was enough? Well there's all this and I still got two quid in my pocket. But take a good look at the colours. Red . . .

QUEENY. Blue . . . green . . .

JOHNNY. Yellow . . . purple . . .

QUEENY. You brought in the rainbow, man!

JOHNNY. And the sizes . . . see this one.

QUEENY [*taking a large length of red from his hands and draping it round her*]. My colour, Johnny.

JOHNNY. That's a curtain you're wearing . . . and what about this for a bed? And cushions to match!

QUEENY. I never seen so much colour.

JOHNNY. How does it make you feel?

QUEENY. Excited.

JOHNNY. Well, don't be scared. Come on, touch it . . . get the feel of it, you'll be handling a lot.

QUEENY. You really think so, Johnny?

JOHNNY. Now that I actually see it I say we can't go wrong. You know when I was walking up the street with this material the women came out of their houses to see what I had. They wanted to buy it there and then. I got two names already. I got to be there this afternoon when they get back with their men's pay . . . and let me tell you they are going to buy. I got scared last night when you offered me the money so suddenly. But now! This is what I've been waiting for, Queeny. I got so many ideas up here my head is bursting. Number one. The place that sold me this also sells feathers and fluff for cushions, you buy it by the box. So we are going to make the cushions complete ourselves. You got a sewing machine?

QUEENY. No. But I can buy one.

JOHNNY. No. You've given your share. The machine comes out of the profits . . . maybe in a month or so. Then you can do some stitching while I'm out selling.

QUEENY. I don't know how to sew.

JOHNNY. So you learn. Other women can, you can. You're the same as them.

QUEENY. Say that again.

JOHNNY. I said you're like the other women. Anything wrong?

QUEENY. Nothing. Nothing at all. I just wanted to hear you say it.

JOHNNY. Now to work.

QUEENY. But you just come in. Aren't you tired? Carrying all that?

JOHNNY. Tired today?

QUEENY. But breakfast. I got something cooking.

JOHNNY. Okay. Bring it in.

[*Queeny goes to the kitchen to fetch his breakfast. Johnny starts sorting out his material.*]

QUEENY [*from the other room*]. When you going to start?

JOHNNY. Straight after I've eaten. This is make-or-break day for me, and I want to know which it is.

QUEENY [*in the doorway*]. Nothing could break today, Johnny. Even if you came home with nothing sold.

JOHNNY. Hey, don't say that!

QUEENY. It's just that I'm so happy.

JOHNNY. We might have something to celebrate tonight.

QUEENY. I got to think about that.

JOHNNY. What?

QUEENY. Our celebration.

JOHNNY. Here?

QUEENY. Of course.

JOHNNY. But isn't this your big night? Pay day?

QUEENY. What do you mean?

JOHNNY. The shebeen.

QUEENY. I'd forgotten.

JOHNNY. There's big money in it. You said so yourself last night.

QUEENY. Big money. [*With bitterness.*] Did you have to remind me?

JOHNNY. We can celebrate tomorrow.

QUEENY. No. This is our day, and I'm not going to let a lot of bums bugger it up. You saw what it was like last night. Tonight's going to be worse. The whole place full of them! . . . moaning and slobbering until it drives you mad.

JOHNNY. Take it easy.

QUEENY. Take it easy! I've taken it far too long and it hasn't been easy. And I'm not taking it tonight. Johnny, the shebeen can go to hell tonight.

JOHNNY. These fellows are your customers. That's not good business.

QUEENY. Don't talk like Sam.

JOHNNY. Sam's got a point there if you want to keep the shebeen.

QUEENY. And what if I don't?

[*Johnny is stuck for words. Queeny comes up to him. She picks up a piece of material to emphasize her next point.*]

We've started this haven't we? Maybe . . .

JOHNNY. Maybe it doesn't work.

QUEENY. It will.

JOHNNY. But suppose . . .

QUEENY. It's going to, Johnny.

JOHNNY. Please! I'm asking you to give me a chance. I'll go out there just now and do my damnedest to sell . . . but don't make me scared to come back. Let's just see how it goes.

QUEENY. But this is our day, Johnny. Look, just for tonight. I'll tell them the police raided me. If I got to start selling again tomorrow, okay. But I can't tonight. Please, Johnny.

JOHNNY. It's your business, Queeny.

QUEENY. You can sell those and leave the rest to me.

[*Johnny cannot argue. She goes back to the kitchen, re-enters with food, and lays it out on the table.*]

QUEENY. Okay.

JOHNNY. You know, I am hungry. When you're excited like this you don't get time to think about food.

QUEENY. That's my job.

JOHNNY. Cooking for me?

QUEENY. I like it. You know I never cooked for any man before?

JOHNNY. Nobody has done any cooking for me.

QUEENY. No one?

JOHNNY. That's what I said.

QUEENY. Your girl friend?

JOHNNY. Never had one.

QUEENY. You're joking.

JOHNNY. I'm not.

QUEENY. Why?

JOHNNY. I've never looked for one.

QUEENY. When you get around to it, what are you going to look for?

JOHNNY. Lots of things.

QUEENY. Tell me.

JOHNNY. She's going to be clean.

QUEENY [*laughing*]. Clean.

JOHNNY. Live and think clean! You can always wash your hands, or your face or your feet. But your mind? Could you wash that if you got to thinking dirt or living like it? I touched real filth once . . . never again!

QUEENY. You had it tough, Johnny?

JOHNNY. No more nor less than anybody else with a black skin. The trouble is a little means so damned much if you think and feel a lot. But there I go talking about my troubles. Tell me about yourself, Queeny. You know I don't even know your real name.

QUEENY. Rose.

JOHNNY. Why do you run away from it?

QUEENY. Who said anything about running away?

JOHNNY. Well, why did you drop it?

QUEENY. People started calling me Queeny. It stuck.

JOHNNY. I'm going to call you Rose.

QUEENY. Don't.

JOHNNY. It's as good as Queeny.

QUEENY. Please, Johnny, don't.

JOHNNY. Okay.

QUEENY. Just let's say I like Queeny better.

JOHNNY. You been here long?

QUEENY. Four or five years. Does that sound long? Maybe it is. But there's been nothing in it . . . nothing I couldn't tell you in one minute. I got fatter, certainly richer, but there's nothing else. You know what's the secret of keeping alive?

JOHNNY. You tell me.

QUEENY. It's to keep wanting things.

JOHNNY. Then I got a long life ahead of me.

QUEENY. That's what I mean. You'll always be doing things, thinking up new ideas, and that's going to keep you going. Me? I just rolled over and died.

JOHNNY. Isn't there anything you want, Queeny?

QUEENY. There is now. But there was a time I thought I had all I wanted when I got this. But when I had it, that was the end. There's been times I never knew what day it was in here . . . and I never needed to know. I'd wake up and think is it Monday or Tuesday, maybe Friday? It didn't make any difference. Giving it a name didn't make it any different from the rest.

I worked too hard and waited too long for this. That is where I made my mistake. Since I was a kid and my father used to drink his pay packet down on a Friday night while we waited hungry at home . . . since those days I said to myself, 'One day you'll have a shebeen and get fat.' Strange the things kids think, huh?

JOHNNY. How many in the family?

QUEENY. Six of us when my mother died. It might have been different if she'd stayed alive. She was one of those people who . . . well, like you say, lived clean. We was so poor we didn't even have any rubbish, but she swept out that room as if it was filthy. When she died I got out.

JOHNNY. The others?

QUEENY. I don't know. I still ask myself that one. You see I was the oldest, the youngest was still drinking from my mother. I should have stayed and tried to help them . . . I mean you know what kids are like, small, helpless, hungry. Now you know something about me. Not so good, is it?

JOHNNY. You mean running away?

QUEENY. And leaving the others.

JOHNNY. You was a kid.

QUEENY. I try to tell myself that, but it doesn't always work. Like you said, you can't wash your mind as easily as your hands. [*Pause.*] But if somebody tried hard enough, could they? . . . Wash off something from the past?

JOHNNY. Depends on the person, I guess.

QUEENY. And other people.

JOHNNY. Why them?

QUEENY. If you were trying to forget something, but others kept reminding you of it . . . wouldn't work, would it?

JOHNNY. [*Pause.*] You may have had it rough, Queeny, but I had my face rubbed in dirt. I know what it smells like, what it tastes like. That's how close I was to it and that's why I hate it. I was a kid. Seventeen years old. It was the big story about the mines. The good food, the clean rooms, the money. My parents bought that one all right. Money! So I came here, ten years ago. I stood just one year in that place. A fellow can't take more. Did you hear what I said? I said a fellow can't take more.

QUEENY. Okay, Johnny, I heard you.

JOHNNY. You might have heard me okay, but do you know what I mean? There's no women in those compounds and they don't let you out. There's big bursting men in those compounds and there's no women. So they take the boys, the young ones, like me. That's what they take.

QUEENY. Okay, Johnny.

JOHNNY. Stop saying that, because it's not okay. It's like dogs, see.

QUEENY. Johnny!

JOHNNY. Yes, dogs, or something else that crawls around the garbage cans or the gutter. Something dirty! I've tried to wash it off, Queeny. I've tried. Every day, I try. But there is always something around that brings it back. Like that bus ride in from Alex this morning. It was hell. It was crowded with men, big men. I could feel the violence in their bodies. Like the nights in the compound when they sat around and spoke about women and got all worked up until... [*Pause. He moves to the suitcase and materials.*] So here we go.

QUEENY. It's the start, Johnny... the clean start. Yours as well as mine. And I still say they look like the rainbow.

JOHNNY [*picking up one piece of material*]. The colours are good...

QUEENY [*mimicking his sales talk.*] And they won't run.

JOHNNY [*laughing*]. Maybe you should also sell?

QUEENY. Not today... I got to prepare for our celebration.

JOHNNY. I'd better start selling and give us something to celebrate.

[*As they get down to business, the old enthusiasm comes back slowly.*]
I'm not going to take it all . . . just a few pieces. We'll see how it goes with them. If I need the others I'll come back.

QUEENY. You got the address of the two women?

JOHNNY. Right here.

QUEENY. What time do you think you'll be back?

JOHNNY. About five.

QUEENY. If I'm not here just make yourself at home.

JOHNNY. While you're about it, find out the price of a good sewing machine . . . who knows?

[*The door opens and Sam comes in.*]

QUEENY [*Watching him inspect the materials*]. Well? [*A note of triumph in her voice.*]

SAM [*giving Queeny a quick look but directing his attention to Johnny*]. So you mean to try it?

QUEENY [*pointing to materials*]. Would that be here if we wasn't?

JOHNNY. That's about it. You look doubtful.

QUEENY. It's a bad habit Sam's got. He doubts everything.

SAM. What you reckon you're going to make on that?

JOHNNY. About fifty per cent if I'm lucky.

SAM. Not much, is it?

QUEENY. It's not a racket, Sam, it's legitimate business.

SAM [*ignoring Queeny*]. Are you lucky?

JOHNNY. No more than anybody else.

SAM. Looks to me like you got a lot of luck.

JOHNNY. We'll see at the end of today.

SAM. We seen a lot already. Yesterday you didn't even know Queeny and today you're in business with her! Ten quid's worth of business! I call that luck.

JOHNNY. Maybe I am.

SAM. You bet you are.

JOHNNY. Anyway I got to be off now . . . see if my luck still holds good. See you later, Queeny.

QUEENY. Five o'clock, Johnny.

[*Johnny exits carrying his suitcase. Sam helps himself to a drink and then sits down.*]

SAM. So I was wrong.

QUEENY. Looks like it, doesn't it?

SAM. Maybe he's playing for more than even I thought.

QUEENY. Meaning?

SAM. You're worth a lot more than ten pounds.

QUEENY [*coming forward*]. Sam, I want you to listen carefully, 'cause I never said anything I meant so much . . . He can have it . . . he can have every penny I got.

SAM. Is it that bad?

QUEENY. Bad? That I found somebody who's worth giving to? It's good, Sam. It feels good. I'm going to enjoy waking up in the morning.

SAM. I do that for nothing.

QUEENY. For nothing, or the cheapest! That's you, that's been you ever since I can remember. And now I feel sorry for you. *Ja*, I actually feel sorry. Yesterday I said I envied you 'cause you had the shop and I just sat around and did nothing. It's changed, Sam, in one day it's changed, and you know how? You've got nobody . . .

SAM. And you've got Johnny.

QUEENY. That's it.

SAM. It's not much if you have a good look at it.

QUEENY. Why you scared, Sam?

SAM. Me?

QUEENY. There's only me and you and I'm not talking to myself. Yes, scared. You're working on him like a man that's scared.

SAM. You're talking nonsense.

QUEENY. You didn't laugh, Sam. If I was wrong you would have laughed.

SAM. What have I got to be scared about?

QUEENY. I don't know and I'm not interested in finding out. You just look scared. I know I'm not.

SAM. We'll see how long it lasts.

QUEENY. It will last as long as it's got to.

SAM. He might not be the settling-down type, Queeny.

QUEENY. Could be, but I'll try and make it that he wants to. But like you said, we don't know. I do know this though, if anybody tries to interfere, they'll wish they was never born.

SAM. Don't look at me. If you get a kick out of it good luck to you. All I'm saying is he might decide to drift, and when he does you'll be glad you still got the shebeen going.

QUEENY. That's finished.

SAM. What do you mean?

QUEENY. What I said. The shebeen is finished. I'm in a legitimate business and it's going to stay that way.

SAM. Are you mad?

QUEENY. Don't shout.

SAM. Legitimate business? Selling rags?

QUEENY. That's how we're starting.

SAM. Starting what? You think you'll ever pick up two hundred per cent profit selling rags? Because that's what you get from the shebeen. And you don't have to work for it.

QUEENY. That's just what I don't like.

SAM. Then keep your rag-bag as a side line.

QUEENY. I'm keeping it, don't worry about that, but it's all I'm keeping.

SAM. So you mean to wreck everything?

QUEENY. What is there to wreck, Sam? You just show me one decent thing that I got to wreck.

SAM. The best shebeen in town . . . the best customers . . .

QUEENY [cutting him short]. I said 'decent'. Go read somewhere what that word means. You're the one that's been to school, remember, you just picked me up in the gutter.

SAM. And I'll be doing that again if you carry on like this. That boy's going to take a powder with all you got and then you'll be back there looking for Sam to pick you up.

QUEENY. Don't.

SAM. Wait till the boys hear about this tonight.

QUEENY. They won't. I'm not selling. I said it's finished and I'm starting from now.

SAM. And that liquor I got?

QUEENY. The liquor *I* bought. I don't give a damn. It can stay here for the rest of my life as far as I'm concerned. Tonight we're going to celebrate.

SAM. Celebrate?

QUEENY. Yes, celebrate! Me and Johnny, right here. 'The boys' can go somewhere else, go moan and vomit on somebody else's floor, 'cause I'm finished with it. I'm going to start to live, Sam.

SAM. That's funny . . . coming from you.

QUEENY. Meaning?

SAM. Nothing.

QUEENY. Don't be scared. I got a lot to remember and one of the things is that no one ever really treated me like a woman, took their hat off when they came in here, said please or thank you or said they liked my smile. I remember that all right, and I remember you. You got fat and rich and smooth on me. You worked me like men work horses and it lasted a long time, so long that I forgot I was a woman. I took this whole Goddamn city to bed with me so that you could get fat and rich. I also made money out of it . . . I remember that too, but it's money I don't like the feel of. It's a greasy coin that stinks of dirty sheets and unwashed men. So if I want to give it away, if I want to give away every penny I got, I don't think I should be ashamed. [*Pause.*] I'm going out now, Sam. When I come back it's going to be my home 'cause that's what it is and that's the way you and everybody else is going to treat it.

[*Queeny leaves. Sam sits meditatively with his glass for a time. Then the door opens and Blackie comes in, still carrying his clock.*]

BLACKIE. Where's Queeny?

SAM. How the hell must I know.

BLACKIE [*seeing the material*]. This chap come?

SAM. Do you think that walked in here by itself?

BLACKIE [*speaking to himself*]. It's no good.

SAM. What do you say?

BLACKIE. It's no good.

SAM [*on the point of making another cutting remark when he stops and picks his words carefully*]. What do you mean?

BLACKIE. This fellow.

SAM. Don't you like him?

BLACKIE. If he comes, I must go.

SAM. You're right and it's all wrong. He doesn't mean any good. He only wants Queeny's money.

BLACKIE. He's no good.

SAM. It would be better if he went.

BLACKIE. Queeny likes him.

SAM. I know but she doesn't see him the way we do. [*Pause.*] You want to get rid of him, Blackie.

BLACKIE. Queeny would be angry.

SAM. I don't mean you must get rough with him. You needn't touch him at all.

BLACKIE. No?

SAM. You needn't lay a hand on him.

BLACKIE. How?

[*Sam goes to the door and sees nobody is listening. He closes it and joins Blackie at the table.*]

SAM. Listen carefully . . .

CURTAIN

Scene 2

Queeny's shebeen late that afternoon. Sam is sitting at the table deep in thought. Blackie is prowling around at the back, obviously nervous. He goes to the window every few seconds and looks out into the street.

SAM [*looking up irritably*]. Why don't you sit down?

BLACKIE. I can't.

SAM. Then do something. Wind your clock if you want to hear the damn thing again. But stop crawling around. It gets on my nerves.

BLACKIE. I don't like it.

SAM. What you worrying about? I fixed it so that she will never know it was us.

BLACKIE. Yes.

SAM. Patrick does the dirty work.

BLACKIE. Maybe he will tell Queeny.

SAM. Tell her what? Don't be a fool. I paid him and I said I'll help him get a job. So Queeny never sells to him again? He can get his liquor somewhere else. And she won't worry about it if I tell her you beat him up. So make it look good. But remember it's only got to look good. Go easy on Patrick. He's doing this because we asked him.

BLACKIE. [*After a few seconds of pacing another thought has struck him.*] She'll want to know how Patrick found out about her.

SAM [*explaining very carefully*]. That woman took on more men in her day than you'll ever know. So one of them saw Queeny around and tells Patrick, one of her old customers. Isn't that possible?

[*Blackie nods his head in grudging agreement. Sam settles back comfortably to enjoy the cunning of his plan.*]

I must give it to myself, it's tidy. Not a loophole. I used what they call psychology. That for your benefit is the head and I been using mine. I could have got somebody to take him down a dark street . . . you might have done it for a price. But that's messy and the police could get round to asking questions. But this way it's me and you and Patrick and each of us got a good reason to shut up.

BLACKIE. Maybe it doesn't work? Maybe this fellow won't care about what Queeny was?

SAM. He will. He's the type. The fastidious kind, that don't like chewing on a bone after all the other dogs taken the meat off.

BLACKIE. I don't like you, Sam.

SAM [*with sarcasm*]. Don't let that worry you. All that's important is that we don't like him.

BLACKIE [*showing his reluctance to implement Sam's plan*]. Maybe I'm wrong, about this chap. Queeny said he was all right.

SAM [*quick to react*]. You mad or something? I explained to you how this chap is going to steal Queeny's cash, didn't I? How you was going to be kicked out because he's come?

[*Blackie is not completely convinced.*]

Look, if I had told you yesterday, just yesterday, that Queeny was going to close up this shebeen, would you have believed me? No. But she has. In one day this Johnny bloke has got her so wrapped up that she's done that.

Queeny uses you around the shebeen. You fetch liquor, you throw out the drunks. But what are you going to do in this cloth business? Sew on curtain rings? And remember we are doing this to protect Queeny.

[*Blackie paces again.*]

So take it easy. This chap is no fool and he'll quickly smell a rat. You got nothing to be nervous about. You're not going to hurt him. Queeny won't be home till late so we got plenty of time. When he comes I'll go across and give Patrick the word. If everything goes right, tonight will be the last we'll see of that bastard.

BLACKIE. Why don't you like him?

SAM. I don't like him cause he's going to steal Queeny's cash. [*That was for Blackie's benefit. The next few words in a more introspective mood.*] And because he's a fancy boy. A straight man that makes like everything else is crooked. Wait till he hears about Queeny.

BLACKIE. Here he comes.

SAM [*joining him at the window*]. He looks happy.

BLACKIE. Must have sold the lot.

SAM. So he was lucky today. That is where it ends. Keep him busy till I come back.

[*Sam hurriedly exits through the street door. Blackie, left alone, shows a moment of panic. He looks around uncertainly for something to do. He*] *sees his clock, goes over to it, and starts winding. The door opens and* Johnny *comes in.*]

JOHNNY. Hello! Where's Queeny?

BLACKIE. Be here just now.

[*Johnny sits down. He is obviously excited and elated.*]

JOHNNY. I sold everything I had with me.

BLACKIE. *Ja.*

JOHNNY. I reckon that's pretty good going.

BLACKIE. Maybe.

JOHNNY. I think so. I mean it's not something that people got to buy. Like soap or medicine. But they bought it. Rags or not they bought every piece I had. And you know, I could have sold the lot . . . I mean the stuff I left behind as well. Hey . . . what about you?

BLACKIE. What about me?

JOHNNY. Wouldn't you like to come out with me next time and give a hand with the selling? You'd get paid. You do sort of help Queeny with things, don't you? It's her money that started this. It's her business as well.

BLACKIE. Me?

JOHNNY. Why not? Looks like I'm going to need somebody. Might as well keep it in the family.

BLACKIE. [*confused*]. I don't know nothing about selling.

JOHNNY. I didn't when I started this morning. It's what you want to do, Blackie . . .

BLACKIE. [*trying to kill the doubts in his mind*]. No!

JOHNNY. Of course you can if you try.

BLACKIE. I said no. I don't even want to try.

JOHNNY [*misinterpreting Blackie's refusal*]. Look, I bet . . .

BLACKIE [*turning on him*]. I don't want to sell your bloody rags. So shut up.

[*Blackie moves to the door but is a few seconds too late. Sam is there.*]

SAM [*sauntering over and dropping into a chair beside Johnny*]. How did it go?

JOHNNY. Okay.

SAM. Just okay or okay fine?

JOHNNY. I sold the lot.

SAM. The lot? That's good going.

JOHNNY. I'm glad, for Queeny's sake. She took a chance giving me ten quid like that.

SAM. Chance?

JOHNNY. The material.

SAM. Oh, that.

JOHNNY [*detecting an undercurrent in Sam's words*]. Well, didn't she?

SAM. Sure, but don't get all worked up about it. Ten pounds is small change to that woman. I don't think she worried too much about that.

JOHNNY. Meaning?

SAM. Maybe she has other ideas. That's all. What did you take?

JOHNNY. The eight pounds I spent on the material and four pounds profit.

SAM. Not bad. What do you say, Blackie? Don't tell me, I know. Queeny's not interested in chicken feed.

JOHNNY. I think she will be.

SAM [*winking at him*]. I get you.

JOHNNY. What do you mean?

SAM. Nothing. Maybe I known Queeny a little longer than you.

[*There is a vigorous knock at the door.*]

SAM. See who it is, Blackie. And remember what Queeny said. She's not selling tonight. [*He turns to Johnny.*] That's right, isn't it?

[*Blackie goes to the door and talks to someone outside. Voices get loud and then* Patrick *comes in.*]

PATRICK [*to Sam*]. Tell him I don't want credit. I got money. [*He sits down.*] How's everybody?

SAM [*ignoring the greeting*]. Blackie wasn't talking about credit. Queeny's not selling.

PATRICK. Look, where is she?

SAM. Not in.

PATRICK. I'm sorry about last night. I didn't mean to mess up her place.

104

SAM. It's got nothing to do with last night. [*Turning to Johnny.*] Isn't that so?

PATRICK. Well then why isn't she selling?

SAM. She said something about celebrating. Anyway it's not your business.

PATRICK. With all the cash she's taken from me it could be.

SAM. Be a good boy and take your few pennies elsewhere, huh.

PATRICK. Few pennies. So my money's not good enough for her any more?

SAM. I just said she's not selling.

PATRICK. It was good enough for her when she first came here. My few pennies were all right then. I bet they were. Because I earned my money honest. Not like some people I know.

SAM. Don't say anything you're going to regret.

PATRICK. I got no regrets. I got nothing to hide.

JOHNNY. What do you mean by that?

PATRICK. Hell, you must be new here to ask questions like that. Go ask Queeny.

JOHNNY. I'm asking you.

SAM. Look, let's just forget what has been said . . .

JOHNNY [*to Patrick*]. I'm asking you, what has Queeny got to hide?

SAM. You'll be sorry, Patrick.

PATRICK. Sorry? Sorry for what? I've got nothing to be ashamed of. I lived my life clean and decent.

SAM. Blackie!

[*The hunchback rushes forward and lifting his clenched fists, cracks them into Patrick's back. Sam sees that Blackie is not bluffing, that he has every intention of killing Patrick. He rushes in and pulls Blackie off. Johnny is riveted to his chair by Patrick's insinuations.*]

SAM. You fool. You bloody crooked fool. Do you want to kill him?

BLACKIE. Yes.

SAM. Listen! That's enough. That's enough. Do you hear?

[*Blackie is brought to his senses. He gives up the struggle with Patrick, and rushes out of the room. Sam turns to Patrick.*]

You all right?

[*Patrick nods his head. He is shaken and Sam helps him to the door and slips something into his hand before he goes. Sam takes out a handkerchief and mops his brow before turning his attention to Johnny.*]

SAM. Thanks for the help.

JOHNNY [*ignoring the sarcasm*]. What did he mean?

SAM. How must I know? You saw him last night. Drinks a lot. Must have had a few tots somewhere else before coming here.

JOHNNY. He was sober. You've known Queeny a long time. What did she do before . . . ?

SAM. Look, I told you I don't know. And even if I did, what sort of friend goes talking behind a back? If Queeny wants you to know, let her tell you.

JOHNNY. Know what?

SAM. I know nothing, absolutely nothing. Does that make you understand? I'm keeping my mouth shut. Anyway, here she comes now. And if you want my advice, don't ask questions.

[*Sam exits quietly through the street door. Johnny waits nervously for Queeny to appear.*]

QUEENY [*entering loaded with parcels*]. Can we celebrate?

JOHNNY. Hello, Queeny.

QUEENY. How did it go?

JOHNNY. It was good.

QUEENY [*her excitement getting the better of her*]. No!

JOHNNY. Yep, the lot.

QUEENY. Everything you took out?

JOHNNY. Everything.

QUEENY. We've done it! We can celebrate . . . and I *mean* celebrate. [*She shows her parcels.*] Fancy candles for the table . . . a new set of knives and forks . . . a chicken . . . Got to see if I can still cook one. And you know what this is? Champagne . . . the real thing. I even bought myself a new dress.

[*She pauses.*] Don't look at me like that. Am I making a fool of myself?

JOHNNY. No, Queeny.

QUEENY. What if I was! I got good reason to stand in the door there and laugh at this damn street till the dogs get tired of barking. Aren't you happy?

JOHNNY. Tired, I guess.

QUEENY. Of course. It must have been hard work. I'll put the kettle on. Don't fiddle with the parcels. There's a surprise for you. Johnny, it's hard for me to believe this has been a day in my life . . . shopping, arguing prices. You know I argued with an Indian about the price of potatoes? And this was the one I hated most of all. Pay day. The big money day. When life started at night and sobered up two hangovers and a hundred brandies later on Monday. Fifteen years is a long time.

JOHNNY. Fifteen? This morning you said five.

QUEENY. Five, of course. What's the matter with me?

[*Picks up one of the parcels.*] Look the other way.

[*A new dress comes out of the parcel. She starts to put it on.*]

JOHNNY. What did you do before this, Queeny?

QUEENY. Just knocked about. Odd jobs.

JOHNNY. Queeny?

QUEENY. *Ja.*

JOHNNY. I need a drink.

QUEENY. Shall we open the champagne now?

JOHNNY. Let's keep that for later. What about brandy?

QUEENY. You asking for brandy?

JOHNNY. I'm all jumpy inside.

QUEENY. I understand. It's in the kitchen in the cupboard. Help yourself.

[*Johnny, still not looking at Queeny, goes into the kitchen and returns with a bottle. He opens it and pours himself a drink which he drinks down, standing in the doorway, then another which he brings into the room with the bottle. Queeny has now finished putting on the new dress.*]

QUEENY. Well, how do you like it?

JOHNNY. It looks good.

QUEENY. Now tell me. Tell me everything that happened to you from the moment you left this morning.

JOHNNY. Well, it's hard. Everything is mixed up. I went to those women I told you about. After that I just kept on going and when I looked again my suitcases was empty. Here, see for yourself. The eight pounds I spent on material plus four pounds profit. That's not bad. Even Sam said so.

QUEENY. I can laugh at him today. Let's call him over.

JOHNNY. No. Leave him alone. I don't like his company, or his talk.

QUEENY. You haven't told me all. Did they buy like you suggested? Table cloths to match the curtains and so on?

JOHNNY. *Ja.* I reckon so.

QUEENY. What's the matter, Johnny? You're not burning up the world like you were this morning.

JOHNNY. Somebody threw cold water on the fire.

QUEENY. I don't get you.

JOHNNY. Well, you know, selling and arguing about prices. It makes you tired.

QUEENY. You look more than just tired.

JOHNNY [*covering up*]. Don't worry, I'll have the fire burning bright again. [*Pours himself another drink.*]

QUEENY. I'll get the coffee. You might really need it. [*The last remark as a joke with a gesture towards the brandy.*]

[*Queeny goes out to the kitchen. Johnny downs the tot. With his face screwed up and his throat burning he puts out his hand for the bottle and pours another.*]

QUEENY [*from the other room*]. What do we do now?

JOHNNY. We said celebrate, didn't we?

QUEENY [*in the doorway*]. You're sounding like your old self again. Maybe that brandy was a good idea. But I meant the business. What do we do now? Buy some more?

JOHNNY. We expand.

QUEENY. Expand?

JOHNNY. We get big. It's when you're small and need people

that you get buggered around. We've got to be so big we don't
need anybody.

QUEENY. Except each other.

JOHNNY. Except each other? Maybe we'll still be buggered
around, by each other. I suppose the only time you're really
safe is when you can tell the rest of the world to go to hell.

QUEENY. That's not true. Remember me when you say that.
Nothing buggers you up like yourself. It's good to need
someone. [*Trying to change the subject.*] Tell me about our
expansion.

JOHNNY. We'll buy more, sell more, and make more money.
Then you'll start taking it serious.

QUEENY [*not understanding his last remark*]. Johnny?

JOHNNY. Four pounds *is* chicken feed, isn't it?

QUEENY. Who said that?

JOHNNY. Blackie.

QUEENY. He said that ... about me?

JOHNNY. Let's forget it.

QUEENY. No! Not if you're going to believe everything you
hear ...

JOHNNY. I didn't say I believed it.

QUEENY. What else did he say?

JOHNNY. Queeny, please.

QUEENY. So that is what I get after all I did for him ...

JOHNNY. He's not ungrateful, Queeny.

QUEENY. I should have known it.

JOHNNY. I offered him a job.

QUEENY. Doing what?

JOHNNY. Helping me.

QUEENY. Well, drop that idea.

JOHNNY. Why?

QUEENY. Because I don't think it's a good idea to have him
around.

JOHNNY. So you'll just get rid of him like that?

QUEENY. Just like that. That's how he came and that's how he can go.

JOHNNY. And when you get tired of selling rags will I also go just like that?

[*Queeny is disturbed.*]

QUEENY. Johnny, we're going wrong.

JOHNNY. You're right [*pulling himself together*].

[*He takes the bottle and pours himself another drink.*]

QUEENY. Easy on that stuff, Johnny. You're not used to it.

JOHNNY. You want me to burn again, don't you?

QUEENY. We got the future to burn up. Tomorrow and the day after and our plans for those days. That stuff will only burn you up.

JOHNNY. The fire needs a spark. That's all this is giving me. Now about these plans. They got to be big. We got to get away from a world that is small. We got to build big so that one of these days we can stand in the street and have a damned good laughing session at the world. We'll laugh ourselves sick, 'cause there's nothing so Goddamn funny only we take it serious.

QUEENY [*trying hard to bring him back to reality*]. The plans, Johnny.

JOHNNY. Plans?

QUEENY. You started off saying you wanted to talk about our plans for the future.

JOHNNY. The future! It's a waste of time talking about that. The only future we've got is tomorrow if we're unlucky enough to wake up.

QUEENY [*still trying*]. I got the prices of sewing machines. I was thinking that for us . . .

JOHNNY. Sewing machines!

QUEENY. You said we got to get a sewing machine, Johnny. I got the prices in my bag.

JOHNNY. Forget the sewing machine. That's a small thought.

QUEENY. I heard big talkers all my life, but I never seen one that was happy. And you were happy this morning, Johnny.

JOHNNY. I'm happy now.

QUEENY. Are you?

JOHNNY [*passing a hand over his eyes*]. I told you I'm tired.

QUEENY. Is it because of what you told me this morning?

JOHNNY. No. I want to forget that tonight.

QUEENY [*pointing to the bottle*]. That's not the way.

JOHNNY. I still got to find that out for myself.

[*Queeny picks up her parcels and takes them to the kitchen. A few seconds later she returns with a small one in her hands.*]

QUEENY. I should have given this to you when I came in. When I was all excited.

[*There is a pause. Queeny is embarrassed.*]

It's a present for you, Johnny. Hell, I'm just making a fool of myself. [*She moves to the back.*]

JOHNNY. Queeny . . .

QUEENY [*stopping*]. Maybe you will like it.

[*She gives it to him. He opens the parcel and takes out a wristwatch.*]

It's just a wristwatch. I thought that maybe when you was going around selling and it comes near lunch . . . [*Her words trail off.*] I just wanted to give you something. It doesn't mean anything else.

[*Johnny goes to the back. A shadow passes the window. It is a man picking out a melancholy little theme on his guitar. Johnny hears the music.*]

JOHNNY [*with a vague gesture towards the window*]. Him.

QUEENY. Who?

JOHNNY. The chap who was playing the guitar.

QUEENY [*listening*]. It's sad.

JOHNNY. It's always sad. When a man walks past a lighted window in an empty street, it's always sad.

QUEENY. Why has it got to be?

JOHNNY. When you're out walking at this hour streets lead nowhere.

QUEENY. You don't have to say it like that.

JOHNNY. It's true.

QUEENY. For you?

JOHNNY. I don't know myself any more.

QUEENY. I know a few things.

JOHNNY. I told you a lot.

QUEENY. I'm not talking about that. I'm talking about a man I met yesterday who got his chance to do something he's been dreaming of for a long time. A man who's got big plans for the future. Doesn't that sound like somebody who's got somewhere to go?

JOHNNY. I seen good-looking apples with worms in them.

QUEENY. What do you mean?

JOHNNY. The apple isn't going to get ripe. And even if it looks like it is, the first person that takes a bite will spit it out ... because they'll find it rotten inside. It only takes one worm to do that to an apple ... and maybe one thought to do it to a man. [*Johnny turns and looks directly at Queeny.*] And you?

QUEENY. I'm trying to be a woman.

JOHNNY. What does that mean?

QUEENY. I'm trying to hold a man, make him want to stay.

JOHNNY [*after a pause*]. Am I the first?

QUEENY [*choosing her words very carefully*]. It's the first time I've ever felt like this about someone.

[*Johnny wants to ask something else. The evasion is obvious but he is not yet drunk enough to force Queeny. He pours himself another drink just a little too hurriedly. Queeny watches his hands and the glass.*]

JOHNNY. Must have been a harder day than I thought.

[*There is a knock at the door. Queeny answers it. It is a customer and she has difficulty in telling him she is not selling. She steps back into the room and slams the door.*]

JOHNNY. It's not going to be easy.

QUEENY. What?

JOHNNY. Keeping it shut. They're going to expect you to sell.

QUEENY. What they expect and what I'm going to do is two different things.

JOHNNY. Looks like it.

QUEENY. I thought you would prefer it this way, Johnny.

JOHNNY. There's worse things in this world than shebeens.

QUEENY. I closed it because it's the only thing you or anybody else can point at in my life.

JOHNNY. You don't have to say that.

QUEENY. Don't I?

JOHNNY. We said we were going to celebrate, remember.

QUEENY. We've gone a long way from that idea.

JOHNNY [*Pause.*] Why did you get mixed up with a bastard like me?

QUEENY. Don't blame yourself, Johnny.

JOHNNY. Then don't blame yourself either. Let's blame the stinking bloody world out there that makes us what we are. Let's blame what sent us into this world, because nobody with any sense would choose to come.

QUEENY. Is that how you feel about it?

JOHNNY. I've felt that way ever since the mines. Ever since they got hold of me and made me worse than an animal. The only difference is that sometimes I get the crazy idea that a man can change the world he lives in. Hell! You can't even change yourself. [*Grabbing the bottle.*] Except that this isn't helping me forget.

QUEENY. Have a cup of coffee instead.

JOHNNY. Who ever heard of celebrating with coffee?

QUEENY. I'd rather not celebrate than see you start on that.

JOHNNY. Don't sell me that line.

QUEENY. Then there's no point in me turning them away at the door.

JOHNNY. This is my last one.

QUEENY. Promise?

JOHNNY. Please, Queeny, don't nag. There's the money we took today, if that's what you're worrying about. [*He shows it to her. Pause.*] I'm sorry.

QUEENY. Is that something else Blackie said and you believed? [*Moving to the door.*] Where is he?

JOHNNY. No! Queeny, please. [*She stops at the door.*] Christ, this is one hell of a way to celebrate.

[*There is a knock at the door. Queeny ignores it. It comes again. she opens the door in a fury.*]

QUEENY [*to the person outside*]. Go to hell. [*She slams the door.*] Let's try to start from the beginning.

JOHNNY. The beginning. Where's that?

QUEENY. Two hours ago when you come home. You had sold everything and you were tired. Be tired, too tired to say anything or think anything. Just want to sit down and rest and wait for the food. Maybe later we'll have some of that champagne.

JOHNNY [*genuinely exhausted*]. That sounds simple. That sounds simple and okay.

QUEENY. Try it, Johnny. Sit down. Or do you want to sleep?

JOHNNY. No, sometimes a man can dream worse things than he can think. There was a time when I couldn't sleep at all, because of my dreams.

QUEENY. It's okay now, Johnny.

JOHNNY. It wasn't then. No. I'll stay awake. It feels like a night for bad dreams.

QUEENY. Dream about today.

JOHNNY. How do you know what today means to me?

QUEENY. You sold everything . . .

JOHNNY. Don't keep on about that like it was the happy ending to a fairy story. So I sold a heap of old rags. But I didn't sell my mind. I still got the same thoughts. I'm the same man as yesterday and the day before that right back to the mines. I never sold myself and bought a brand new person. [*Pause.*] Here we go again. You make the supper. I'll be okay.

[*Queeny goes to the kitchen. Johnny prowls around nervously. The shadow of the man with the guitar passes the window again. We hear the music. It seems to drive Johnny to the point of desperation. He rushes to the window.*]

[*Queeny comes back. Johnny sees the bottle of champagne.*]

JOHNNY. Let's have the champagne now.

QUEENY. Go ahead.

[*While Johnny works out the cork, she fetches two glasses. Johnny drinks his straight down.*]

QUEENY. Aren't we supposed to touch the glasses together?

JOHNNY. Of course, I forgot. [*Pours himself another glass.*] To ourselves, since nobody else gives a damn.

QUEENY. To ourselves and the business.

[*There is a knock at the door.*]

JOHNNY. Can't you stop that damned knocking?

QUEENY. The only way I can do that is to leave the door open and let them come in.

[*The knock comes again.*]

JOHNNY. Well, answer it, tell him to go to hell like you did the others, but shut him up.

QUEENY. You're shouting.

[*We hear the knock again.*]

JOHNNY. Okay, I'm shouting . . . but it's because that's getting on my nerves.

[*Queeny goes across and opens the door.*]

QUEENY. Nobody here.

JOHNNY. You don't keep customers by keeping them waiting.

QUEENY. Then I'd better not answer the door.

JOHNNY. You sure you want to lose them?

QUEENY. Meaning?

JOHNNY. Next Friday you might think it better business to open again.

QUEENY. Why should I want to do that?

[*Johnny is saved from answering by another knock at the door.*]

JOHNNY. Christ, there it goes again.

QUEENY. You didn't answer my question.

JOHNNY. If you'll tell him to shut up.

QUEENY. I asked you . . .

JOHNNY. Well, stop asking me . . . You might get an answer you . . .

[*He moves suddenly and knocks over the bottle of champagne. It spills over the table cloth, then drips onto the floor. They watch as if mesmerized. The knocking is heard again.*]

QUEENY. I told Sam I was closing down because I was sick of drunks messing up my place. [*She speaks quietly.*]

JOHNNY [*moving suddenly*]. I need some fresh air.

QUEENY. Johnny!

JOHNNY [*a cry of desperation*]. The window ... I'm only going to the window ... Don't suffocate me, Queeny ...

QUEENY. What's happening, Johnny? What's gone wrong?

[*Pause. Johnny gets a grip on himself.*]

JOHNNY. I got the smell of filth again. Queeny, I wanted to start today more than anything else in my life. I thought I'd been given my chance to start from the beginning ... I want to do that ... Jesus knows, I want to do that. I told you about myself this morning, Queeny. It wasn't just that I owed you a start ... I looked at you like I've never looked at another woman before ... I don't want to run away from it but ... Queeny, I been honest with you ... you got to be honest with me. But tell me ... I got to know ...

QUEENY. Who ... ?

JOHNNY. Queeny, listen ...

QUEENY. Who told you?

JOHNNY. Nobody told me anything.

QUEENY. Blackie!

JOHNNY. He didn't say a thing.

QUEENY. It was Blackie.

JOHNNY. If you go out without telling me, I won't be here when you come back.

QUEENY. Why must you know?

JOHNNY. I got to stop myself thinking.

QUEENY. Will it make any difference what I tell you?

JOHNNY. Don't ask me that. I'm not God. I didn't make myself.

QUEENY. I didn't ask you any questions about yourself.

JOHNNY. Can't you see, Queeny, I had to tell you, just like I got to know now?

QUEENY. But you're asking me. You're asking me for something
I've been trying to hide away from myself. Give me time,
Johnny. Give me time to live with myself and find the right
words, and tell you when I know I got to, when I can.

JOHNNY. And what must I do?

QUEENY. Wait. You got to wait.

JOHNNY. Wait. You know what that word means . . . wait? That
means days, weeks, months, maybe years. I just had two hours
of it and it's driving me mad. And you know why? Because you
don't stop thinking when you're waiting. [*Pause*.] Queeny, let
me go. Let me walk out of that door.

QUEENY. No.

JOHNNY. If I stay I got to know.

QUEENY. You said this morning . . .

JOHNNY. Don't stall, Queeny! Tell me or let me go.

[*Evasions are past. Queeny realizes that she can no longer avoid the
truth.*]

QUEENY. Where do I begin?

JOHNNY. There is a name for everything.

QUEENY. Nongogo.

JOHNNY. Jesus!

QUEENY. Yes . . . Nongogo . . . a woman for two and six. Don't
you think that was a bargain? Me for two and six? And you're
seeing me when I'm older and fat. You should have seen me
then . . . Maybe you would have joined the queue.

JOHNNY. No!

QUEENY. Yes . . . I'm telling you yes!

JOHNNY. Stop it.

QUEENY. You wanted to know so I'm telling you, Johnny, and
now you got to listen. I did it because I was hungry, because I
had sworn to myself I was going to make enough to tell the rest
of the world to go to hell. And nothing makes money like Sam
organizing the business. We started with queues around the
mine dumps at night. I can also tell you a few things about
compounds, Johnny. But we ended big . . . one man at a time.
That's how I got here and Sam got his shop across the street

and that's the ten pounds that bought you rags and the first decent thing I've ever had in my life. Because if you think I liked it or wanted it that way you're so far away from knowing what a woman is, you can forget them. I'm a woman, Johnny. I never stopped being one, but no one's given me a chance. I've had men but never one who treated me like I mattered far more than just a night in bed. Because that man I'll love. If he'll just take me, for what I want to be, and not what I was, I'll make him happy. God's been generous in what he's given me. In body, in feelings, in the need for love ... give me a chance ...

JOHNNY. Stop using words that mean nothing. Love, chance ... God made me without the one and my life's had nothing of the other. Why didn't you say you were filth ... like me? When I walked in here last night, why didn't you recognize another piece of trash? Why did I have to think you were different?

QUEENY. Different from what? The respectable people out there? Respectable? They were my customers ... the ones that lived cleanest and hated filth ... like you! I've found Bibles in their pockets when they lay sleeping in my bed, with pictures of their pretty wives and nice clean children. And I bet Daddy took them all to church on Sundays.

JOHNNY. Don't drag everything into the gutter with you, Queeny.

QUEENY. I'm not the landlord of that strip of muck, Johnny. Everybody owns a plot down there.

JOHNNY. Some of us try to crawl out of it.

QUEENY. What do you think I've been doing for five years? It had ended, Johnny, it was dead and buried when you walked in here. But you won't let it stay that way, will you? You'd be worse than Sam, who just sighs when he passes the grave. You've dug it up. You've performed a miracle, Johnny. The miracle of Jesus and the dead body. You've brought it back to life. The warmth of your hate, the breath of your disgust, has got it living again. I'm not too old ... not *too* fat ... even you looked at me like you never looked at another woman. God's put a lot of men onto this earth. There are a lot of streets I haven't walked, lamp-posts I haven't stood under, faces I haven't smiled at.

[*Hands on her hips, she starts laughing at Johnny and walks up to him provocatively. He turns and goes out, with Queeny laughing loudly. When Johnny has gone, Queeny goes to the door, flings it open, and shouts out into the street.*]

QUEENY. Where's everybody? This damn place is a graveyard! I've got a locker full of booze and it's not diluted!

[*Queeny goes back into the room. She goes to the mirror, puts on lipstick . . . rouge . . . earrings . . . bracelets, and dolls herself up into the real tart.*]

SAM [*appearing at the door*]. Did I hear right?

QUEENY. What did you hear, Sam?

SAM. I heard something that sounded like the old Queeny.

QUEENY. There's nothing wrong with your hearing.

[*Sam laughs. He goes back into the street.*]

SAM. [*off stage*]. Come on . . . I'm telling you it's all right.

[*Sam comes back rubbing his hands.*]

SAM. We still got time. It's only nine. When the word gets around that Queeny's back in business, they'll be back for the ball.

[*Patrick enters hesitantly.*]

SAM. Come in.

PATRICK. Is this on the level?

QUEENY. The only level we worry about here is that in the brandy bottle. Where's Blackie? Blackie!

SAM [*to Patrick*]. Didn't I tell you?

PATRICK. You sure did.

QUEENY. What did you call the kid, Patrick?

PATRICK. Kid? It was twins.

[*Blackie appears.*]

QUEENY. Where have you been? I got customers and you're keeping them waiting.

[*Blackie backs away uncertainly . . . Sam and Patrick laugh at the expression on his face.*]

QUEENY [*pouring the rest of the champagne*]. Have some of this while you're waiting.

PATRICK. What is it?

SAM. Champagne.

PATRICK. Lemonade!

SAM. You got no taste.

[*Blackie has brought in the liquor.*]

SAM [*pours the drinks*]. You had us worried.

PATRICK. You sure did.

SAM. It's like old times again.

PATRICK. It sure is. What happened to that salesman, Queeny?

QUEENY. Man? There was no man here.

CURTAIN

THE COAT

**An Acting Exercise from Serpent Players
of New Brighton**

CHARACTERS

LAVRENTI
MARIE
ANIKO
JINGI
HAEMON

THE COAT was first presented as a public reading in the Dunne Hall of the Hill Presbyterian Church, Port Elizabeth, on 28 November 1966, directed by Athol Fugard with the following cast, who adopted their character names from their roles in earlier successful Serpent Players productions:

LAVRENTI (*Caucasian Chalk Circle*)	Mulligan Mbikwane
MARIE (*Woyzeck*)	Mabel Magada
ANIKO (*Caucasian Chalk Circle*)	Nomhle Nkonyeni
JINGI (*Mandragola/The Cure*)	Humphrey Njikelane
HAEMON (*Antigone*)	John Kani

THE COAT was revived 2–6 May 1990 at the University of Witwatersrand Theatre, Johannesburg, directed by Maishe Maponya, with a cast including George Modise and Adelaide de Broize.

Five chairs on an empty stage. The actors—three men and two women—walk on and sit down. One of the men comes forward and addresses the audience.

LAVRENTI. We are a group of actors from New Brighton. Aniko, Marie, Haemon, Jingi . . . [*the actors nod as they are introduced*] . . . and I am Lavrenti.

New Brighton. I often wonder what that name means to outsiders, like you. I am using the word in its purely descriptive sense—we live inside and you live outside. That world where your servants go at the end of the day, that ugly scab of pondokkies and squalor that spoils the approach to Port Elizabeth. If you are interested in knowing something about it we might be able to help you, because we accepted the chance to come here tonight so that we could tell you about a coat, a man's coat, which came back to New Brighton in a stranger's shopping bag.

Allow me a short word of explanation.

There are many confused and even contradictory reasons for our existence as a group. The hunger for applause, boredom, conceit, desperation, even money at one stage—though we have now learnt enough to know that here in Port Elizabeth, Theatre is not the way you make it, but lose it. We have talked about this question of motives more times than I care to remember. But during all that talking we have discovered one thing which we all have in common, something on top of all the other reasons, or should I say at the bottom, because it hasn't been all that strong. We want to use the theatre. For what? Here it gets a bit confused again. Some of us say to understand the world we live in, but we also boast a few idealists who think that Theatre might have something to do with changing it.

These attitudes imply something of a purpose to our work. This in turn has involved us in the life and people of New Brighton. It is the only world we know. It is real. We want our work to be real. So we study and try to understand that world—the shopkeepers and the housewives who complain about the shopkeepers; the labourers coming home tired at night and the bus conductors who don't wait for those labourers at bus stops; the tsotsis who molest the young lovers, the young lovers themselves . . . as one of us once put it, its problems and its pleasures.

It was in this way that we first heard and talked about the coat.

To begin with, I don't think any of us believed we had anything to learn from it. That was a mistake of course—but remember we are still only beginners, still learning the first lessons and making the first mistakes.

We discovered that the coat was real. I don't mean that we didn't believe it had ever existed. We knew it had. When I say 'real' I mean we discovered that it was the cause and effect of things. We came to believe in it so strongly that we decided to use tonight to show you what had happened when we discussed and examined it. There are certain facts; we will give you them. There are a lot of questions; we tried to find the answers. Listen and judge for yourself.

Just before we start let me answer any of you who might be asking: Why the coat? Why not the man who wore the coat? Isn't he real? Isn't a real man a better subject for an actor's exercise? Of course he is. The man would have been better, but it was the coat that came back.

One other point. We thought it might help you to follow and understand us if we had a coat something like the original to work with. Likewise the shopping bag.

Marie brought back the coat.

[*Lavrenti sits down. Marie comes forward. She carries a brown-paper shopping bag.*]

MARIE. I brought the coat back with me from Cradock, a hundred and sixty miles away.* I had gone to Cradock for my husband's trial. The coat isn't his. It belongs to another New Brighton man. There have been a lot of our men in the

Cradock cells. The charges are mostly the same: membership of a banned organisation, distributing pamphlets, addressing a meeting and so on. They go to Robben Island afterwards. The lucky ones get three years. Most of them get five or seven.

When we got to Cradock, I went straight to the Magistrate's Court. I was lucky, because all the white people were having tea, so they let me see him in the Court Room. When the court is working they do not let you in. Nobody is allowed in. Only the officials. I saw my husband in the Court Room. He looked all right. He said that his case hadn't started yet. They were still busy with two other men. One of them was the owner of the coat. He was wearing it.

[*She thinks very hard.*]

They, the two men, were sitting in the dock. There were lots of policemen and white men about, coming and going and drinking their tea. The two men sat very still. They looked about fifty. I asked my husband their names. He said that he didn't know. They were in another cell. In court they were called number one accused and number two accused.

Then I went out to the cafe to buy them food. When I came back the Court was busy so I had to wait. I waited at the back near the cells. At lunchtime they came out but nothing had happened yet. They were still busy on the case of the two men. They let me see my husband. I gave him the food. We talked softly.

The Court started again at two o'clock. When I saw them at teatime the case of the two men had finished. They each got five years. My husband's case then started but when he came out at five o'clock it wasn't finished. I went around to the cells to say goodbye because I had to go home. I could only get one day off from my work.

[*Marie speaks slowly now, concentrating hard on giving every detail, trying to be as clear and factual as possible.*]

While I was talking to him the two men came past. The one with the coat came up to me quickly and asked me to see his wife and children. He gave me the address. He asked me to tell them what had happened to him. Then he took off his coat and said I must give it to his wife. 'Tell her to use it,' he said. 'Tell them I will come back.'

I said goodbye to them. Outside I folded up the coat and put it in the shopping bag in which I had brought my husband's clean clothes. I brought it back with me to New Brightòn.

On the way back—I think it was near Cookhouse—the van with the prisoners passed us. It was going very fast. One man was looking out through the back window. I think it was him, the one who gave me the coat.

I went to the address the next day. It was in Mnqandi Street. I knocked on the door and an old woman opened it. She was alone. It was the wife. I told her why I had come and gave her the coat. In front of me she went through all the pockets. All she found was a little piece of brown paper with some powder inside. She told me she had got it from a witchdoctor to keep the sentence small. She said it had worked, because she had heard about other men who had got twenty years.

I gave her the message from her husband—that she must use the coat and wait for him—then said goodbye and left.

LAVRENTI [*coming forward*]. What sort of coat was it?

MARIE. Oh, just an old coat. A man's sportscoat.

LAVRENTI. Torn?

MARIE. I don't think it was torn. It might have had patches, but it wasn't torn.

LAVRENTI. So it was worth something?

MARIE. Certainly. One rand, one rand fifty. Something like that.

LAVRENTI [*to the audience*]. Those were our facts. The first thing we did was to improvise the little scene where the coat was handed over. We wanted to see it, that moment, when it passed from the hands of a stranger to the wife, because that is when the coat starts to live again, where it comes back into our lives.

Aniko will take the part of the wife. So then here it is: The Scene In Which The Wife Gets Back Her Husband's Coat.

[*Lavrenti sits down, Aniko joins Marie.*]

MARIE. Hello, Mama.

ANIKO. Hello, my child.

MARIE. How are you, Mama?

ANIKO. I am all right, my child. I am all right. How are you?

MARIE. Carrying on, Mama. Trying to carry on. These are hard times.

ANIKO. Yes, these are hard times, but we must carry on. There is nothing else for people like us to do.

MARIE. I came to see you, Mama, because your husband asked me. I saw him yesterday at Cradock. My husband is also one of those up there.

ANIKO. Yes.

MARIE. Your husband got five years, Mama.

ANIKO. Yes.

MARIE. He asked me to tell you and to say he was all right.

ANIKO. Five years.

MARIE. He gave me his coat, Mama, and told me to give it to you. He said you must use it, and wait for him.

[*Marie takes out the coat.*]

Here it is.

ANIKO. Yes, that's his coat. [*She takes it*]. He'll be cold now, without it.

MARIE. They wouldn't have let him keep it. They take everything away and give you prison clothes.

ANIKO. Short trousers.

MARIE. And a shirt.

ANIKO. He's an old man for short trousers. [*She examines the coat.*] It's a good coat.

MARIE. There is still a lot of use in it, Mama. Maybe it will fit one of your sons?

ANIKO. Is there anything in the pockets?

MARIE. I didn't look, Mama. I bring it just as he gave it to me.

ANIKO [*going through the pockets*]. He got it last year. From a baas at his work. He used to do some jobs for him in the garden on

Saturdays. One day he gave him this coat. What did he look like, my child, yesterday?

MARIE. He looked all right, Mama. They say the food isn't too bad.

ANIKO. Where is he now?

MARIE. I think here in Port Elizabeth. At the Rooihel. The van with the prisoners passed me on the road when I was coming back. They will write and tell you where they are going to take him. Some of them go to Robben Island.

[*Aniko finds a little twist of brown paper in one of the pockets.*]

ANIKO. *Ja*, he kept it.

MARIE. What, Mama?

ANIKO. They told me to get some medicine to keep the number of years of his sentence small. I gave it to him when he was here at the Rooihel. It worked. It was strong. There are families in this street who won't see their men for ten years.

I will wait for him. I will keep this coat for him.

[*Marie hesitates, on the verge of saying something, but changes her mind.*]

MARIE. Goodbye, Mama.

ANIKO. Goodbye and God bless you, my child.

[*Marie walks back to her chair.*]

LAVRENTI. You hesitated there, as if you wanted to say something.

MARIE. Yes, I know. I wanted to tell her it was silly to keep the coat all that time if she could use it. Five years is long.

LAVRENTI. Why didn't you?

MARIE. I don't know. I felt sorry for her.

LAVRENTI. [*to Aniko, who is still by herself.*]

So now the coat is with the old woman. What did you, as the wife, feel when you got it back?

ANIKO. I'm not sure. I wasn't really in it yet, you know, in the part.

LAVRENTI. What do you think she felt? Was she sad, or . . .

JINGI. Of course she was sad. She's lost her husband for five years.

HAEMON. But remember she said she thought he might have got longer. She must have also been a little bit relieved.

ANIKO. Can I work it out? Give me a chair.

[*Lavrenti moves forward Aniko's chair.*]

The Scene Where The Old Woman Is Alone With The Coat. When Marie left she hung it up . . .*Ja!* . . . and then she said a prayer.

Thanks God it's all over. After waiting for so long, now I know I only have to wait for five years. It could have been longer. God, please give me strength to wait, and look after him in gaol. Thanks God.

Ja, then she goes on with her housework. I am alone in the house. I look at the coat, I think about the man. His name is Temba. Temba's coat.

[*Aniko has moved slowly into the character of the old woman.*]

Ja, Temba. Five years. One two three four five years. It's easy to count it. But how long is five years? It's a long time in a man's life. You will be older when you come back to Mnqandi Street. We will be older. Our daughter is ten. She will be fifteen. Our son is sixteen. He will be a man. *Ja*, Temba. He must be a man before his time.

I must look for work now. Do washing for a white madam. Joyce next door will help me to find work. Five years! A lot of things can happen. Lots of things do happen. Six months ago you were still walking down Mnqandi Street in the early morning with the other men to work. At night you came back. And now?

Where are you now? Cradock. Robben Island. Where is Robben Island? Far away I think.

And your coat. Temba's coat. You said you will come back. You said we must wait. Will they let you come back, Temba? When your five years is past will they open the gates and let you out?

Ai! The white people. What is it all about? What is the matter with them? They have got everything. And now they also take our men away.

You will look older when you come back to us. What did you

look like the last time I saw you? When was the last time I saw you? In gaol. At the Rooihel.

I stood with food and waited outside the big doors with the other women. We stood a long time. Then they opened the door and let us in . . . one by one. You were still wearing this coat. You asked about the children. You said you were all right.

[*Pause. She thinks hard.*]

It's hard to remember what you looked like. Sometimes here in the house, at night, you looked tired. We were getting old, Temba.

And now? We must wait. We must live without you for five years. It will be hard. But I can do washing. Joyce must help me find a white madam with washing . . .

[*Aniko breaks off with a weary gesture and turns to the other actors. She speaks as herself.*]

Tired, fellows. I think she feels tired. Looking for washing is hell, man. Those old women walk, *Boetie*. And all that waiting there at the gaol! *Ai*, no!

LAVRENTI. So?

ANIKO. So you asked me what I think the old girl feels and I'm saying she feels *moeg*.

JINGI. And sad.

ANIKO. I felt tired.

JINGI. It looked sad.

MARIE. But don't you think she asked too many questions? Everything was a question.

ANIKO. That's what made me tired. Every time I thought something, there was a question. Questions without answers is hell, man.

LAVRENTI. Let's get back to the coat. His message was: Tell her to use it. Let's see it being used. How does she use it? Go on, use it.

[*Pause, Aniko thinks.*]

ANIKO. It's night time and cold. Raining maybe. We're all

asleep. Then I hear one of the children on the floor—the girl—shivering. I get up and take her father's coat and put it on her like a blanket.

JINGI. Were they as poor as that? No beds, no blankets?

MARIE. No, I don't think they were so poor.

JINGI. Exactly! Mnqandi Street is a good address.

LAVRENTI. Hang on. That's no criticism. Aniko can't be limited to facts which she doesn't know. She was giving us *her* old woman, and there are enough old women and their children sleeping on the floor to make that possible.

ANIKO. What do you mean, possible? It *happens*, man.

HAEMON. I've got a better idea for using the coat. Can we try it?

LAVRENTI. Go ahead.

[*Haemon joins Aniko, taking his chair with him.*]

HAEMON. I am the son at school. My father is now in gaol serving his five years. My mother is struggling to support us. I can see she is worried. So I am going to ask her to let me leave school and get a job.

MARIE. How does the coat come into it?

HAEMON. I'm coming to that. I've heard about a job and I want to go and apply. But my own coat is torn. You must be smart to get a job. So I am going to ask her to lend me my father's coat.

ANIKO. We are in the house?

HAEMON. Yes. It's supper time. I've got my samp and beans and I'm sitting next to the stove where it's warm. You're sitting at the table. I can see you are worried.

LAVRENTI. Right. So then. The Scene Where The Son Borrows The Father's Coat To Look For A Job.

[*Aniko and Haemon take up positions. He eats in silence for a few seconds and watches his mother. Then he gets up and moves his chair beside her.*]

HAEMON. You look worried tonight, Mama.

ANIKO. I am just thinking, my boy.

HAEMON. Have we got this week's rent, Mama?

ANIKO. Yes, I think we will have it.

HAEMON. And food, Mama?

ANIKO. What are you worrying about these things for! Worry about your lessons at school. I haven't let you go hungry yet.

HAEMON. But I must worry, Mama. You are alone. I am my father's son.

ANIKO. He will be back with us one day.

HAEMON. We still have a long time to wait.

ANIKO. Yes.

HAEMON. We are struggling, Mama.

ANIKO. So are a lot of other people in New Brighton.

HAEMON. Yes, but you are alone. They have got uncles, and families ... you are alone.

ANIKO. My sister sent me two rand last week from East London.

HAEMON. Will she send you two rand again this week, and next week ... ?

ANIKO. No. She can't. She is poor. But why are you going on like this? I know all these things. But I am trying my best.

HAEMON. I want to get a job, Mama. I want to leave school and get a job.

ANIKO. No.

HAEMON. Please, Mama ...

ANIKO. No!

HAEMON. Please just listen to me, Mama.

ANIKO. No! You go to school. You learn. If your father had gone to school maybe he wouldn't be where he is now. You learn to read and write.

HAEMON. I can already read and write, Mama.

ANIKO. Then learn more. Learn all you can and keep yourself out of gaol. This world is too clever now for old people like your father and me, but you can learn about it.

HAEMON. Mama ...

THE COAT

ANIKO. I said, no! Have you lost your manners that you do not listen to a big person any more?

HAEMON. Mama, I am my father's son. I am your son. Just listen to me once.

We need money, Mama. You said yourself that we must see that we are here when father comes back. But how can we stay here if we don't pay the rent? How can we be alive if we don't eat? How can we eat without money? Please, Mama! Listen to me. If I get a job it will be easier. I won't stop learning. I will go to night school. I can still write my exams.

ANIKO. The last time I saw your father in gaol he asked me how you were getting on at school. He said to me: 'He must learn. The white man's world is a strange one. Tell him to be clever.'

HAEMON. I can do all that at night school, Mama. Other boys do it. They work during the day and study at night. I will do what my father wants. But I also want to be here when he comes back.

ANIKO. You don't even know if you can get a job.

HAEMON. I can, Mama. George Ngxokolo told me about one. It's at the same place where he works. One of the white madams called him and said he must look for a good boy for them in New Brighton.

ANIKO. How much is the pay?

HAEMON. Five rands a week.

ANIKO. That will help.

HAEMON. Can I go tomorrow and see them?

ANIKO. Your father will not forgive me.

HAEMON. Father will understand, Mama. When I tell him how you struggled and all our troubles, he will understand.

ANIKO. What time must you be at this place?

HAEMON. Early, Mama. George said I must be there early to show them I will always be early.

ANIKO. I will give you busfare.

HAEMON. George also said I must look smart.

ANIKO. Your other shirt is clean.

HAEMON. But my jacket is so old, Mama.

ANIKO. It's all we've got.

HAEMON [*hesitantly*]. Couldn't I borrow father's jacket? Just to get the job! I'll look after it. It will help me get the job.

ANIKO. Yes, you can borrow it.

HAEMON [*turning to the other actors*]. That's all.

LAVRENTI [*to Haemon*]. Put on the coat.

[*Haemon puts it on.*]

JINGI. It fits.

LAVRENTI. I like this. We've got the coat being worn, being used.

JINGI. I've got reservations about that scene though.

MARIE. I thought it was right. What was wrong with it?

JINGI. I think Haemon was too advanced for his age.

HAEMON. How?

JINGI. How old were you supposed to be?

HAEMON. Sixteen years.

JINGI. And you want to tell me that a sixteen-year-old boy will discuss things with his mother like that? Will worry and care like that?

MARIE. Yes.

JINGI. Never.

ANIKO. *Boet* Jingi! I know of a case in our street, man, just like that. There are older boys in the family but they do nothing. It's the young one who helps his mother. He sells newspapers at night, during weekends he gets garden jobs in Newton Park. In fact I think he is younger than fifteen.

HAEMON. Yes, you get them.

JINGI. What percentage?

HAEMON. I don't know.

JINGI. Exactly.

HAEMON. But you get them.

JINGI. They're a very small minority, my friend.

HAEMON. So what?

JINGI. So what are we trying to do? Aren't we trying to find out something about New Brighton?

LAVRENTI. Yes, we are.

JINGI. Then let's concern ourselves with the majority. And I'm saying that the majority of young boys and girls, and men and women for that matter, don't give a damn about what is going on, not even in their own homes. They don't help their mothers the way Haemon showed us.

HAEMON. So what must we do about those that do? Pretend they don't exist?

JINGI. If we are concerned with New Brighton, and understanding it . . .

HAEMON. But loyalty to your parents, understanding, sympathy, self-sacrifice . . . these are also a part of New Brighton. Aren't they?

JINGI. Look, Haemon, I challenge you . . .

HAEMON [to the others]. He's not answering my question. Is New Brighton all bad? Don't people, the young people, have any good points?

LAVRENTI [to Jingi]. Answer his question.

JINGI. Yes, they do. A few of them.

HAEMON. Well I think we must understand them just as much as the others. Maybe they are the most important of all.

MARIE. Hear! Hear!

HAEMON. Why concern ourselves with New Brighton at all if there is nothing good to say about it?

I think that woman's son, the son who stands by his mother and tries to help, is more important than ten of the other kind. You can show the other kind if you want to. I showed you the son who I believed in.

LAVRENTI. Let's get back to the improvisation. I wonder whether the wife would have given the coat away so easily, even to her son.

JINGI. Same here.

ANIKO. You fellows better listen better next time. I didn't give it away. I lent it to him.

HAEMON. *Ewe*, Mama.

LAVRENTI. All right, it's not a criticism. Let's make it a question. Would the wife give away the coat?

MARIE. No.

LAVRENTI. Even if she was pressed? Aniko?

ANIKO. What do you mean pressed? Hard-up?

LAVRENTI. Yes.

ANIKO. *Ai, Boet* Lavrenti! You want to see this old woman in trouble, hey!

LAVRENTI. Well, what do you think?

ANIKO. Maybe. Maybe no. I don't know.

JINGI. Suppose one of your children is sick?

ANIKO. Then I'll buy medicine.

JINGI. But you haven't got any money. You're broke.

LAVRENTI. Hang on. Give her the coat.

[*Haemon takes off the coat and gives it to Aniko. He stands a little to one side but doesn't sit.*]

Okay, Jingi.

JINGI [*to Aniko*]. One of your children is sick. The ten-year-old girl. The doctor has told you she must get some certain kind of medicine straight away. But you're broke. It's the end of the week, so Haemon hasn't got his pay yet. But you've got the coat. You could sell it. Marie told us it was worth about one rand, one rand fifty. That will be enough for medicine, with enough left over for a bucket of entrails. The child is sick. She needs medicine and good food. What do you say? The child is crying, man! Listen to her! There in the other room crying 'Mama! Mama!' Here is one rand fifty. Give me the coat and it's yours.

ANIKO. No, man. Maybe there is something else. I've got two pots. Take one.

JINGI. One old pot? What's that worth? Two bob! And anyway it's got a hole in it and no lid.

ANIKO. There must be something else! My zinc bath ... No. I need it for the washing.

JINGI. What are you worrying about? What's your problem? The coat hangs there, useless in the wardrobe. Nobody wears it. Nobody is going to be cold. You could save up and buy him a much better one for when he comes back. Times will change. He didn't say you must keep it for him. He said: 'Use it. Tell her to use it.' Those were his words. Well now his daughter is sick. There in the other room. Wouldn't he be the first one to tell you to sell it? Here it is in my hand. One rand fifty. Give me the coat and it's yours. What about it?

[*Aniko looks at the outstretched, clenched fist of Jingi. She is about to hand over the coat when Haemon jumps forward.*]

HAEMON. No, Mama! I'll borrow from my baas at work. He will lend it to me.

ANIKO [*clutching the coat to herself and turning away from Jingi*]. Thank you, my son.

[*Marie claps her hands and laughs. Lavrenti smiles. Jingi drops his hand and with a hopeless gesture to the other actors returns to his seat. Lavrenti gets up.*]

LAVRENTI [*to Haemon*]. You cheated.

JINGI. *Ja*! That was a sure case of interference.

HAEMON. She is my mother. It was my father's coat.

LAVRENTI. But we wanted her on the spot, man.

HAEMON. Then you shouldn't have told me to try on the coat.

LAVRENTI. What difference did that make?

HAEMON. I thought about my father.

LAVRENTI. You are complicating matters with your loyalty.

HAEMON. That's right.

LAVRENTI [*smiling*]. Okay, okay, we get you. But let's try again. Because I think it's a good question. Would she ever sell that coat? Come on, let's try and work out a situation in which she is really in a tight corner and the only way out is to sell the coat. Jingi had a good try with that idea of the sick child but there were too many loopholes.

JINGI. What about hunger? Starvation? Food. A hungry person will do anything for food.

MARIE. Her neighbours wouldn't let her starve. We've heard about this woman, Joyce . . . she wouldn't let this old woman starve.

JINGI. What? There are plenty of families that go to sleep at night with only a mug of hot water in their bellies and their neighbours don't give a damn.

LAVRENTI. Hold it. Hold it. Let's not get back to that argument.

MARIE. What about funeral expenses? Suppose the little girl had died from her illness, and the old woman needed money for funeral expenses? You know how fussy our people are about burials and all that.

ANIKO. No, man. *Sis*, Marie! Jeesus! I'll commit suicide. That's my answer. My husband is in gaol, now my daughter dies! I don't want to live anymore. What's the matter with you people? Why don't you just get a big lorry to knock her down and kill her and get it over with?

LAVRENTI. We want her alive. She's no good to us dead.

ANIKO. Then have pity on her.

LAVRENTI. There's not much of that in life, sister. But anyway you're right, let's not exaggerate the circumstances. Just a nice straightforward case of destitution. Hardly enough money for one meal, no money for clothes or . . . Come on!

JINGI. Rent.

LAVRENTI. *Ja*, rent! That's a thought. There's a nice, typical New Brighton predicament. How about it?

JINGI. She's fallen two months behind in her rent. The Headman has brought around the final notice. If she doesn't pay up straight away she gets out. We could have a scene where she sits and thinks about the final notice.

ANIKO. I can't read.

MARIE. So you call in Joyce from next door. Maybe she can. You discuss things with her.

LAVRENTI. And then?

JINGI. Then she goes to the Administration Offices to plead with the Headman to give her a week to find some money. He

138

tells her that she must pay something straight away. I've got it! He's a member of one of those money-lending societies that get rich on the poor people . . . so he sends her along to his society to sell her coat.

LAVRENTI. We've got it. Okay, Aniko? Marie will be your neighbour, Jingi will be the Headman at the Administration Offices. Then you go to borrow money from the Society and Marie will be that woman as well.

ANIKO. What about Haemon? I want Haemon. He helps me.

HAEMON. Yes, you must reckon with the two of us now.

LAVRENTI. We want her alone.

HAEMON. That's not fair.

LAVRENTI. Fair doesn't come into it. We're black.

HAEMON. But she *has* got a son.

LAVRENTI. Look man, this is an experiment . . . a theatre laboratory. We are allowed to isolate a factor for examination. So let's us assume that for some reason or other you cannot interfere in this one. Okay?

HAEMON. Not even to give her moral support?

LAVRENTI. All right, if you want to. That's useless enough.

LAVRENTI. Right.

The Scene Where The Wife Is Faced With Selling Her Husband's Coat To Pay Her Rent.

[*Lavrenti sits down. Haemon sits down by himself to one side. Aniko is alone.*]

ANIKO. Sis Joyce! Sis Joyce!

MARIE [*seated*]. What is it?

ANIKO. Come here please, Sis Joyce!

MARIE [*joining Aniko*]. What is wrong?

ANIKO. *Haai* Sis Joyce! Is it true? Do they want to throw me out of my house? The Headman brought me this paper. Is it true?

MARIE. *Tula*, Sissy. *Tula*. Let me read it.

[*Reading*] That unless the arrears of twenty-four rand are paid immediately you will be evicted from the house . . .

Hey hey hey! Haven't you been paying your rent?

ANIKO. These last four months have been terrible, Sis Joyce. Every week I said, this week I will pay the rent, even if I go hungry. But when the children come home and they are hungry, but I see they are too frightened to ask if there is any food . . . what must a mother do? Then the little girl was sick, John lost his job . . . Is it true that they want to throw me out? Does the paper say so?

MARIE. Yes, if you don't pay them what you owe.

ANIKO. What must I do?

MARIE. Go to the Headman at the Office. Speak to him, Sissy. Ask him to speak with the Superintendent. Plead with him. Sis Nkonyeni got this paper one time and she went there and spoke to them and they gave her more time to find the money.

ANIKO. I will go straight away.

[*Marie sits down.*]

It took me thirty minutes to get to the Administration Offices. One long walk, straight, straight down from Mnqandi Street. It's a rough road. I was in a hurry.

I tripped and fell, I got up and carried on. Past the White Location until I came to the offices.

There are people in the yard, sitting and waiting. It is a hot day. There is no shade. I sat with them and waited. The ones who were before you, go in. They look worried. When they come out they still look worried. Some of them get a piece of paper inside. They walk away looking at it. Then your turn comes.

[*Jingi moves forward his chair, sits down, and pretends to write. Aniko moves up to him, he looks up at her and goes on writing. He keeps her waiting a long time.*]

JINGI. Have you got the money?

Hey! I'm speaking to you. Have you got the money? Twenty-four rand.

ANIKO. No . . .

JINGI. Then what are you wasting my time for? Go and find the money.

ANIKO. Please, Sibonda . . . please give me till the end of this month. My son is looking for a job . . . I know he will find one, he is a good boy. I am going to do washing. I will have some money at the end of the month.

JINGI. This rent must be paid no later than the date shown on your notice.

ANIKO. *Ag sies tog*, my father! Can't you please speak to the Superintendent for me. I can't speak his language.

JINGI. I can't bother him! He's a busy man. Do you think he's got time to sit around and listen to sad stories. Pay your rent or get out of the house.

ANIKO. Won't you take me to him, let me speak to him?

JINGI. You want me to lose my job?

ANIKO [*turning to leave*]. Oh my God, what am I going to do now?

JINGI. Anyway, where's your husband?

ANIKO. In gaol for five years. On Robben Island.

JINGI. Haven't you got anybody to help you raise the money?

ANIKO. No.

JINGI. Not even two rand?

ANIKO. Two rand? I thought the paper said twenty-four.

JINGI. I know what the paper said! But if you could put down two rand I might be able to get you another week.

ANIKO. Two rand?

JINGI. Yes, two rand. Are you deaf?

ANIKO. I haven't got two rand.

JINGI. Why don't you borrow from the societies?

ANIKO. I don't know any of them.

JINGI. Look, I'll help you. There is a society at No. 5 Nikwe Street . . . June Molefe . . . tell her I sent you. She will lend you money if you have something to put down as security . . . your sewing machine, or kitchen chairs . . .

ANIKO. I don't have those.

JINGI. You must have something.

ANIKO. A man's coat.

JINGI. That will do, if it's still in good condition.

ANIKO. How much is the interest?

JINGI. Twenty-five cents a week on every two rand.

ANIKO. You will give me another week if I pay two rand?

JINGI. Yes, but don't say I said so.

ANIKO. I will go and see June.

JINGI. I will keep this order until you come back.

[*Aniko moves away. Jingi rejoins the other actors.*]

ANIKO. I walked back all the way to Mnqandi Street to fetch the coat. It was a long walk. I was tired. I cried. The streets of New Brighton made me cry. A child saw I was crying and asked me why. He had two oranges. Buy an orange, Mama, he said. One cent each. I didn't have words for him. I didn't have words for myself. I just walked.

At the house I drank a glass of water, took the coat and started to walk to Nikwe Street. I passed Avenue A, then the Roman Church but I didn't look at it. Then into Pendla Road and up into Jolobe Road, past the Newell High School. But I didn't see anything. All I knew was that the roads are full of stones.

I reached number five Nikwe Street. I knocked on the door . . .

[*Marie moves forward.*]

. . . a woman opened it. I told her my business. She took the coat . . .

[*Marie takes the coat and examines it.*]

. . . and said she would lend me two rand. She gave me the coat to hold, went away and came back with the money.

MARIE [*holding out her hand*]. Two rand, Mama.

[*Aniko holds the coat. She doesn't move.*]

Two rand for the coat, Mama.

[*Still Aniko doesn't move.*]

Are you all right, Mama?

ANIKO [*turning to the other actors who are watching her expectantly*]. Don't just sit there and pity her.

LAVRENTI. What else can we do?

ANIKO. But a man wore this coat!

[*pause*]

You think it's easy? Just hand it over and take the money! This is all that's left of him. It came back to New Brighton empty, but there was a man in it once ... my husband, my children's father.

LAVRENTI. What are you trying to tell us? We know the facts.

ANIKO. No you don't. There are other facts. Life isn't just eating samp and beans, with meat once a week, or washing the white man's underpants and sleeping in council houses. We are a nation with men, and one of them wore this coat. Can I not struggle a little for him? When he comes back can I not say: Yes, it was hard for us as well. But we waited. We had faith. Here is your coat, my husband. We kept it for you.

LAVRENTI. That's moving, Aniko ... but how much of that is you, how much the wife? We're not interested in what you would *like* to see happen, but in what *does* happen.

Where is that husband going to come back to if you leave the house? And if you do leave it you know they'll most probably endorse you out and back into the reserves. How will you live there? Where will your son find work or carry on with his studies?

ANIKO [*after a pause*]. Then I must sell it?

LAVRENTI. Work it out. Do you want that house for another week?

ANIKO. Yes.

JINGI. Won't another week give you and your son a chance to raise the money for your back rent?

ANIKO. Yes.

LAVRENTI. Don't you want to be in that house, waiting, when your husband comes back?

ANIKO. Yes.

LAVRENTI. What do you think that coat is going to look like in five years time? All you'll have left to give him is a moth-eaten, useless old rag.

ANIKO [*wearily*]. Yes yes yes ... YES, to all your questions, yes to all my feelings, my worries, yes to my children, yes to you my husband.

LAVRENTI. Go back to June Molefe at Number Five Nikwe Street.

[*Aniko turns and moves back to Marie. Marie holds out her hand again.*]

MARIE. Two rand, Mama. Two rand for the coat.

[*Aniko hands over the coat and takes the money.*]

LAVRENTI. Okay.

[*The actors sit around in their chairs.*]

JINGI. One thought struck me, isn't there some organisation that has been paying the rents of these wives who have their husbands on Robben Island?

MARIE. It's been banned.

JINGI. Yes, but the churches have taken over, haven't they?

LAVRENTI. It would still be easy for them to miss one woman. There's over a thousand families in New Brighton with husbands and fathers on the Island.

ANIKO. You fellows sure gave that old woman a workout. First this, then that ...

HAEMON. Wasn't there a man in the Bible who suffered a series of calamities?

JINGI. Job. He was tested by God.

LAVRENTI. How about it, Aniko? You think God was testing the old girl?

ANIKO. We aren't prophets, man, we're people.

HAEMON. I wonder now if we spent too much time on the coat. We didn't say anything about the man. From the moment I put on that coat I started to think about my father. And what about Cradock?

LAVRENTI. At the start we said that our concern was with New Brighton.

HAEMON. Cradock has become a part of New Brighton.*

LAVRENTI. That's interesting geography.

HAEMON. I think we should have said something about Cradock and that Court Room.

JINGI. *You* can. I don't know anything about it.

HAEMON. We didn't know anything about the coat, but we guessed.

LAVRENTI. [*correcting him*]. We had facts and we investigated.

HAEMON. There are facts about Cradock. We could do the same thing there. The real drama is surely the man who wore the coat.

MARIE. The wives wait. That is also drama.

LAVRENTI. We didn't do too badly. Because it was just a coat we struck a good balance between reason and emotion. Our boredom kept us objective.

HAEMON. Are you saying that we must be bored with these things before we can understand them, or do anything about them?

LAVRENTI. Let's take that up next time.

[*The actors leave the stage.*]

SIZWE BANSI IS DEAD

devised by
Athol Fugard, John Kani, and Winston Ntshona

CHARACTERS

STYLES
SIZWE BANSI
BUNTU

SIZWE BANZI IS DEAD (original spelling) was first performed at
The Space, Cape Town, on 8 October 1972, directed by Athol Fugard
(lighting: Brian Astbury) with the following cast:

STYLES and BUNTU	John Kani
SIZWE BANSI	Winston Ntshona

The play was performed at St Stephen's Hall, New Brighton, Port
Elizabeth, for one night only on 23 August 1973, with the same cast
and director. The first London production, which became part of a
'South African Season' with THE ISLAND, at The Theatre Upstairs,
Royal Court, with the same cast and director (design: Douglas Heap),
was on 20 September 1973.

The first American production, at the Long Wharf Theater, New
Haven, on 10 October 1974, was followed by a Broadway season with
THE ISLAND at the Edison Theater, New York, with the original cast
and director, from 13 December 1974. The first Australian production
was at the Seymour Centre, York Theatre, New South Wales, as part of
a season with THE ISLAND, with the original cast and director, on
29 March 1976. The first 'open' production in South Africa, with the
original cast and director, was at the Market Theatre, Johannesburg, in
September 1979.

The play was televised with the original cast for the BBC in 1974
(director John Davies); and for CBS cable production (director Merrill
Brockway) in 1981.

Styles's Photographic Studio in the African township of New Brighton, Port Elizabeth. Positioned prominently, the name-board:

> *Styles Photographic Studio. Reference Books; Passports;*
> *Weddings; Engagements; Birthday Parties and Parties.*
>
> *Prop.—Styles.*

Underneath this a display of photographs of various sizes. Centre stage, a table and chair. This is obviously used for photographs because a camera on a tripod stands ready a short distance away.

There is also another table, or desk, with odds and ends of photographic equipment and an assortment of 'props' for photographs.

The setting for this and subsequent scenes should be as simple as possible so that the action can be continuous.

Styles walks on with a newspaper. A dapper, alert young man wearing a white dustcoat and a bowtie. He sits down at the table and starts to read the paper.

STYLES [*reading the headlines*]. 'Storm buffets Natal. Damage in many areas . . . trees snapped like . . . what? . . . matchsticks. . . .'

[*He laughs.*]

They're having it, boy! And I'm watching it . . . in the paper.

[*Turning the page, another headline.*]

'China: A question-mark on South West Africa.' What's China want there? *Yo!* They better be careful. China gets in there . . . !
[*Laugh.*] I'll tell you what happens. . . .

[*Stops abruptly. Looks around as if someone might be eavesdropping on his intimacy with the audience.*]

No comment.

[*Back to his paper.*]

What's this? . . . *Ag!* American politics. Nixon and all his votes. Means buggerall to us.

[*Another page, another headline.*]

'Car plant expansion. 1·5 million rand plan.' *Ja.* I'll tell you what *that* means . . . more machines, bigger buildings . . . never any expansion to the pay-packet. Makes me fed-up. I know

149

what I'm talking about. I worked at Ford one time. We used to read in the newspaper ... big headlines! ... 'So and so from America or London made a big speech: "... going to see to it that the conditions of their non-white workers in Southern Africa were substantially improved."' The talk ended in the bloody newspaper. Never in the pay-packet.

Another time we read: Mr Henry Ford Junior Number two or whatever the hell he is ... is visiting the Ford Factories in South Africa!

[*Shakes his head ruefully at the memory.*]

Big news for us, man! When a big man like that visited the plant there was usually a few cents more in the pay-packet at the end of the week.

Ja, a Thursday morning. I walked into the plant ... 'Hey! What's this?' ... Everything was quiet! Those big bloody machines that used to make so much noise they made my head go around ... ? Silent! Went to the notice-board and read: Mr Ford's visit today!

The one in charge of us ... [*laugh*] hey! I remember him. General Foreman Mr 'Baas' Bradley. Good man that one, if you knew how to handle him ... he called us all together:

[*Styles mimics Mr 'Baas' Bradley. A heavy Afrikaans accent.*]

'Listen, boys, don't go to work on the line. There is going to be a General Cleaning first.'

I used to like General Cleaning. Nothing specific, you know, little bit here, little bit there. But that day! Yessus ... in came the big machines with hot water and brushes—sort of electric mop—and God alone knows what else. We started on the floors. The oil and dirt under the machines was thick, man. All the time the bosses were walking around watching us:

[*Slapping ...s hands together as he urges on the 'boys'.*]

'Come on, boys! It's got to be spotless! Big day for the plant!' Even the *big* boss, the one we only used to see lunch-times, walking to the canteen with a big cigar in his mouth and his hands in his pockets ... that day? Sleeves rolled up, running around us:

'Come on! Spotless, my boys! Over there, John. . . .' I thought: What the hell is happening? It was beginning to feel like hard work, man. I'm telling you we cleaned that place—spot-checked after fifteen minutes! . . . like you would have thought it had just been built.

First stage of General Cleaning finished. We started on the second. Mr 'Baas' Bradley came in with paint and brushes. I watched.

W—h—i—t—e   l—i—n—e

[*Mr 'Baas' Bradley paints a long white line on the floor.*]

What's this? Been here five years and I never seen a white line before. Then:

[*Mr 'Baas' Bradley at work with the paint-brush.*]

CAREFUL THIS SIDE. TOW MOTOR IN MOTION.

[*Styles laughs.*]

It was nice, man. Safety-precautions after six years. Then another gallon of paint.

Y—e—l—l—o—w   l—i—n—e—

NO SMOKING IN THIS AREA. DANGER!

Then another gallon:

G—r—e—e—n   l—i—n—e—

I noticed that that line cut off the roughcasting section, where we worked with the rough engine blocks as we got them from Iscor. Dangerous work that. Big machines! One mistake there and you're in trouble. I watched them and thought: What's going to happen here? When the green line was finished, down they went on the floor—Mr 'Baas' Bradley, the lot!—with a big green board, a little brush, and a tin of white paint.

EYE PROTECTION AREA. Then my big moment:

'Styles!'

'Yes, sir!'

[*Mr 'Baas' Bradley's heavy Afrikaans accent*] 'What do you say in your language for this? Eye Protection Area.'

It was easy, man!

'*Gqokra Izi Khuselo Zamehlo Kule Ndawo.*'

Nobody wrote it!

'Don't bloody fool me, Styles!'

'No, sir!'

'Then spell it . . . slowly.'

[*Styles has a big laugh.*]

Hey! That was my moment, man. Kneeling there on the floor . . . foreman, general foreman, plant supervisor, plant manager . . . and Styles? Standing!

[*Folds his arms as he acts out his part to the imaginary figures crouched on the floor.*]

'G—q—o—k—r—a' . . . and on I went, with Mr 'Baas' Bradley painting and saying as he wiped away the sweat:

'You're not fooling me, hey!'

After that the green board went up. We all stood and admired it. Plant was looking nice, man! Colourful!

Into the third phase of General Cleaning.

'Styles!'

'Yes, sir!'

'Tell all the boys they must now go to the bathroom and wash themselves clean.'

We needed it! Into the bathroom, under the showers . . . hot water, soap . . . on a Thursday! Before ten? *Yo!* What's happening in the plant? The other chaps asked me: 'What's going on, Styles?' I told them: 'Big-shot cunt from America coming to visit you.' When we finished washing they gave us towels . . . [*laugh*].

Three hundred of us, man! We were so clean we felt shy! Standing there like little ladies in front of the mirror. From there to the General Store.

Handed in my dirty overall.

'Throw it on the floor.'

'Yes, sir!'

New overall comes, wrapped in plastic. Brand new, man! I normally take a thirty-eight but this one was a forty-two. Then next door to the tool room . . . brand new tool bag, set of spanners, shifting spanner, torque wrench—all of them brand new—and because I worked in the dangerous hot test section I was also given a new asbestos apron and fire-proof gloves to replace the ones I had lost about a year ago. I'm telling you I walked back heavy to my spot. Armstrong on the moon!* Inside the plant it was general meeting again. General Foreman Mr 'Baas' Bradley called me.

'Styles!'

'Yes, sir.'

'Come translate.'

'Yes, sir!'

[*Styles pulls out a chair. Mr 'Baas' Bradley speaks on one side, Styles translates on the other.*]

'Tell the boys in your language, that this is a very big day in their lives.'

'Gentlemen, this old fool says this is a hell of a big day in our lives.'

The men laughed.

'They are very happy to hear that, sir.'

'Tell the boys that Mr Henry Ford the Second, the owner of this place, is going to visit us. Tell them Mr Ford is the big Baas. He owns the plant and everything in it.'

'Gentlemen, old Bradley says this Ford is a big bastard. He owns everything in this building, which means you as well.'

A voice came out of the crowd:

'Is he a bigger fool than Bradley?'

'They're asking, sir, is he bigger than you?'

'Certainly . . . [*blustering*] . . . certainly. He is a very big baas. He's a . . . [*groping for words*] . . . he's a Makulu Baas.'

I loved that one!

'Mr "Baas" Bradley says most certainly Mr Ford is bigger than him. In fact Mr Ford is the grandmother baas of them all . . . that's what he said to me.'

'Styles, tell the boys that when Mr Henry Ford comes into the plant I want them all to look happy. We will slow down the speed of the line so that they can sing and smile while they are working.'

'Gentlemen, he says that when the door opens and his grandmother walks in you must see to it that you are wearing a mask of smiles. Hide your true feelings, brothers. You must sing. The joyous songs of the days of old before we had fools like this one next to me to worry about.' [*To Bradley.*] 'Yes, sir!'

'Say to them, Styles, that they must try to impress Mr Henry Ford that they are better than those monkeys in his own country, those niggers in Harlem who know nothing but strike, strike.'

Yo! I liked that one too.

'Gentlemen, he says we must remember, when Mr Ford walks in, that we are South African monkeys, not American monkeys. South African monkeys are much better trained....' Before I could even finish, a voice was shouting out of the crowd:

'He's talking shit!' I had to be careful!

[*Servile and full of smiles as he turns back to Bradley.*]

'No, sir! The men say they are much too happy to behave like those American monkeys.'

Right! Line was switched on nice and slow—and we started working.

[*At work on the Assembly Line; singing.*]

'*Tshotsholoza . . . tshotsholoza . . . kulezondawo. . . .*'

We had all the time in the world, man! . . . torque wrench out . . . tighten the cylinder-head nut . . . wait for the next one . . . [*Singing*] '*Vyabaleka . . . vyabaleka . . . kulezondawo. . . .*' I kept my eye on the front office. I could see them—Mr 'Baas' Bradley, the line supervisor—through the big glass window, brushing their hair, straightening the tie. There was some General Cleaning going on there too.

[*He laughs.*]

We were watching them. Nobody was watching us. Even the old Security Guard. The one who every time he saw a black man walk past with his hands in his pockets he saw another spark-plug walk out of the plant. Today? To hell and gone there on the other side polishing his black shoes.

Then, through the window, I saw three long black Galaxies zoom up. I passed the word down the line: He's come!

Let me tell you what happened. The big doors opened; next thing the General Superintendent, Line Supervisor, General Foreman, Manager, Senior Manager, Managing Director ... the bloody lot were there ... like a pack of puppies!

[*Mimics a lot of fawning men retreating before an important person.*]

I looked and laughed! 'Yessus, Styles, they're all playing your part today!' They ran, man! In came a tall man, six foot six, hefty, full of respect and dignity ... I marvelled at him! Let me show you what he did.

[*Three enormous strides*] One ... two ... three ... [*Cursory look around as he turns and takes the same three strides back.*]

One ... two ... three ... OUT! Into the Galaxy and gone! That's all. Didn't talk to me, Mr 'Baas' Bradley, Line Supervisor, or anybody. He didn't even look at the plant! And what did I see when those three Galaxies disappeared? The white staff at the main switchboard.

'Double speed on the line! Make up for production lost!'

It ended up with us working harder that bloody day than ever before. Just because that big. ... [*shakes his head.*]

Six years there. Six years a bloody fool.

[*Back to his newspaper. A few more headlines with appropriate comment, then. . . .*]

[*Reading*] 'The Mass Murderer! Doom!'

[*Smile of recognition.*]

'For fleas ... Doom. Flies ... Doom. Bedbugs ... Doom. For cockroaches and other household pests. The household insecticide ... Doom.' Useful stuff. Remember, Styles? *Ja.*

[*To the audience.*] After all that time at Ford I sat down one day. I said to myself:

'Styles, you're a bloody monkey, boy!'

'What do you mean?'

'You're a monkey, man.'

'Go to hell!'

'Come on, Styles, you're a monkey, man, and you know it. Run up and down the whole bloody day! Your life doesn't belong to you. You've sold it. For what, Styles? Gold wristwatch in twenty-five years time when they sign you off because you're too old for anything any more.'

I was right. I took a good look at my life. What did I see? A bloody circus monkey! Selling most of his time on this earth to another man. Out of every twenty-four hours I could only properly call mine the six when I was sleeping. What the hell is the use of that?

Think about it, friend. Wake up in the morning, half-past six, out of the pyjamas and into the bath-tub, put on your shirt with one hand, socks with the other, realize you got your shoes on the wrong bloody feet, and all the time the seconds are passing and if you don't hurry up you'll miss the bus. . . . 'Get the lunch, dear. I'm late. My lunch, please, darling!' . . . then the children come in . . . 'Daddy, can I have this? Daddy, I want money for that.' 'Go to your mother. I haven't got time. Look after the children, please, sweetheart!!' . . . grab your lunch . . . 'Bye Bye!!' and then run like I-don't-know-what for the bus stop. You call that living? I went back to myself for another chat:

'Suppose you're right. What then?'

'Try something else.'

'Like what?'

Silly question to ask. I knew what I was going to say. Photographer! It was my hobby in those days. I used to pick up a few cents on the side taking cards at parties, weddings, big occasions. But when it came to telling my wife and parents that I wanted to turn professional . . . !!

My father was the worst.

'You call that work? Click-click with a camera. Are you mad?' I tried to explain. 'Daddy, if I could stand on my own two feet and not be somebody else's tool, I'd have some respect for myself. I'd be a man.'

'What do you mean? Aren't you one already? You're circumcised, you've got a wife. . . .'

Talk about the generation gap!

Anyway I thought: To hell with them. I'm trying it. It was the Christmas shutdown, so I had lots of time to look around for a studio. My friend Dhlamini at the Funeral Parlour told me about a vacant room next door. He encouraged me. I remember his words. 'Grab your chance, Styles. Grab it before somebody in my line puts you in a box and closes the lid.' I applied for permission to use the room as a studio. After some time the first letter back:

'Your application has been received and is being considered.' A month later: 'The matter is receiving the serious consideration of the Board.' Another month: 'Your application is now on the director's table.' I nearly gave up, friends. But one day, a knock at the door—the postman—I had to sign for a registered letter. 'We are pleased to inform you. . . .'

[*Styles has a good laugh.*]

I ran all the way to the Administration Offices, grabbed the key, ran all the way back to Red Location, unlocked the door, and walked in!

What I found sobered me up a little bit. Window panes were all broken; big hole in the roof, cobwebs in the corners. I didn't let that put me off though. Said to myself: 'This is your chance, Styles. Grab it.' Some kids helped me clean it out. The dust! *Yo!* When the broom walked in the Sahara Desert walked out! But at the end of that day it was reasonably clean. I stood here in the middle of the floor, straight! You know what that means? To stand straight in a place of your own? To be your own . . . General Foreman, Mr 'Baas', Line Supervisor—the lot! I was tall, six foot six and doing my own inspection of the plant.

So I'm standing there—here—feeling big and what do I see on the walls? Cockroaches. *Ja*, cockroaches . . . in *my* place. I don't mean those little things that run all over the place when you pull out the kitchen drawer. I'm talking about the big bastards, the paratroopers as we call them. I didn't like them. I'm not afraid of them but I just don't like them! All over. On the floors, the walls. I heard the one on the wall say: 'What's going on? Who opened the door?' The one on the floor answered: 'Relax. He won't last. This place is condemned.' That's when I thought: Doom.

Out of here and into the Chinaman's shop. 'Good day, sir.
I've got a problem. Cockroaches.'
The Chinaman didn't even think, man, he just said: 'Doom!'
I said: 'Certainly.' He said: 'Doom, seventy-five cents a tin.'
Paid him for two and went back. *Yo!* You should have seen me!
Two-tin Charlie!

[*His two tins at the ready, forefingers on the press-buttons, Styles gives
us a graphic re-enactment of what happened. There is a brief respite to
'reload'—shake the tins—and tie a handkerchief around his nose after
which he returns to the fight. Styles eventually backs through the
imaginary door, still firing, and closes it. Spins the tins and puts them
into their holsters.*]

I went home to sleep. *I* went to sleep. Not *them* [*the cockroaches*].
What do you think happened here? General meeting under
the floorboards. All the bloody survivors. The old professor
addressed them: 'Brothers, we face a problem of serious pollu-
tion . . . contamination! The menace appears to be called
Doom. I have recommended a general inoculation of the whole
community. Everybody in line, please. [*Inoculation proceeds.*]
Next . . . next . . . next . . .' While poor old Styles is smiling in
his sleep! Next morning I walked in. . . . [*He stops abruptly.*] . . .
What's this? Cockroach walking on the floor? Another one on
the ceiling? Not a damn! Doom did it yesterday. Doom does it
today. [*Whips out the two tins and goes in fighting. This time, however,
it is not long before they peter out.*] Pssssssssss . . . pssssss . . .
psssss . . . pss [*a last desperate shake, but he barely manages to get out a
squirt*].
Pss.

No bloody good! The old bastard on the floor just waved his
feelers in the air as if he was enjoying air-conditioning.

I went next door to Dhlamini and told him about my problem. He laughed. 'Doom? You're wasting your time, Styles.
You want to solve your problem, get a cat. What do you think
a cat lives on in the township? Milk? If there's any the baby
gets it. Meat? When the family sees it only once a week? Mice?
The little boys got rid of them years ago. Insects, man, township cats are insect-eaters. Here. . . .'

He gave me a little cat. I'm... I'm not too fond of cats normally. This one was called Blackie... I wasn't too fond of that name either. But... Kitsy! Kitsy! Kitsy... little Blackie followed me back to the studio.

The next morning when I walked in what do you think I saw? Wings. I smiled. Because one thing I do know is that no cockroach can take his wings off. He's dead!

[*Proud gesture taking in the whole of his studio.*]

So here it is!

[*To his name-board.*]

'Styles Photographic Studio. Reference Books; Passports; Weddings; Engagements; Birthday Parties and Parties. Proprietor: Styles.'

When you look at this, what do you see? Just another photographic studio? Where people come because they've lost their Reference Book and need a photo for the new one? That I sit them down, set up the camera... 'No expression, please.'... click-click... 'Come back tomorrow, please'... and then kick them out and wait for the next? No, friend. It's more than just that. This is a strong-room of dreams. The dreamers? My people. The simple people, who you never find mentioned in the history books, who never get statues erected to them, or monuments commemorating their great deeds. People who would be forgotten, and their dreams with them, if it wasn't for Styles. That's what I do, friends. Put down, in my way, on paper the dreams and hopes of my people so that even their children's children will remember a man... 'This was our Grandfather'... and say his name. Walk into the houses of New Brighton and on the walls you'll find hanging the story of the people the writers of the big books forget about.

[*To his display-board.*]

This one [*a photograph*] walked in here one morning. I was just passing the time. Midweek. Business is always slow then. Anyway, a knock at the door. Yes! I must explain something. I get two types of knock here. When I hear... [*knocks solemnly on the table*]... I don't even look up, man. 'Funeral parlour is next door.' But when I hear... [*energetic rap on the table... he laughs*] ... that's *my* sound, and I shout 'Come in!'

In walked a chap, full of smiles, little parcel under his arm. I can still see him. man!

[*Styles acts both roles.*]

'Mr Styles?'

I said: 'Come in!'

'Mr Styles, I've come to take a snap, Mr Styles.'

I said: 'Sit down! Sit down, my friend!'

'No, Mr Styles. I want to take the snap standing. [*Barely containing his suppressed excitement and happiness*] Mr Styles, take the card, please!'

I said: 'Certainly, friend.'

Something you mustn't do is interfere with a man's dream. If he wants to do it standing, let him stand. If he wants to sit, let him sit. Do exactly what they want! Sometimes they come in here, all smart in a suit, then off comes the jacket and shoes and socks... [*adopts a boxer's stance*] ... 'Take it, Mr Styles. Take it!' And I take it. No questions! Start asking stupid questions and you destroy that dream. Anyway, this chap I'm telling you about... [*laughing warmly as he remembers*] ... I've seen a lot of smiles in my business, friends, but that one gets first prize. I set up my camera, and just as I was ready to go... 'Wait, wait, Mr Styles! I want you to take the card with this.' Out of his parcel came a long piece of white paper... looked like some sort of document... he held it in front of him. [*Styles demonstrates.*] For once I didn't have to say, 'Smile!' Just: 'Hold it!' ... and, click... finished. I asked him what the document was.

'You see, Mr Styles, I'm forty-eight years old. I work twenty-two years for the municipality and the foreman kept on saying to me if I want promotion to Boss-boy I must try to better my education. I didn't write well, Mr Styles. So I took a course with the Damelin Correspondence College. Seven years, Mr Styles! And at last I made it. Here it is. Standard Six Certificate, School Leaving, Third Class! I made it, Mr Styles.

I made it. But I'm not finished. I'm going to take up for the Junior Certificate, then Matric . . . and you watch, Mr Styles. One day I walk out of my house, graduate, self-made! Bye-bye, Mr Styles' . . . and he walked out of here happy, man, self-made.

[*Back to his display-board; another photograph.*]

My best. Family Card. You know the Family Card? Good for business. Lot of people and they all want copies.

One Saturday morning. Suddenly a hell of a noise outside in the street. I thought: What's going on now? Next thing that door burst open and in they came! First the little ones, then the five- and six-year-olds. . . . I didn't know what was going on, man! Stupid children, coming to mess up my place. I was still trying to chase them out when the bigger boys and girls came through the door. Then it clicked. Family Card!

[*Changing his manner abruptly.*]

'Come in! Come in!'

[*Ushering a crowd of people into his studio.*]

. . . now the young men and women were coming in, then the mothers and fathers, uncles and aunties . . . the eldest son, a mature man, and finally . . .

[*Shaking his head with admiration at the memory.*]

the Old Man, the Grandfather! [*The 'old man' walks slowly and with dignity into the studio and sits down in the chair.*]

I looked at him. His grey hair was a sign of wisdom. His face, weather-beaten and lined with experience. Looking at it was like paging the volume of his history, written by himself: He was a living symbol of Life, of all it means and does to a man. I adored him. He sat there—half smiling, half serious—as if he had already seen the end of his road.

The eldest son said to me: 'Mr Styles, this is my father, my mother, my brothers and sisters, their wives and husbands, our children. Twenty-seven of us, Mr Styles. We have come to take a card. My father . . . ,' he pointed to the old man, '. . . my father always wanted it.'

I said: 'Certainly. Leave the rest to me.' I went to work.

[*Another graphic re-enactment of the scene as he describes it.*]

The old lady here, the eldest son there. Then the other one, with the other one. On this side I did something with the daughters, aunties, and one bachelor brother. Then in front of it all the eight-to-twelves, standing, in front of them the four-to-sevens, kneeling, and finally right on the floor everything that was left, sitting. Jesus, it was hard work, but finally I had them all sorted out and I went behind the camera.

[*Behind his camera.*]

Just starting to focus . . .

[*Imaginary child in front of the lens; Styles chases the child back to the family group.*]

'. . . Sit down! Sit down!'

Back to the camera, start to focus again. . . . Not One Of Them Was Smiling! I tried the old trick. 'Say cheese, please.' At first they just looked at me. 'Come on! Cheese!' The children were the first to pick it up.

[*Child's voice.*] 'Cheese. Cheese. Cheese.' Then the ones a little bit bigger—'Cheese'—then the next lot—'Cheese'—the uncles and aunties—'Cheese'—and finally the old man himself—'Cheese'! I thought the roof was going off, man! People outside in the street came and looked through the window. They joined in: 'Cheese.' When I looked again the mourners from the funeral parlour were there wiping away their tears and saying 'Cheese'. Pressed my little button and there it was—New Brighton's smile, twenty-seven variations. Don't you believe those bloody fools who make out we don't know how to smile!

Anyway, you should have seen me then. Moved the bachelor this side, sister-in-laws that side. Put the eldest son behind the old man. Reorganized the children. . . . [*Back behind his camera.*] 'Once again, please! Cheese!' Back to work . . . old man and old woman together, daughters behind them, sons on the side. Those that were kneeling, now standing, those that were standing, now kneeling. . . . Ten times, friends! Each one different!

[*An exhausted Styles collapses in a chair.*]

When they walked out finally I almost said, Never Again! A week later the eldest son came back for the cards. I had them ready. The moment he walked through that door I could see he was in trouble. He said to me: 'Mr Styles, we almost didn't make it. My father died two days after the card. He will never see it.' 'Come on,' I said. 'You're a man. One day or the other everyone of us must go home. Here. . . .' I grabbed the cards. 'Here. Look at your father and thank God for the time he was given on this earth.' We went through them together. He looked at them in silence. After the third one, the tear went slowly down his cheek.

But at the same time . . . I was watching him carefully . . . something started to happen as he saw his father there with himself, his brothers and sisters, and all the little grandchildren. He began to smile. 'That's it, brother,' I said. 'Smile! Smile at your father. Smile at the world.'

When he left, I thought of him going back to his little house somewhere in New Brighton, filled that day with the little mothers in black because a man had died. I saw my cards passing from hand to hand. I saw hands wipe away tears, and then the first timid little smiles.

You must understand one thing. We own nothing except ourselves. This world and its laws, allows us nothing, except ourselves. There is nothing we can leave behind when we die, except the memory of ourselves. I know what I'm talking about, friends—I had a father, and he died.

[*To the display-board.*]

Here he is. My father. That's him. Fought in the war. Second World War. Fought at Tobruk. In Egypt. He fought in France so that this country and all the others could stay Free. When he came back they stripped him at the docks—his gun, his uniform, the dignity they'd allowed him for a few mad years because the world needed men to fight and be ready to sacrifice themselves for something called Freedom. In return they let him keep his scoff-tin and gave him a bicycle. Size twenty-eight. I remember, because it was too big for me. When he died, in a rotten old suitcase amongst some of his old rags, I found that photograph. That's all. That's all I have from him.

[*The display-board again.*]

Or this old lady. Mrs Matothlana. Used to stay in Sangocha Street. You remember! Her husband was arrested. . . .

[*Knock at the door.*]

Tell you about it later. Come in!

[A man *walks nervously into the studio. Dressed in an ill-fitting new double-breasted suit. He is carrying a plastic bag with a hat in it. His manner is hesitant and shy. Styles takes one look at him and breaks into an enormous smile.*]

[*An aside to the audience.*] A Dream!

[*To the man.*] Come in, my friend.

MAN. Mr Styles?

STYLES. That's me. Come in! You have come to take a card?

MAN. Snap.

STYLES. Yes, a card. Have you got a deposit?

MAN. Yes.

STYLES. Good. Let me just take your name down. You see, you pay deposit now, and when you come for the card, you pay the rest.

MAN. Yes.

STYLES [*to his desk and a black book for names and addresses*]. What is your name? [*The man hesitates, as if not sure of himself.*]

Your name, please?

[*Pause.*]

Come on, my friend. You must surely have a name?

MAN [*pulling himself together, but still very nervous*]. Robert Zwelinzima.

STYLES [*writing*]. 'Robert Zwelinzima.' Address?

MAN [*swallowing*]. Fifty, Mapija Street.

STYLES [*writes, then pauses*]. 'Fifty, Mapija?'

MAN. Yes.

STYLES. You staying with Buntu?

MAN. Buntu.

STYLES. Very good somebody that one. Came here for his Wedding Card. Always helping people. If that man was white they'd call him a liberal.

[*Now finished writing. Back to his customer.*]

All right. How many cards do you want?

MAN. One card.

STYLES [*disappointed*]. Only one?

MAN. One.

STYLES. How do you want to take the card?

[*The man is not sure of what the question means.*]

You can take the card standing . . .

[*Styles strikes a stylish pose next to the table.*]

sitting . . .

[*Another pose . . . this time in the chair.*]

anyhow. How do you want it?

MAN. Anyhow.

STYLES. Right. Sit down.

[*Robert hesitates.*]

Sit down!

[*Styles fetches a vase with plastic flowers, dusts them off, and places them on the table. Robert holds up his plastic bag.*]

What you got there?

[*Out comes the hat.*]

Aha! Stetson. Put it on, my friend.

[*Robert handles it shyly.*]

You can put it on, Robert.

[*Robert pulls it on. Styles does up one of his jacket buttons.*]

What a beautiful suit, my friend! Where did you buy it?

MAN. Sales House.

STYLES. [*quoting a sales slogan*]. 'Where the Black world buys the best. Six months to pay. Pay as you wear.'

[*Nudges Robert.*]

. . . and they never repossess!

[*They share a laugh.*]

What are you going to do with this card?

[*Chatting away as he goes to his camera and sets it up for the photo. Robert watches the preparations apprehensively.*]

MAN. Send it to my wife.

STYLES. Your wife!

MAN. Nowetu.

STYLES. Where's your wife?

MAN. King William's Town.

STYLES [*exaggerated admiration*]. At last! The kind of man I like. Not one of those foolish young boys who come here to find work and then forget their families back home. A man, with responsibility!

Where do you work?

MAN. Feltex.

STYLES. I hear they pay good there.

MAN. Not bad.

[*He is now very tense, staring fixedly at the camera. Styles straightens up behind it.*]

STYLES. Come on, Robert! You want your wife to get a card with her husband looking like he's got all the worries in the world on his back? What will she think? 'My poor husband is in trouble!' You must smile!

[*Robert shamefacedly relaxes a little and starts to smile.*]

That's it!

[*He relaxes still more. Beginning to enjoy himself. Uncertainly produces a very fancy pipe from one of his pockets.*
Styles now really warming to the assignment.]

Look, have you ever walked down the passage to the office with the big glass door and the board outside: 'Manager—Bestuurder'. Imagine it, man, you, Robert Zwelinzima, behind a desk in an office like that! It can happen, Robert. Quick promotion to Chief Messenger. I'll show you what we do.

[*Styles produces a Philips class-room map of the world, which he hangs behind the table as a backdrop to the photo.*]

Look at it, Robert. America, England, Africa, Russia, Asia!

[*Carried away still further by his excitement, Styles finds a cigarette, lights it, and gives it to Robert to hold. The latter is now ready for the 'card' . . . pipe in one hand and cigarette in the other. Styles stands behind his camera and admires his handiwork.*]

Mr Robert Zwelinzima, Chief Messenger at Feltex, sitting in his office with the world behind him. Smile, Robert. Smile!

[*Studying his subject through the viewfinder of the camera.*]

Lower your hand, Robert . . . towards the ashtray . . . more . . . now make a four with your legs. . . .

[*He demonstrates behind the camera. Robert crosses his legs.*]

Hold it, Robert. . . . Keep on smiling . . . that's it. . . . [*presses the release button—the shutter clicks.*]

Beautiful! All right, Robert.

[*Robert and his smile remain frozen.*]

Robert. You can relax now. It's finished!

MAN. Finished?

STYLES. Yes. You just want the one card?

MAN. Yes.

STYLES. What happens if you lose it? Hey? I've heard stories about those postmen, Robert. *Yo!* Sit on the side of the road and open the letters they should be delivering! 'Dear wife . . .'—one rand this side, letter thrown away.'Dear wife . . .'—another rand this side, letter thrown away. You want that to happen to you? Come on! What about a movie, man?

MAN. Movie?

STYLES. Don't you know the movie?

MAN. No.

STYLES. Simple! You just walk you see . . .

[*Styles demonstrates; at a certain point freezes in mid-stride.*]

. . . and I take the card! Then you can write to your wife: 'Dear wife, I am coming home at Christmas. . . .' Put the card in your letter and post it. Your wife opens the letter and what does she see? Her Robert, walking home to her! She shows it to the children. 'Look, children, your daddy is coming!' The children jump and clap their hands: 'Daddy is coming! Daddy is coming!'

MAN [*excited by the picture Styles has conjured up*]. All right!

STYLES. You want a movie?

MAN. I want a movie.

STYLES. That's my man! Look at this, Robert.

[*Styles reverses the map hanging behind the table to reveal a gaudy painting of a futuristic city.*]

City of the Future! Look at it. Mr Robert Zwelinzima, man about town, future head of Feltex, walking through the City of the Future!

MAN [*examining the backdrop with admiration. He recognizes a landmark*]. OK.

STYLES. OK Bazaars... [*the other buildings*] ... Mutual Building Society, Barclays Bank... the lot!

What you looking for, Robert?

MAN. Feltex.

STYLES. Yes... well, you see, I couldn't fit everything on, Robert. But if I had had enough space Feltex would have been here.

[*To his table for props.*]

Walking-stick... newspaper....

MAN [*diffidently*]. I don't read.

STYLES. That is not important, my friend. You think all those monkeys carrying newspapers can read? They look at the pictures.

[*After 'dressing' Robert with the props he moves back to his camera.*]

This is going to be beautiful, Robert. My best card. I must send one to the magazines.

All right, Robert, now move back. Remember what I showed you. Just walk towards me and right in front of the City of the Future. I'll take the picture. Ready? Now come, Robert....

[*Pipe in mouth, walking-stick in hand, newspaper under the other arm, Robert takes a jaunty step and then freezes, as Styles had shown him earlier.*]

Come, Robert. . . .

[*Another step.*]

Just one more, Robert. . . .

[*Another step.*]

Stop! Hold it, Robert. Hold it!

[*The camera flash goes off; simultaneously a blackout except for one light on Robert, frozen in the pose that will appear in the picture. We are in fact looking at the photograph. It 'comes to life' and dictates the letter that will accompany it to Nowetu in King William's Town.*]

MAN. Nowetu . . .

[*Correcting himself.*]

Dear Nowetu,

I've got wonderful news for you in this letter. My troubles are over, I think. You won't believe it, but I must tell you. Sizwe Bansi, in a manner of speaking, is dead! I'll tell you what I can.

As you know, when I left the Railway Compound I went to stay with a friend of mine called Zola. A very good friend that, Nowetu. In fact he was even trying to help me find some job. But that's not easy, Nowetu, because Port Elizabeth is a big place, a very big place with lots of factories but also lots of people looking for a job like me. There are so many men, Nowetu, who have left their places because they are dry and have come here to find work!

After a week with Zola, I was in big trouble. The headman came around, and after a lot of happenings which I will tell you when I see you, they put a stamp in my passbook which said I must leave Port Elizabeth at once in three days time. I was very much unhappy, Nowetu. I couldn't stay with Zola because if the headman found me there again my troubles would be even bigger. So Zola took me to a friend of his called Buntu, and asked him if I could stay with him until I decided what to do. . . .

[*Buntu's house in New Brighton. Table and two chairs. Robert, in a direct continuation of the preceding scene, is already there, as Buntu, jacket slung over his shoulder, walks in. Holds out his hand to Robert.*]

BUNTU. Hi. Buntu.

[*They shake hands.*]

MAN. Sizwe Bansi.

BUNTU. Sit down.

[*They sit.*]

Zola told me you were coming. Didn't have time to explain anything. Just asked if you could spend a few nights here. You can perch yourself on that sofa in the corner. I'm alone at the moment. My wife is a domestic . . . sleep-in at Kabega Park . . . only comes home weekends. Hot today, hey?

[*In the course of this scene Buntu will busy himself first by having a wash—basin and jug of water on the table—and then by changing from his working clothes preparatory to going out. Sizwe Bansi stays in his chair.*]

What's your problem, friend?

MAN. I've got no permit to stay in Port Elizabeth.

BUNTU. Where do you have a permit to stay?

MAN. King William's Town.

BUNTU. How did they find out?

MAN [*tells his story with the hesitation and uncertainty of the illiterate. When words fail him he tries to use his hands.*]

I was staying with Zola, as you know. I was very happy there. But one night . . . I was sleeping on the floor . . . I heard some noises and when I looked up I saw torches shining in through the window . . . then there was a loud knocking on the door. When I got up Zola was there in the dark . . . he was trying to whisper something. I think he was saying I must hide. So I crawled under the table. The headman came in and looked around and found me hiding under the table . . . and dragged me out.

BUNTU. Raid?

MAN. Yes, it was a raid. I was just wearing my pants. My shirt was lying on the other side. I just managed to grab it as they were pushing me out. . . . I finished dressing in the van. They drove straight to the administration office . . . and then from there they drove to the Labour Bureau. I was made to stand in the passage there, with everybody looking at me and shaking their heads like they knew I was in big trouble. Later I was taken into an office and made to stand next to the door.... The white man behind the desk had my book and he also looked at me and shook his head. Just then one other white man came in with a card....

BUNTU. A card?

MAN. He was carrying a card.

BUNTU. Pink card?

MAN. Yes, the card was pink.

BUNTU. Record card. Your whole bloody life is written down on that. Go on.

MAN. Then the first white man started writing something on the card ... and just then somebody came in carrying a....

[demonstrates what he means by banging a clenched fist on the table.]

BUNTU. A stamp?

MAN. Yes, a stamp. [Repeats the action.] He was carrying a stamp.

BUNTU. And then?

MAN. He put it on my passbook.

BUNTU. Let me see your book?

[Sizwe produces his passbook from the back-pocket of his trousers. Buntu examines it.]

Shit! You know what this is? [The stamp.]

MAN. I can't read.

BUNTU. Listen ... [reads]. 'You are required to report to the Bantu Affairs Commissioner, King William's Town, within three days of the above-mentioned date for the....' You should have been home yesterday! ... 'for the purpose of repatriation to home district.' Influx Control.

You're in trouble, Sizwe.

MAN. I don't want to leave Port Elizabeth.

BUNTU. Maybe. But if that book says go, you go.

MAN. Can't I maybe burn this book and get a new one?

BANTU. Burn that book? Stop kidding yourself, Sizwe! Anyway, suppose you do. You must immediately go apply for a new one. Right? And until that new one comes, be careful the police don't stop you and ask for your book. Into the Courtroom, brother. Charge: Failing to produce Reference Book on Demand. Five rand or five days. Finally the new book comes. Down to the Labour Bureau for a stamp . . . it's got to be endorsed with permission to be in this area. White man at the Labour Bureau takes the book, looks at it—doesn't look at you!—goes to the big machine and feeds in your number . . .

[*Buntu goes through the motions of punching out a number on a computer.*]

. . . card jumps out, he reads: 'Sizwe Bansi. Endorsed to King William's Town. . . .' Takes your book, fetches that same stamp, and in it goes again. So you burn that book, or throw it away, and get another one. Same thing happens.

[*Buntu feeds the computer; the card jumps out.*]

'Sizwe Bansi. Endorsed to King William's Town. . . .' Stamp goes in the third time. . . . But this time it's also into a van and off to the Native Commissioner's Office; card around your neck with your number on it; escort on both sides and back to King William's Town. They make you pay for the train fare too!

MAN. I think I will try to look for some jobs in the garden.

BUNTU. You? Job as a garden-boy? Don't you read the newspapers?

MAN. I can't read.

BUNTU. I'll tell you what the little white ladies say: 'Domestic vacancies. I want a garden-boy with good manners and a wide knowledge of seasons and flowers. Book in order.' Yours in order? Anyway what the hell do you know about seasons and flowers? [*After a moment's thought.*] Do you know any white man who's prepared to give you a job?

MAN. No. I don't know any white man.

BUNTU. Pity. We might have been able to work something then. You talk to the white man, you see, and ask him to write a letter saying he's got a job for you. You take that letter from the white man and go back to King William's Town, where you show it to the Native Commissioner there. The Native Commissioner in King William's Town reads that letter from the white man in Port Elizabeth who is ready to give you the job. He then writes a letter back to the Native Commissioner in Port Elizabeth. So you come back here with the two letters. Then the Native Commissioner in Port Elizabeth reads the letter from the Native Commissioner in King William's Town together with the first letter from the white man who is prepared to give you a job, and he says when he reads the letters: Ah yes, this man Sizwe Bansi can get a job. So the Native Commissioner in Port Elizabeth then writes a letter which you take with the letters from the Native Commissioner in King William's Town and the white man in Port Elizabeth, to the Senior Officer at the Labour Bureau, who reads all the letters. Then he will put the right stamp in your book and give you another letter from himself which together with the letters from the white man and the two Native Affairs Commissioners, you take to the Administration Office here in New Brighton and make an application for Residence Permit, so that you don't fall victim of raids again. Simple.

MAN. Maybe I can start a little business selling potatoes and. . . .

BUNTU. Where do you get the potatoes and . . . ?

MAN. I'll buy them.

BUNTU. With what?

MAN. Borrow some money. . . .

BUNTU. Who is going to lend money to a somebody endorsed to hell and gone out in the bush? And how you going to buy your potatoes at the market without a Hawker's Licence? Same story, Sizwe. You won't get that because of the bloody stamp in your book.

There's no way out, Sizwe. You're not the first one who has tried to find it. Take my advice and catch that train back to King William's Town. If you need work so bad go knock on the door of the Mines Recruiting Office. Dig gold for the white man.* That's the only time they don't worry about Influx Control.

MAN. I don't want to work on the mines. There is no money there. And it's dangerous, under the ground. Many black men get killed when the rocks fall. You can die there.

BUNTU [*stopped by the last remark into taking possibly his first real look at Sizwe*].

You don't want to die.

MAN. I don't want to die.

BUNTU [*stops whatever he is doing to sit down and talk to Sizwe with an intimacy that was not there before.*]

You married, Sizwe?

MAN. Yes.

BUNTU. How many children?

MAN. I've got four children.

BUNTU. Boys? Girls?

MAN. I've got three boys and one girl.

BUNTU. Schooling?

MAN. Two are schooling. The other two stay at home with their mother.

BUNTU. Your wife is not working.

MAN. The place where we stay is fifteen miles from town. There is only one shop there. Baas van Wyk. He has already got a woman working for him. King William's Town is a dry place, Mr Buntu ... very small and too many people. That is why I don't want to go back.

BUNTU. *Ag*, friend ... I don't know! I'm also married. One child.

MAN. Only one?

BUNTU. *Ja*, my wife attends this Birth Control Clinic rubbish. The child is staying with my mother.

[*Shaking his head.*] *Hai*, Sizwe! If I had to tell you the trouble I had before I could get the right stamps in my book, even though I was born in this area! The trouble I had before I could get a decent job ... born in this area! The trouble I had to get this two-roomed house ... born in this area!

174

MAN. Why is there so much trouble, Mr Buntu?

BUNTU. Two weeks back I went to a funeral with a friend of mine. Out in the country. An old relative of his passed away. Usual thing ... sermons in the house, sermons in the church, sermons at the graveside. I thought they were never going to stop talking!

At the graveside service there was one fellow, a lay preacher ... short man, neat little moustache, wearing one of those old-fashioned double-breasted black suits. ... *Haai!* He was wonderful. While he talked he had a gesture with his hands ... like this ... that reminded me of our youth, when we learnt to fight with kieries. His text was 'Going Home'. He handled it well, Sizwe. Started by saying that the first man to sign the Death Contract with God, was Adam, when he sinned in Eden. Since that day, wherever Man is, or whatever he does, he is never without his faithful companion, Death. So with Outa Jacob ... the dead man's name ... he has at last accepted the terms of his contract with God.

But in his life, friends, he walked the roads of this land. He helped print those footpaths which lead through the bush and over the veld ... footpaths which his children are now walking. He worked on farms from this district down to the coast and north as far as Pretoria. I knew him. He was a friend. Many people knew Outa Jacob. For a long time he worked for Baas van der Walt. But when the old man died his young son Hendrik said: 'I don't like you. Go!' Outa Jacob picked up his load and put it on his shoulders. His wife followed. He went to the next farm ... through the fence, up to the house ...: 'Work, please, Baas.' Baas Potgieter took him. He stayed a long time there too, until one day there was trouble between the Madam and his wife. Jacob and his wife were walking again. The load on his back was heavier, he wasn't so young any more, and there were children behind them now as well. On to the next farm. No work. The next one. No work. Then the next one. A little time there. But the drought was bad and the farmer said: 'Sorry, Jacob. The cattle are dying. I'm moving to the city.' Jacob picked up his load yet again. So it went, friends. On and on ... until he arrived there. [*The grave at his feet.*] Now at last it's over. No matter how hard-arsed the boer on this farm wants to be, he cannot move Outa Jacob. He has reached Home.

[*Pause.*]

That's it, brother. The only time we'll find peace is when they dig a hole for us and press our face into the earth.

[*Putting on his coat.*]

Ag, to hell with it. If we go on like this much longer we'll do the digging for them.

[*Changing his tone.*]

You know Sky's place, Sizwe?

MAN. No.

BUNTU. Come. Let me give you a treat. I'll do you there.

[*Exit Buntu.*

Blackout except for a light on Sizwe. He continues his letter to Nowetu.]

MAN. Sky's place? [*Shakes his head and laughs.*] Hey, Nowetu! When I mention that name again, I get a headache ... the same headache I had when I woke up in Buntu's place the next morning. You won't believe what it was like. You cannot! It would be like you walking down Pickering Street in King William's Town and going into Koekemoer's Café to buy bread, and what do you see sitting there at the smart table and chairs? Your husband, Sizwe Bansi, being served ice-cream and cool drinks by old Mrs Koekemoer herself. Such would be your surprise if you had seen me at Sky's place. Only they weren't serving cool drinks and ice-cream. No! First-class booze, Nowetu. And it wasn't old Mrs Koekemoer serving me, but a certain lovely and beautiful lady called Miss Nkonyeni. And it wasn't just your husband Sizwe sitting there with all the most important people of New Brighton, but *Mister* Bansi.

[*He starts to laugh.*]

Mister Bansi!

[*As the laugh gets bigger, Sizwe rises to his feet.*]

176

[*The street outside Sky's shebeen in New Brighton. Our man is amiably drunk. He addresses the audience.*]

MAN. Do you know who I am, friend? Take my hand, friend. Take my hand. I am Mister Bansi, friend. Do you know where I come from? I come from Sky's place, friend. A most wonderful place. I met everybody there, good people. I've been drinking, my friends—brandy, wine, beer.... Don't you want to go in there, good people? Let's all go to Sky's place. [*Shouting.*] Mr Buntu! Mr Buntu!

[*Buntu enters shouting goodbye to friends at the shebeen. He joins Sizwe. Buntu, though not drunk, is also amiably talkative under the influence of a good few drinks.*]

BUNTU [*discovering the audience*]. Hey, where did you get all these wonderful people?

MAN. I just found them here, Mr Buntu.

BUNTU. Wonderful!

MAN. I'm inviting them to Sky's place, Mr Buntu.

BUNTU. You tell them about Sky's?

MAN. I told them about Sky's place, Mr Buntu.

BUNTU [*to the audience*]. We been having a time there, man!

MAN. They know it. I told them everything.

BUNTU [*laughing*]. Sizwe! We had our fun there.

MAN. Hey ... hey....

BUNTU. Remember that Member of the Advisory Board?

MAN. Hey.... hey... Mr Buntu! You know I respect you, friend. You must call me nice.

BUNTU. What do you mean?

MAN [*clumsy dignity*]. I'm not just Sizwe no more. *He* might have walked in, but Mr Bansi walked out!

BUNTU [*playing along*]. I am terribly sorry, Mr Bansi. I apologize for my familiarity. Please don't be offended.

[*Handing over one of the two oranges he is carrying.*]

Allow me ... with the compliments of Miss Nkonyeni.

MAN [*taking the orange with a broad but sheepish grin*]. Miss Nkonyeni!

BUNTU. Sweet dreams, Mr Bansi.

MAN [*tears the orange with his thumbs and starts eating it messily*]. Lovely lady, Mr Buntu.

BUNTU [*leaves Sizwe with a laugh. To the audience*]. Back there in the shebeen a Member of the Advisory Board hears that he comes from King William's Town. He goes up to Sizwe. 'Tell me, Mr Bansi, what do you think of Ciskeian Independence?'

MAN [*interrupting*]. *Ja*, I remember that one. Bloody Mister Member of the Advisory Board. Talking about Ciskeian Independence!

[*To the audience.*]

I must tell you, friend . . . when a car passes or the wind blows up the dust, Ciskeian Independence makes you cough. I'm telling you, friend . . . put a man in a pondok and call that Independence? My good friend, let me tell you . . . Ciskeian Independence is shit!*

BUNTU Or that other chap! Old Jolobe. The fat tycoon man! [*to the audience*] Comes to me . . . [*pompous voice*] . . . 'Your friend, Mr Bansi, is he on an official visit to town?' 'No,' I said, 'Mr Bansi is on an official walkout!' [*Buntu thinks this is a big joke.*]

MAN [*stubbornly*]. I'm here to stay.

BUNTU [*looking at his watch*]. Hey, Sizwe. . . .

MAN [*reproachfully*]. Mr Buntu!

BUNTU. [*correcting himself*]. Mr Bansi, it is getting late. I've got to work tomorrow. Care to lead the way, Mr Bansi?

MAN. You think I can't? You think Mr Bansi is lost?

BUNTU. I didn't say that.

MAN. You are thinking it, friend. I'll show you. This is Chinga Street.

BUNTU. Very good! But which way do we . . . ?

MAN [*setting off*]. This way.

BUNTU [*pulling him back*]. Mistake. You're heading for Site and Service and a lot of trouble with the tsotsis.

MAN [*the opposite direction*]. That way.

BUNTU. Lead on. I'm right behind you.

MAN. *Ja*, you are right, Mr Buntu. There is Newell High School. Now....

BUNTU. Think carefully!

MAN. . . . when we were going to Sky's we had Newell in front. So when we leave Sky's we put Newell behind.

BUNTU. Very good!

[*An appropriate change in direction. They continue walking, and eventually arrive at a square, with roads leading off in many directions. Sizwe is lost. He wanders around, uncertain of the direction to take.*]

MAN. *Haai*, Mr Buntu . . . !

BUNTU. Mbizweni Square.

MAN. *Yo!* Cross-roads to hell, wait . . . [*Closer look at landmark.*] . . . that building . . . Rio Cinema! So we must. . . .

BUNTU. Rio Cinema? With a white cross on top, bell outside, and the big show on Sundays?

MAN [*sheepishly*]. You're right, friend. I've got it, Mr Buntu. That way.

[*He starts off. Buntu watches him.*]

BUNTU. Goodbye. King William's Town a hundred and fifty miles. Don't forget to write.

MAN [*hurried about-turn*]. *Haai . . . haai. . . .*

BUNTU. Okay, Sizwe, I'll take over from here. But just hang on for a second I want to have a piss. Don't move!

[*Buntu disappears into the dark.*]

MAN. *Haai*, Sizwe! You are a country fool! Leading Mr Buntu and Mr Bansi astray. You think you know this place New Brighton? You know nothing!

[*Buntu comes running back.*]

BUNTU [*urgently*]. Let's get out of here.

MAN. Wait, Mr Buntu, I'm telling that fool Sizwe. . . .

BUNTU. Come on! There's trouble there . . . [*pointing in the direction from which he has come*] . . . let's move.

MAN. Wait, Mr Buntu, wait. Let me first tell that Sizwe. . . .

BUNTU. There's a dead man lying there!

MAN. Dead man?

BUNTU. I thought I was just pissing on a pile of rubbish, but when I looked carefully I saw it was a man. Dead. Covered in blood. Tsotsis must have got him. Let's get the hell out of here before anybody sees us.

MAN. Buntu ... Buntu. ...

BUNTU. Listen to me, Sizwe! The tsotsis might still be around.

MAN. Buntu. ...

BUNTU. Do you want to join him?

MAN. I don't want to join him.

BUNTU. Then come.

MAN. Wait, Buntu.

BUNTU. Jesus! If Zola had told me how much trouble you were going to be!

MAN. Buntu ... we must report that man to the police station.

BUNTU. Police Station! Are you mad? You drunk, passbook not in order ... 'We've come to report a dead man, Sergeant.' 'Grab them!' Case closed. We killed him.

MAN. Mr Buntu, ... we can't leave him. ...

BUNTU. Please, Sizwe!

MAN. Wait. Let's carry him home.

BUNTU. Just like that! Walk through New Brighton streets, at this hour, carrying a dead man! Anyway we don't know where he stays. Come.

MAN. Wait, Buntu, ... listen. ...

BUNTU. Sizwe!

MAN. Buntu, we can know where he stays. That passbook of his will talk. It talks, friend, like mine. His passbook will tell you.

BUNTU [after a moment's desperate hesitation]. You really want to land me in the shit, hey!

[Disappears into the dark again.]

MAN. It will tell you in good English where he stays. My passbook talks good English too ... big words that Sizwe can't read and doesn't understand. Sizwe wants to stay here in New Brighton and find a job; passbook says, 'No! Report back.'

Sizwe wants to feed his wife and children; passbook says, 'No.

Endorsed out.'

Sizwe wants to. . . .

[*Buntu reappears, a passbook in his hand. Looks around furtively and moves to the light under a lamp-post.*]

They never told us it would be like that when they introduced it. They said: Book of Life! Your friend! You'll never get lost! They told us lies.

[*He joins Buntu, who is examining the book.*]

BUNTU. *Haai!* Look at him [*the photograph in the book, reading*]. 'Robert Zwelinzima. Tribe: Xhosa. Native Identification Number. . . .'

MAN. Where does he stay, Buntu?

BUNTU [*paging through the book*]. Worked at Dorman Long seven years . . . Kilomet Engineering . . . eighteen months . . . Anderson Hardware two years . . . now unemployed. Hey, look, Sizwe! He's one up on you. He's got a work-seeker's permit.

MAN. Where does he stay, Buntu?

BUNTU. Lodger's Permit at 42 Mdala Street. From there to Sangocha Street . . . now at. . . .

[*Pause. Closes the book abruptly.*]

To hell with it I'm not going *there*.

MAN. Where, Buntu?

BUNTU [*emphatically*]. I Am Not Going There!

MAN. Buntu. . . .

BUNTU. You know where he is staying now? Single Men's Quarters! If you think I'm going there this time of the night you got another guess coming.

[*Sizwe doesn't understand.*]

Look, Sizwe . . . I stay in a house, there's a street name and a number. Easy to find. Ask anybody . . . Mapija Street? That way. You know what Single Men's Quarters is? Big bloody concentration camp with rows of things that look like train carriages. Six doors to each! Twelve people behind each door! You want me to go there now? Knock on the first one: 'Does

Robert Zwelinzima live here?' 'No!' Next one: 'Does Robert . . . ?' 'Bugger off, we're trying to sleep!' Next one: 'Does Robert Zwelinzima . . . ?' They'll fuck us up, man! I'm putting this book back and we're going home.

MAN. Buntu!

BUNTU [half-way back to the alleyway]. What?

MAN. Would you do that to me, friend? If the tsotsis had stabbed Sizwe, and left him lying there, would you walk away from him as well?

[The accusation stops Buntu.]

Would you leave me lying there, wet with your piss? . . . I wish I was dead. I wish I was dead because I don't care a damn about anything any more.

[Turning away from Buntu to the audience.]

What's happening in this world, good people? Who cares for who in this world? Who wants who?

Who wants me, friend? What's wrong with me? I'm a man. I've got eyes to see. I've got ears to listen when people talk. I've got a head to think good things. What's wrong with me?

[Starts to tear off his clothes.]

Look at me! I'm a man. I've got legs. I can run with a wheelbarrow full of cement! I'm strong! I'm a man. Look! I've got a wife. I've got four children. How many has he made, lady? [The man sitting next to her.] Is he a man? What has he got that I haven't . . . ?

[A thoughtful Buntu rejoins them, the dead man's reference book still in his hand.]

BUNTU. Let me see your book?

[Sizwe doesn't respond.]

Give me your book!

MAN. Are you a policeman now, Buntu?

BUNTU. Give me your bloody book, Sizwe!

MAN [handing it over]. Take it, Buntu. Take this book and read it carefully, friend, and tell me what it says about me. Buntu, does that book tell you I'm a man?

[*Buntu studies the two books. Sizwe turns back to the audience.*]

That bloody book . . . ! People, do you know? No! Wherever you go . . . it's that bloody book. You go to school, it goes too. Go to work, it goes too. Go to church and pray and sing lovely hymns, it sits there with you. Go to hospital to die, it lies there too!

[*Buntu has collected Sizwe's discarded clothing.*]

BUNTU. Come!

[*Buntu's house, as earlier. Table and two chairs. Buntu pushes Sizwe down into a chair. Sizwe still muttering, starts to struggle back into his clothes. Buntu opens the two reference books and places them side by side on the table. He produces a pot of glue, then very carefully tears out the photograph in each book. A dab of glue on the back of each and then Sizwe's goes back into Robert's book, and Robert's into Sizwe's. Sizwe watches this operation, at first uninterestedly, but when he realizes what Buntu is up to, with growing alarm. When he is finished, Buntu pushes the two books in front of Sizwe.*]

MAN [*shaking his head emphatically*]. Yo! Haai, haai. No, Buntu.

BUNTU. It's a chance.

MAN. Haai, haai, haai . . .

BUNTU. It's your only chance!

MAN. No, Buntu! What's it mean? That me, Sizwe Bansi. . . .

BUNTU. Is dead.

MAN. I'm not dead, friend.

BUNTU. We burn this book . . . [*Sizwe's original*] . . . and Sizwe Bansi disappears off the face of the earth.

MAN. What about the man we left lying in the alleyway?

BUNTU. Tomorrow the Flying Squad passes there and finds him. Check in his pockets . . . no passbook. Mount Road Mortuary. After three days, nobody has identified him. Pauper's Burial. Case closed.

MAN. And then?

BUNTU. Tomorrow I contact my friend Norman at Feltex. He's a boss-boy there. I tell him about another friend, Robert Zwelinzima, book in order, who's looking for a job. You roll up later, hand over the book to the white man. Who does Robert Zwelinzima look like? You! Who gets the pay on Friday? You, man!

MAN. What about all that shit at the Labour Bureau, Buntu?

BUNTU. You don't have to go there. This chap had a work-seeker's permit, Sizwe. All you do is hand over the book to the white man. *He* checks at the Labour Bureau. They check with their big machine. 'Robert Zwelinzima has the right to be employed and stay in this town.'

MAN. I don't want to lose my name, Buntu.

BUNTU. You mean you don't want to lose your bloody passbook! You love it, hey?

MAN. Buntu. I cannot lose my name.

BUNTU [*leaving the table*]. All right, I was only trying to help. As Robert Zwelinzima you could have stayed and worked in this town. As Sizwe Bansi...? Start walking, friend. King William's Town. Hundred and fifty miles. And don't waste any time! You've got to be there by yesterday. Hope you enjoy it.

MAN. Buntu....

BUNTU. Lots of scenery in a hundred and fifty miles.

MAN. Buntu!...

BUNTU. Maybe a better idea is just to wait until they pick you up. Save yourself all that walking. Into the train with the escort! Smart stuff, hey. Hope it's not too crowded though. Hell of a lot of people being kicked out, I hear.

MAN. Buntu!...

BUNTU. But once you're back! Sit down on the side of the road next to your pondok with your family... the whole Bansi clan on leave... for life! Hey, that sounds okay. Watching all the cars passing, and as you say, friend, cough your bloody lungs out with Ciskeian Independence.

MAN [*now really desperate*]. Buntu!!!

BUNTU. What you waiting for? Go!

MAN. Buntu.

BUNTU. What?

MAN. What about my wife, Nowetu?

BUNTU. What about her?

MAN [*maudlin tears*]. Her loving husband, Siwze Bansi, is dead!

BUNTU. So what! She's going to marry a better man.

MAN [*bridling*]. Who?

BUNTU. You ... Robert Zwelinzima.

MAN [*thoroughly confused*]. How can I marry my wife, Buntu?

BUNTU. Get her down here and I'll introduce you.

MAN. Don't make jokes, Buntu. Robert ... Sizwe ... I'm all mixed up. Who am I?

BUNTU. A fool who is not taking his chance.

MAN. And my children! Their father is Sizwe Bansi. They're registered at school under Bansi. . . .

BUNTU. Are you really worried about your children, friend, or are you just worried about yourself and your bloody name? Wake up, man! Use that book and with your pay on Friday you'll have a real chance to do something for them.

MAN. I'm afraid. How do I get used to Robert? How do I live as another man's ghost?

BUNTU. Wasn't Sizwe Bansi a ghost?

MAN. No!

BUNTU. No? When the white man looked at you at the Labour Bureau what did he see? A man with dignity or a bloody passbook with an N.I. number? Isn't that a ghost? When the white man sees you walk down the street and calls out, 'Hey, John! Come here' ... to you, Sizwe Bansi ... isn't that a ghost? Or when his little child calls you 'Boy' ... you a man, circumcised, with a wife and four children ... isn't that a ghost? Stop fooling yourself. All I'm saying is be a real ghost, if that is what they want, what they've turned us into. Spook them into hell, man!

[*Sizwe is silenced. Buntu realizes his words are beginning to reach the other man. He paces quietly, looking for his next move. He finds it.*]

Suppose you try my plan. Friday. Roughcasting section at Feltex. Paytime. Line of men—non-skilled labourers. White man with the big box full of pay-packets.

185

'John Kani!' 'Yes, sir!' Pay-packet is handed over. 'Thank you, sir.'

Another one. [*Buntu reads the name on an imaginary pay-packet.*] 'Winston Ntshona!' 'Yes, sir!' Pay-packet over. 'Thank you, sir!' Another one. 'Fats Bokhilane!' '*Hier is ek, my baas!*' Pay-packet over. '*Dankie, my baas!*'

Another one. 'Robert Zwelinzima!'

[*No response from Sizwe.*]

'Robert Zwelinzima!'

MAN. Yes, sir.

BUNTU [*handing him the imaginary pay-packet*]. Open it. Go on.

[*Takes back the packet, tears it open, empties its contents on the table, and counts it.*]

Five . . . ten . . . eleven . . . twelve . . . and ninety-nine cents. In *your* pocket!

[*Buntu again paces quietly, leaving Sizwe to think. Eventually. . . .*]

Saturday. Man in overalls, twelve rand ninety-nine cents in the back pocket, walking down Main Street looking for Sales House. Finds it and walks in. Salesman comes forward to meet him.

'I've come to buy a suit.' Salesman is very friendly.

'Certainly. Won't you take a seat. I'll get the forms. I'm sure you want to open an account, sir. Six months to pay. But first I'll need all your particulars.'

[*Buntu has turned the table, with Sizwe on the other side, into the imaginary scene at Sales House.*]

BUNTU [*pencil poised, ready to fill in a form*]. Your name, please, sir?

MAN [*playing along uncertainly*]. Robert Zwelinzima.

BUNTU [*writing*]. 'Robert Zwelinzima.' Address?

MAN. Fifty, Mapija Street.

BUNTU. Where do you work?

MAN. Feltex.

BUNTU. And how much do you get paid?

MAN. Twelve . . . twelve rand ninety-nine cents.

BUNTU. N.I. Number, please?

[*Sizwe hesitates.*]

Your Native Identity number please?

[*Sizwe is still uncertain. Buntu abandons the act and picks up Robert Zwelinzima's passbook. He reads out the number.*]

N—I—3—8—1—1—8—6—3.

Burn that into your head, friend. You hear me? It's more important than your name.

N.I. number . . . three. . . .

MAN. Three.

BUNTU. Eight.

MAN. Eight.

BUNTU. One.

MAN. One.

BUNTU. One.

MAN. One.

BUNTU. Eight.

MAN. Eight.

BUNTU. Six.

MAN. Six.

BUNTU. Three.

MAN. Three.

BUNTU. Again. Three.

MAN. Three.

BUNTU. Eight.

MAN. Eight.

BUNTU. One.

MAN. One.

BUNTU. One.

MAN. One.

BUNTU. Eight.

MAN. Eight.

BUNTU. Six.

MAN. Six.

BUNTU. Three.

MAN. Three.

BUNTU [*picking up his pencil and returning to the role of the salesman*]. N.I. number, please.

MAN [*pausing frequently, using his hands to remember*]. Three ... eight ... one ... one ... eight ... six ... three. ...

BUNTU [*abandoning the act*]. Good boy.

[*He paces. Sizwe sits and waits.*]

Sunday. Man in a Sales House suit, hat on top, going to church. Hymn book and bible under the arm. Sits down in the front pew. Priest in the pulpit.

[*Buntu jumps on to a chair in his new role. Sizwe kneels.*]

The Time has come!

MAN. Amen!

BUNTU. Pray, brothers and sisters. ... Pray. ... Now!

MAN. Amen.

BUNTU. The Lord wants to save you. Hand yourself over to him, while there is still time, while Jesus is still prepared to listen to you.

MAN [*carried away by what he is feeling*]. Amen, Jesus!

BUNTU. Be careful, my brothers and sisters. ...

MAN. Hallelujah!

BUNTU. Be careful lest when the big day comes and the pages of the big book are turned, it is found that your name is missing. Repent before it is too late.

MAN. Hallelujah! Amen.

BUNTU. Will all those who have not yet handed in their names for membership of our burial society please remain behind.

[*Buntu leaves the pulpit and walks around the audience with a register.*]

Name, please, sir? Number? Thank you.

Good afternoon, sister. Your name, please?

Address? Number? God bless you.

[*He has reached Sizwe.*]

Your name, please, brother?

MAN. Robert Zwelinzima.

BUNTU. Address?

MAN. Fifty, Mapija Street.

BUNTU. N.I. number.

MAN [*again tremendous effort to remember*]. Three . . . eight . . . one . . . one . . . eight . . . six . . . three. . . .

[*They both relax.*]

BUNTU [*after pacing for a few seconds*]. Same man leaving the church . . . walking down the street.

[*Buntu acts out the role while Sizwe watches. He greets other members of the congregation.*]

'God bless you, Brother Bansi. May you always stay within the Lord's mercy.'

'Greetings, Brother Bansi. We welcome you into the flock of Jesus with happy spirits.'

'God bless you, Brother Bansi. Stay with the Lord, the Devil is strong.'

Suddenly. . . .

[*Buntu has moved to behind Sizwe. He grabs him roughly by the shoulder.*]

Police!

[*Sizwe stands up frightened. Buntu watches him carefully.*]

No, man! Clean your face.

[*Sizwe adopts an impassive expression. Buntu continues as the policeman.*]

What's your name?

MAN. Robert Zwelinzima.

BUNTU. Where do you work?

MAN. Feltex.

BUNTU. Book!

[*Sizwe hands over the book and waits while the policeman opens it, looks at the photograph, then Sizwe, and finally checks through its stamps and endorsements. While all this is going on Sizwe stands quietly, looking down at his feet, whistling under his breath. The book is finally handed back.*]

Okay.

[*Sizwe takes his book and sits down.*]

MAN [*after a pause*]. I'll try it, Buntu.

BUNTU. Of course you must, if you want to stay alive.

MAN. Yes, but Sizwe Bansi is dead.

BUNTU. What about Robert Zwelinzima then? That poor bastard I pissed on out there in the dark. So *he's* alive again. Bloody miracle, man.

Look, if someone was to offer me the things I wanted most in my life, the things that would make me, my wife, and my child happy, in exchange for the name Buntu . . . you think I wouldn't swop?

MAN. Are you sure, Buntu?

BUNTU [*examining the question seriously*]. If there was just me . . . I mean, if I was alone, if I didn't have anyone to worry about or look after except myself . . . maybe then I'd be prepared to pay some sort of price for a little pride. But if I had a wife and four children wasting away their one and only life in the dust and poverty of Ciskeian Independence . . . if I had four children waiting for me, their father, to do something about their lives . . . *ag*, no, Sizwe. . . .

MAN. Robert, Buntu.

BUNTU [*angry*]. All right! Robert, John, Athol, Winston. . . . Shit on names, man! To hell with them if in exchange you can get a piece of bread for your stomach and a blanket in winter. Understand me, brother, I'm not saying that pride isn't a way for us. What I'm saying is shit on our pride if we only bluff ourselves that we are men.

Take your name back, Sizwe Bansi, if it's so important to you. But next time you hear a white man say 'John' to you, don't say '*Ja, Baas?*' And next time the bloody white man says to you, a man, 'Boy, come here,' don't run to him and lick his arse like we all do. Face him and tell him: 'White man. I'm a Man!' *Ag, kak!* We're bluffing ourselves.

It's like my father's hat. Special hat, man! Carefully wrapped in plastic on top of the wardrobe in his room. God help the child who so much as touches it! Sunday it goes on his head, and a man, full of dignity, a man I respect, walks down the street. White man stops him: 'Come here, kaffir!' What does he do?

[*Buntu whips the imaginary hat off his head and crumples it in his hands as he adopts a fawning, servile pose in front of the white man.*]

'What is it, Baas?'

If that is what you call pride, then shit on it! Take mine and give me food for my children.

[*Pause.*]

Look, brother, Robert Zwelinzima, that poor bastard out there in the alleyway, if there *are* ghosts, he is smiling tonight. He is here, with us, and he's saying: 'Good luck, Sizwe! I hope it works.' He's a brother, man.

MAN. For how long, Buntu?

BUNTU. How long? For as long as you can stay out of trouble. Trouble will mean police station, then fingerprints off to Pretoria to check on previous convictions . . . and when they do that . . . Siswe Bansi will live again and you will have had it.

MAN. Buntu, you know what you are saying? A black man stay out of trouble? Impossible, Buntu. Our skin is trouble.

BUNTU [*wearily*]. You said you wanted to try.

MAN. And I will.

BUNTU [*picks up his coat*]. I'm tired, . . . Robert. Good luck. See you tomorrow.

[*Exit Buntu, Sizwe picks up the passbook, looks at it for a long time, then puts it in his back pocket. He finds his walking-stick, newspaper, and pipe and moves downstage into a solitary light. He finishes the letter to his wife.*]

MAN. So Nowetu, for the time being my troubles are over. Christmas I come home. In the meantime Buntu is working a plan to get me a Lodger's Permit. If I get it, you and the children can come here and spend some days with me in Port Elizabeth. Spend the money I am sending you carefully. If all goes well I will send some more each week.

I do not forget you, my dear wife.

Your loving husband,
Sizwe Bansi.

[*As he finishes the letter, Sizwe returns to the pose of the photo. Styles'
Photographic Studio. Styles is behind the camera.*]

STYLES. Hold it, Robert. Hold it just like that. Just one more.
Now smile, Robert.... Smile.... Smile....

[*Camera flash and blackout.*]

THE ISLAND

devised by

Athol Fugard, John Kani, and Winston Ntshona

CHARACTERS

JOHN
WINSTON

THE ISLAND was given its first performance under the title DIE HODOSHE SPAN at The Space, Cape Town, on 2 July 1973, directed by Athol Fugard (lighting: Brian Astbury) with John Kani and Winston Ntshona, described in the cast list thus:

JOHN Bonisile Kani
WINSTON Zola Ntshona

The first London production was as part of a 'South African Season' with SIZWE BANSI IS DEAD, at The Theatre Upstairs, Royal Court, with the same cast and director (design: Douglas Heap) on 12 December 1973.

The first American production was in a season with SIZWE BANSI IS DEAD at the Edison Theater, New York, with the original cast and director, from 13 November 1974. The first Australian production was at the Seymour Centre, York Theatre, New South Wales, as part of a season with SIZWE BANSI IS DEAD, with the same cast and director, from 31 March 1976. The first 'open' production in South Africa, with the original cast and director, was at The Market Theatre, Johannesburg, on 20 June 1977.

The play was televised with the original cast for Radio-Telefis-Éireann (director: Louis Lentin) after a performance directed by Barney Simon at the Gate Theatre, Dublin, in April 1986.

SCENE ONE

Centre stage: a raised area representing a cell on Robben Island.*
Blankets and sleeping-mats—the prisoners sleep on the floor—are neatly
folded. In one corner are a bucket of water and two tin mugs.

The long drawn-out wail of a siren. Stage-lights come up to reveal a
*moat of harsh, white light around the cell. In it the two prisoners—*John
stage-right and Winston *stage-left—mime the digging of sand. They*
wear the prison uniform of khaki shirt and short trousers.* Their heads are
shaven. It is an image of back-breaking and grotesquely futile labour.
Each in turns fills a wheelbarrow and then with great effort pushes it to
where the other man is digging, and empties it. As a result, the piles of
sand never diminish. Their labour is interminable. The only sounds are
their grunts as they dig, the squeal of the wheelbarrows as they circle the
cell, and the hum of Hodoshe, the green carrion fly.

A whistle is blown. They stop digging and come together, standing side
by side as they are handcuffed together and shackled at the ankles. Another
whistle. They start to run . . . John mumbling a prayer, Winston muttering
a rhythm for their three-legged run.

They do not run fast enough. They get beaten . . . Winston receiving a
bad blow to the eye and John spraining an ankle. In this condition they
arrive finally at the cell door. Handcuffs and shackles are taken off. After
being searched, they lurch into their cell. The door closes behind them. Both
men sink to the floor.

A moment of total exhaustion until slowly, painfully, they start to
explore their respective injuries . . . Winston his eye, and John his ankle.
Winston is moaning softly and this eventually draws John's attention away
from his ankle. He crawls to Winston and examines the injured eye. It
needs attention. Winston's moaning is slowly turning into a sound of
inarticulate outrage, growing in volume and violence. John urinates into
one hand and tries to clean the other man's eye with it, but Winston's
anger and outrage are now uncontrollable. He breaks away from John and
crawls around the cell, blind with rage and pain. John tries to placate
him . . . the noise could bring back the warders and still more trouble.
Winston eventually finds the cell door but before he can start banging on it
John pulls him away.

WINSTON [*calling*]. Hodoshe!

JOHN. Leave him, Winston. Listen to me, man! If he comes now we'll be in bigger shit.

WINSTON. I want Hodoshe. I want him now! I want to take him to the office. He must read my warrant. I was sentenced to Life, brother, not bloody Death!

JOHN. Please, Winston! He made us run. . . .

WINSTON. I want Hodoshe!

JOHN. He made us run. He's happy now. Leave him. Maybe he'll let us go back to the quarry tomorrow. . . .

[*Winston is suddenly silent. For a moment John thinks his words are having an effect, but then he realizes that the other man is looking at his ear. Winston touches it. It is bleeding. A sudden spasm of fear from John, who puts a hand to his ear. His fingers come away with blood on them. The two men look at each other.*]

WINSTON. *Nyana we Sizwe!*

[*In a reversal of earlier roles Winston now gets John down on the floor of the cell so as to examine the injured ear. He has to wipe blood and sweat out of his eyes in order to see clearly. John winces with pain. Winston keeps restraining him.*]

WINSTON [*eventually*]. It's not too bad. [*Using his shirt-tail he cleans the injured ear.*]

JOHN [*through clenched teeth as Winston tends his ear*]. Hell, *ons was gemoer vandag!* [*A weak smile.*] News bulletin and weather forecast! Black Domination was chased by White Domination. Black Domination lost its shoes and collected a few bruises. Black Domination will run barefoot to the quarry tomorrow. Conditions locally remain unchanged—thunderstorms with the possibility of cold showers and rain. Elsewhere, fine and warm!

[*Winston has now finished tending John's ear and settles down on the floor beside him. He clears his nose, ears, and eyes of sand.*]

WINSTON. Sand! Same old sea sand I used to play with when I was young. St George's Strand. New Year's Day. Sand dunes. Sand castles. . . .

JOHN. *Ja*, we used to go there too. Last. . . . [*Pause and then a small laugh. He shakes his head.*] The Christmas before they arrested me, we were down there. All of us. Honeybush. My little Monde played in the sand. We'd given her one of those little buckets and spades for Christmas.

WINSTON. *Ja.*

JOHN. Anyway, it was Daddy's turn today. [*Shaking his head ruefully.*] *Haai*, Winston, this one goes on the record. 'Struesgod! I'm a man, brother. A man! But if Hodoshe had kept us at those wheelbarrows five minutes longer...! There would have been a baby on the Island tonight. I nearly cried.

WINSTON. *Ja.*

JOHN. There was no end to it, except one of us!

WINSTON. That's right.

JOHN. This morning when he said: 'You two! The beach!'... I thought, Okay, so it's my turn to empty the sea into a hole. He likes that one. But when he pointed to the wheelbarrows, and I saw his idea...! [*Shaking his head.*] I laughed at first. Then I wasn't laughing. Then I hated you. You looked so stupid, *broer!*

WINSTON. That's what he wanted.

JOHN. It was going to last forever, man! Because of *you*. And for *you*, because of *me. Moer!* He's cleverer than I thought.

WINSTON. If he was God, he would have done it.

JOHN. What?

WINSTON. Broken us. Men get tired. Hey! There's a thought. We're still alive because Hodoshe got tired.

JOHN. Tomorrow?

WINSTON. We'll see.

JOHN. If he takes us back there... If I hear that wheelbarrow ...of yours again, coming with another bloody load of... eternity!

WINSTON [*with calm resignation*]. We'll see.

[*Pause. John looks at Winston.*]

JOHN [*with quiet emphasis, as if the other man did not fully understand the significance of what he had said*]. I *hated* you, Winston.

WINSTON [*meeting John's eyes*]. *I* hated *you.*

[*John puts a hand on Winston's shoulder. Their brotherhood is intact. He gets slowly to his feet.*]

JOHN. Where's the *lap*?

WINSTON. Somewhere. Look for it.

JOHN. Hey! You had it last.

[*Limping around the cell looking for their wash-rag.*]

WINSTON. *Haai*, man! You got no wife here. Look for the rag yourself.

JOHN [*finding the rag beside the water bucket*]. Look where it is. Look! Hodoshe comes in here and sees it. 'Whose *lappie* is that?' Then what do you say?

WINSTON. 'It's his rag, sir.'

JOHN. Yes? Okay. 'It's my rag, sir.' When you wash, use your shirt.

WINSTON. Okay, okay! 'It's our rag, sir!'

JOHN. That will be the bloody day!

[*John, getting ready to wash, starts to take off his shirt. Winston produces a cigarette butt, matches, and flint from their hiding-place under the water bucket. He settles down for a smoke.*]

Shit, today was long. Hey, Winston, suppose the watch of the chap behind the siren is slow! We could still be there, man! [*He pulls out three or four rusty nails from a secret pocket in his trousers. He holds them out to Winston.*] Hey, there.

WINSTON. What?

JOHN. With the others.

WINSTON [*taking the nails*]. What's this?

JOHN. Necklace, man. With the others.

WINSTON. Necklace?

JOHN. Antigone's necklace.*

WINSTON. *Ag*, shit, man!

[*Slams the nails down on the cell floor and goes on smoking.*]

Antigone! Go to hell, man, John.

JOHN. Hey, don't start any nonsense now. You promised. [*Limps over to Winston's bed-roll and produces a half-completed necklace made of nails and string.*] It's nearly finished. Look. Three fingers, one

198

nail. . . . three fingers, one nail. . . . [*Places the necklace beside Winston who is shaking his head, smoking aggressively, and muttering away.*] Don't start any nonsense now, Winston. There's six days to go to the concert. We're committed. We promised the chaps we'd do something. This *Antigone* is just right for us. Six more days and we'll make it.

[*He continues washing.*]

WINSTON. Jesus, John! We were down on the beach today. Hodoshe made us run. Can't you just leave a man . . . ?

JOHN. To hell with you! Who do you think ran with you? I'm also tired, but we can't back out now. Come on! Three fingers. . . .

WINSTON. . . . one nail! [*Shaking his head.*] Haai . . . haai . . . haai!

JOHN. Stop moaning and get on with it. Shit, Winston! What sort of progress is this? [*Abandoning his wash.*] Listen. Listen! Number 42 is practising the Zulu War Dance. Down there they're rehearsing their songs. It's just in this *moer* cell that there's always an argument. Today you want to do it, tomorrow you don't want to do it. How the hell must I know what to report to the chaps tomorrow if we go back to the quarry?

[*Winston is unyielding. His obstinacy gets the better of John, who eventually throws the wash-rag at him.*]

There! Wash!

[*John applies himself to the necklace while Winston, still muttering away in an undertone, starts to clean himself.*]

How can I be sure of anything when you carry on like this? We've still got to learn the words, the moves. Shit! It could be so bloody good, man.

[*Winston mutters protests all the way through this speech of John's. The latter holds up the necklace.*]

Nearly finished! Look at it! Three fingers. . . .

WINSTON. . . . one nail.

JOHN. *Ja!* Simple. Do you still remember all I told you yesterday? Bet you've bloody forgotten. How can I carry on like this? I can't move on, man. Over the whole bloody lot again! Who Antigone is . . . who Creon is. . . .

WINSTON. Antigone is mother to Polynices. . . .

JOHN. *Haai, haai, haai* . . . shit, Winston! [*Now really exasperated.*] How many times must I tell you that Antigone is the sister to the two brothers? Not the mother. That's another play.*

WINSTON. Oh.

JOHN. That's all you know! 'Oh.' [*He abandons the necklace and fishes out a piece of chalk from a crack in the floor.*] Come here. This is the last time. 'Struesgod. The last time.

WINSTON. *Ag*, no, John.

JOHN. Come! I'm putting this plot down for the last time! If you don't learn it tonight I'm going to report you to the old men* tomorrow. And remember, *broer*, those old men will make Hodoshe and his tricks look like a little boy.

WINSTON. Jesus Christ! Learn to dig for Hodoshe, learn to run for Hodoshe, and what happens when I get back to the cell? Learn to read *Antigone!*

JOHN. Come! And shut up! [*He pulls the reluctant Winston down beside him on the floor. Winston continues to clean himself with the rag while John lays out the 'plot' of Antigone.*] If you would just stop moaning, you would learn faster. Now listen!

WINSTON. Okay, do it.

JOHN. Listen! It is the Trial of Antigone. Right?

WINSTON. So you say.

JOHN. First, the accused. Who is the accused?

WINSTON. Antigone.

JOHN. Coming from you that's bloody progress. [*Writing away on the cell floor with his chalk.*] Next the State. Who is the State?

WINSTON. Creon.

JOHN. King Creon. Creon is the State. Now . . . what did Antigone do?

WINSTON. Antigone buried her brother Eteocles.

JOHN. No, no, no! Shit, Winston, when are you going to remember this thing? I told you, man, Antigone buried

Polynices. The traitor! The one who I said was on *our* side. Right?

WINSTON. Right.

JOHN. Stage one of the Trial. [*Writing on the floor.*] The State lays its charges against the Accused . . . and lists counts . . . you know the way they do it. Stage two is Pleading. What does Antigone plead? Guilty or Not Guilty?

WINSTON. Not Guilty.

JOHN [*trying to be tactful*]. Now look, Winston, we're not going to argue. Between me and you, in this cell, we know she's Not Guilty. But in the play she pleads Guilty.

WINSTON. No, man, John! Antigone is Not Guilty. . . .

JOHN. In the play. . . .

WINSTON [*losing his temper*]. To hell with the play! Antigone had every right to bury her brother.

JOHN. Don't say 'To hell with the play'. We've got to do the bloody thing. And in the play she pleads Guilty. Get that straight. Antigone pleads. . . .

WINSTON [*giving up in disgust*]. Okay, do it your way.

JOHN. It's not my way! In the play. . . .

WINSTON. Guilty!

JOHN. Yes, Guilty!

[*Writes furiously on the floor.*]

WINSTON. Guilty.

JOHN. Stage three, Pleading in Mitigation of Sentence. Stage four, Sentence, State Summary, and something from you . . . Farewell Words. Now learn that.

WINSTON. Hey?

JOHN [*getting up*]. Learn that!

WINSTON. But we've just done it!

JOHN. *I've* just done it. Now *you* learn it.

WINSTON [*throwing aside the wash-rag with disgust before applying himself to learning the 'plot'*]. Learn to run, learn to read. . . .

JOHN. And don't throw the rag there! [*Retrieving the rag and placing it in its correct place.*] Don't be so bloody difficult, man.

We're nearly there. You'll be proud of this thing when we've done it.

[*Limps to his bed-roll and produces a pendant made from a jam-tin lid and twine.*] Look. Winston, look! Creon's medallion. Good, hey! [*Hangs it around his neck.*] I'll finish the necklace while you learn that.

[*He strings on the remaining nails.*] Jesus, Winston! June 1965.*

WINSTON. What?

JOHN. This, man. *Antigone*. In New Brighton. St Stephen's Hall. The place was packed, man! All the big people. Front row ... dignitaries. Shit, those were the days. Georgie was Creon. You know Georgie?

WINSTON. The teacher?

JOHN. That's him. He played Creon. Should have seen him, Winston. Short and fat, with big eyes, but by the time the play was finished he was as tall as the roof.

[*Onto his legs in an imitation of Georgie's Creon.*]

'My Councillors, now that the Gods have brought our City safe through a storm of troubles to tranquillity....' And old Mulligan! Another short-arsed teacher. With a beard! He used to go up to the Queen.... [*Another imitation.*] 'Your Majesty, prepare for grief, but do not weep.'

[*The necklace in his hands.*]

Nearly finished!

Nomhle played Antigone. A bastard of a lady that one, but a beautiful bitch. Can't get her out of my mind tonight.

WINSTON [*indicating the 'plot'*]. I know this.

JOHN. You sure?

WINSTON. This? ... it's here. [*Tapping his head.*]

JOHN. You're not bullshitting, hey? [*He rubs out the 'plot' and then paces the cell.*] Right. The Trial of Antigone. Who is the Accused?

WINSTON. Antigone.

JOHN. Who is the State?

WINSTON. King Creon.

JOHN. Stage one.

WINSTON [*supremely self-confident*]. Antigone lays charges. . . .

JOHN. NO, SHIT, MAN, WINSTON!!!

[*Winston pulls John down and stifles his protests with a hand over his mouth.*]

WINSTON. Okay . . . okay . . . listen, John . . . listen. . . . The State lays charges against Antigone.

[*Pause.*]

JOHN. Be careful!

WINSTON. The State lays charges against Antigone.

JOHN. Stage two.

WINSTON. Pleading.

JOHN. What does she plead? Guilty or Not Guilty?

WINSTON. Guilty.

JOHN. Stage three.

WINSTON. Pleading in Mitigation of Sentence.

JOHN. Stage four.

WINSTON. State Summary, Sentence, and Farewell Words.

JOHN [*very excited*]. He's got it! That's my man. See how easy it is, Winston? Tomorrow, just the words.

[*Winston gets onto his legs, John puts away the props. Mats and blankets are unrolled. The two men prepare for sleep.*]

JOHN. Hell, I hope we go back to the quarry tomorrow. There's still a lot of things we need for props and costumes. Your wig! The boys in Number Fourteen said they'd try and smuggle me a piece of rope from the jetty.

WINSTON. *Ja*, I hope we're back there. I want to try and get some tobacco through to Sipho.

JOHN. Sipho?

WINSTON. Back in solitary.

JOHN. Again!

WINSTON. *Ja*.

JOHN. Oh hell!

WINSTON. Simon passed the word.

JOHN. What was it this time?

WINSTON. Complained about the food I think. Demanded to see the book of Prison Regulations.

JOHN. Why don't they leave him alone for a bit?

WINSTON. Because he doesn't leave them alone.

JOHN. You're right. I'm glad I'm not in Number Twenty-two with him. One man starts getting hard-arsed like that and the whole lot of you end up in the shit.

[*Winston's bed is ready. He lies down.*]

You know what I'm saying?

WINSTON. *Ja.*

JOHN. What?

WINSTON. What 'What'?

JOHN. What am I saying?

WINSTON. *Haai,* Johnny, man! I'm tired now! Let a man. . . .

JOHN. I'm saying Don't Be Hard-Arsed! You! When Hodoshe opens that door tomorrow say '*Ja, Baas*' the right way. I don't want to be back on that bloody beach tomorrow just because you feel like being difficult.

WINSTON [*wearily*]. Okay, man, Johnny.

JOHN. You're not alone in this cell. I'm here too.

WINSTON. Jesus, you think I don't know that!

JOHN. People must remember their responsibilities to others.

WINSTON. I'm glad to hear you say that, because I was just going to remind you that it is your turn tonight.

JOHN. What do you mean? Wasn't it my turn last night?

WINSTON [*shaking his head emphatically*]. *Haai, haai.* Don't you remember? Last night I took you to bioscope.

JOHN. Hey, by the way! So you did. Bloody good film too. 'Fastest Gun in the West'. Glenn Ford.

[*Whips out a six-shooter and guns down a few bad-men.*]

You were bullshitting me a bit, though. How the hell can Glenn Ford shoot backwards through his legs? I tried to work that one out on the beach.

[*He is now seated on his bed-roll. After a moment's thought he holds up an empty mug as a telephone-receiver and starts to dial. Winston watches him with puzzlement.*]

Operator, put me through to New Brighton, please ... yes, New Brighton, Port Elizabeth. The number is 414624.... Yes, mine is local ... local. ...

WINSTON [*recognizing the telephone number*]. The Shop!

[*He sits upright with excitement as John launches into the telephone conversation.*]

JOHN. That you, Scott? Hello, man! Guess who! ... You got it! You bastard! Hell, shit, Scott, man ... how things with you? No, still inside. Give me the news, man ... you don't say! No, we don't hear anything here ... not a word.... What's that? Business is bad? ... You bloody undertaker! People aren't dying fast enough! No, things are fine here....

[*Winston, squirming with excitement, has been trying unsuccessfully to interrupt John's torrent of words and laughter. He finally succeeds in drawing John's attention.*]

WINSTON. Who else is there? Who's with Scott?

JOHN. Hey, Scott, who's there with you? ... Oh no! ... call him to the phone, man. ...

WINSTON. Who's it?

JOHN [*ignoring Winston*]. Just for a minute, man, please, Scott....

[*Ecstatic response from John as another voice comes over the phone.*]

Hello there, you beautiful bastard ... how's it, man? ...

WINSTON. Who the hell is it, man?

JOHN [*hand over the receiver*]. Sky!

[*Winston can no longer contain his excitement. He scrambles out of his bed to join John, and joins in the fun with questions and remarks whispered into John's ear. Both men enjoy it enormously.*]

How's it with Mangi? Where's Vusi? How are the chaps keeping, Sky? Winston? ... All right, man. He's here next to me. No, fine, man, fine, man ... small accident today when he collided with Hodoshe, but nothing to moan about. His right eye bruised, that's all. Hey, Winston's asking how are the punkies doing? [*Big laugh.*] You bloody lover boy! Leave something for us, man!

[*John becomes aware of Winston trying to interrupt again: to Winston.*]

Okay . . . okay. . . .

[*Back to the telephone.*] Listen, Sky, Winston says if you get a chance, go down to Dora Street, to his wife. Tell V., Winston says he's okay, things are fine. Winston says she must carry on . . . nothing has happened . . . tell her to take care of everything and everybody. . . . *Ja*. . . .

[*The mention of his wife guillotines Winston's excitement and fun. After a few seconds of silence, he crawls back heavily to his bed and lies down. A similar shift in mood takes place in John.*]

And look, Sky, you're not far from Gratten Street. Cross over to it, man, drop in on number thirty-eight, talk to Princess, my wife. How is she keeping? Ask her for me. I haven't received a letter for three months now. Why aren't they writing? Tell her to write, man. I want to know how the children are keeping. Is Monde still at school? How's my twin baby, my Father and Mother? Is the old girl sick? They mustn't be afraid to tell me. I want to know. I know it's an effort to write, but it means a lot to us here. Tell her . . . this was another day. They're not very different here. We were down on the beach. The wind was blowing. The sand got in our eyes. The sea was rough. I couldn't see the mainland properly. Tell them that maybe tomorrow we'll go to the quarry. It's not so bad there. We'll be with the others. Tell her also . . . it's starting to get cold now, but the worst is still coming.

[*Slow fade to blackout.*]

SCENE TWO

The cell, a few days later.

John is hidden under a blanket. Winston is in the process of putting on Antigone's wig and false breasts.

JOHN. Okay?

WINSTON [*still busy*]. No.

JOHN. Okay?

WINSTON. No.

JOHN. Okay?

WINSTON. No.

[*Pause*]

JOHN. Okay?

[*Winston is ready. He stands waiting. John slowly lifts the blanket and looks. He can't believe his eyes. Winston is a very funny sight. John's amazement turns into laughter, which builds steadily. He bangs on the cell wall.*]

Hey, Norman. Norman! Come this side, man. I got it here. *Poes!*

[*John launches into an extravagant send-up of Winston's Antigone. He circles 'her' admiringly, he fondles her breasts, he walks arm in arm with her down Main Street, collapsing with laughter between each 'turn'. He climaxes everything by dropping his trousers.*]

Speedy Gonzales! Here I come!

[*This last joke is too much for Winston who has endured the whole performance with mounting but suppressed anger. He tears off the wig and breasts, throws them down on the cell floor, and storms over to the water bucket where he starts to clean himself.*]

WINSTON. It's finished! I'm not doing it. Take your Antigone and shove it up your arse!

JOHN [*trying to control himself*]. Wait, man. Wait. . . .

[*He starts laughing again.*]

WINSTON. There is nothing to wait for, my friend. I'm not doing it.

JOHN. Please, Winston!

WINSTON. You can laugh as much as you like, my friend, but just let's get one thing straight, I'm *not* doing Antigone. And in case you want to know why... I'm a man, not a bloody woman.

JOHN. When did I say otherwise?

WINSTON. What were you laughing at?

JOHN. I'm not laughing now.

WINSTON. What are you doing, crying?

[*Another burst of laughter from John.*]

There you go again, more laughing! Shit, man, you want me to go out there tomorrow night and make a bloody fool of myself? You think I don't know what will happen after that? Every time I run to the quarry... 'Nyah... nyah.... Here comes Antigone!... Help the poor lady!...' Well, you can go to hell with your Antigone.

JOHN. I wasn't laughing at you.

WINSTON. Then who were you laughing at? Who else was here that dressed himself as a lady and made a bloody fool of himself?

JOHN [*now trying very hard to placate the other man*]. Okay Winston, Okay! I'm not laughing any more.

WINSTON. You can go to hell with what you're saying.

JOHN. Look, Winston, try to understand, man, ... this is Theatre.

WINSTON. You call laughing at me, Theatre? Then go to hell with your Theatre!

JOHN. Please, Winston, just stop talking and listen to me.

WINSTON. No! You get this, brother, ... I am not doing your Antigone! I would rather run the whole day for Hodoshe. At least I know where I stand with him. All *he* wants is to make me a 'boy'... not a bloody woman.

JOHN. Okay, okay....

WINSTON. Nothing you can say....

JOHN [*shouting the other man down*]. Will you bloody listen!

208

WINSTON [*throwing the wash-rag down violently*]. Okay. I'm listening.

JOHN. Sure I laughed. *Ja . . . I laughed*. But can I tell you why I laughed? I was preparing you for . . . stage fright! You think I don't know what I'm doing in this cell? This is preparation for stage fright! I know those bastards out there. When you get in front of them, sure they'll laugh . . . 'Nyah, nyah!' . . . they'll laugh. But just remember this, brother, nobody laughs forever! There'll come a time when they'll stop laughing, and that will be the time when our Antigone hits them with her words.

WINSTON. You're day-dreaming, John. Just get it into your head that I'm not doing Antigone. It's as simple as that.

JOHN [*realizing for the first time that Winston needs to be handled very carefully*]. Hey, Winston! Hold on there, man. We've only got one more day to go! They've given us the best spot in the programme. We end the show! You can't back out now.

WINSTON. You think I can't? Just wait and see.

JOHN. Winston! You want to get me into trouble? Is that what you want?

WINSTON. Okay, I won't back out.

JOHN [*delighted with his easy victory*]. That's my man!

WINSTON [*retrieving the wig and false breasts off the floor and slamming them into John's hands*]. Here's Antigone . . . take these titties and hair and play Antigone. I'm going to play Creon. Do you understand what I'm saying? Take your two titties. . . . I'll have my balls and play Creon. [*Turns his back on a flabbergasted John, fishes out a cigarette-butt and matches from under the water bucket, and settles down for a smoke.*]

JOHN [*after a stunned silence*]. You won't make it! I thought about that one, days ago. It's too late now to learn Creon's words.

WINSTON [*smoking*]. I hate to say it, but that is just too bad. I am not doing Antigone.

[*John is now furious. After a moment's hesitation he stuffs on the wig and false breasts and confronts Winston.*]

JOHN. Look at me. Now laugh.

[*Winston tries, but the laugh is forced and soon dies away.*]

Go on.

[*Pause.*]

Go on laughing! Why did you stop? Must I tell you why? Because behind all this rubbish is me, and you know it's me. You think those bastards out there won't know it's you? Yes, they'll laugh. But who cares about that as long as they laugh in the beginning and listen at the end. That's all we want them to do ... listen at the end!

WINSTON. I don't care what you say, John. I'm not doing Antigone.

JOHN. Winston ... you're being difficult. You promised. ...

WINSTON. Go to hell, man. Only last night you tell me that this Antigone is a bloody ... what you call it ... legend! A Greek one at that. Bloody thing never even happened. Not even history! Look, brother, I got no time for bullshit. Fuck legends. Me? ... I live my life here! I know why I'm here, and it's history, not legends. I had my chat with a magistrate in Cradock and now I'm here. Your Antigone is a child's play, man.

JOHN. Winston! That's Hodoshe's talk.

WINSTON. You can go to hell with that one too.

JOHN. Hodoshe's talk, Winston! That's what he says all the time. What he wants us to say all our lives. Our convictions, our ideals ... that's what he calls them ... child's play. Everything we fucking do is 'child's play' ... when we ran that whole day in the sun and pushed those wheelbarrows, when we cry, when we shit ... child's play! Look, brother, ... I've had enough. No one is going to stop me doing Antigone. ...

[*The two men break apart suddenly, drop their trousers, and stand facing the wall with arms outstretched. Hodoshe calls John.*]

Yes, sir!

[*He then pulls up his trousers and leaves the cell. When he has left, Winston pulls up his trousers and starts muttering with savage satisfaction at the thought of John in Hodoshe's hands.*]

WINSTON. There he goes. Serves him right. I just hope Hodoshe teaches him a lesson. Antigone is important! Antigone this!

Antigone that! Shit, man. Nobody can sleep in this bloody cell because of all that bullshit. Polynices! Eteocles! The other prisoners too. Nobody gets any peace and quiet because of that bloody Antigone! I hope Hodoshe gives it to him.

[*He is now at the cell door. He listens, then moves over to the wig on the floor and circles it. He finally picks it up. Moves back to the cell door to make sure no one is coming. The water bucket gives him an idea. He puts on the wig and, after some difficulty, manages to see his reflection in the water. A good laugh, which he cuts off abruptly. He moves around the cell trying out a few of Antigone's poses. None of them work. He feels a fool. He finally tears off the wig and throws it down on the floor with disgust.*]

Ag, voetsek!

[*Hands in pockets, he paces the cell with grim determination.*]

I'm not going to do it. And I'm going to tell him. When he comes back. For once he must just shut that big bloody mouth of his and listen. To me! I'm not going to argue, but 'struesgod that . . . !

[*The wig on the floor. He stamps on it.*]

Shit, man! If he wants a woman in the cell he must send for his wife, and I don't give a damn how he does it. I didn't walk with those men and burn my bloody passbook in front of that police station, and have a magistrate send me here for life so that he can dress me up like a woman and make a bloody fool of me. I'm going to tell him. When he walks through that door.

[*John returns. Winston is so involved in the problem of Antigone that at first he does not register John's strangely vacant manner.*]

Listen, *broer*, I'm not trying to be difficult, but this Antigone! No! Please listen to me, John. 'Struesgod I can't do it. I mean, let's try something else, like singing or something. You always got ideas. You know I can sing or dance. But not Antigone. Please, John.

JOHN [*quietly*]. Winston. . . .

WINSTON [*still blind to the other man's manner*]. Don't let's argue, man. We're been together in this cell too long now to quarrel about rubbish. But you know me. If there's one thing I can't stand it's people laughing at me. If I go out there tomorrow night and those bastards start laughing I'll fuck up the first one I lay my hands on. You saw yourself what happened in here when you started laughing . I wanted to *moer* you, John. I'm not joking. I really wanted to. . . . Hey, are you listening to me? [*Looking squarely at John.*]

JOHN. Winston . . . I've got something to tell you.

WINSTON. [*registering John's manner for the first time*]. What's the matter? Hodoshe? What happened? Are we in shit? Solitary?

JOHN. My appeal was heard last Wednesday. Sentence reduced. I've got three months to go.

[*Long silence. Winston is stunned. Eventually. . . .*]

WINSTON. Three. . . .

JOHN. . . . months to go.

WINSTON. Three. . . .

JOHN. *Ja.* That's what Prinsloo said.

WINSTON. John!

[*Winston explodes with joy. The men embrace. They dance a jig in the cell. Winston finally tears himself away and starts to hammer on the cell walls so as to pass on the news to other prisoners.*]

Norman! Norman!! John. Three months to go. *Ja.* . . . Just been told. . . .

[*Winston's excitement makes John nervous. He pulls Winston away from the wall.*]

JOHN. Winston! Not yet, man. We'll tell them at the quarry tomorrow. Let me just live with it for a little while.

WINSTON. Okay okay. . . . How did it happen?

[*He pulls John down to the floor. They sit close together.*]

JOHN. Jesus, I'm so mixed up, man! *Ja* . . . the door opened and I saw Hodoshe. Ooo God, I said to myself. Trouble! Here we go again! All because of you and the noise you were making. Went down the corridor straight to Number Four . . . Solitary and Spare Diet!! But at the end, instead of turning right, we turned left into the main block, all the way through it to Prinsloo's office.

WINSTON. Prinsloo!

JOHN. I'm telling you. Prinsloo himself, man. We waited outside for a little bit, then Hodoshe pushed me in. Prinsloo was behind his desk, busy with some papers. He pulled out one and said to me: 'You are very lucky. Your lawyers have been working on your case. The sentence has been reduced from ten years, to three.'

WINSTON. What did Hodoshe say?

JOHN. Nothing. But he looked unhappy.

[*They laugh.*]

Hey, something else. Hodoshe let me walk back here by myself! He didn't follow me.

WINSTON. Of course. You are free.

JOHN. *Haai*, Winston, not yet. Those three months . . . ! Or suppose it's a trick.

WINSTON. What do you mean?

JOHN. Those bastards will do anything to break you. If the wheelbarrows and the quarry don't do it, they'll try something else. Remember that last visit of wives, when they lined up all the men on the other side. . . . 'Take a good look and say goodbye! Back to the cells!'

WINSTON. You say you saw Prinsloo?

JOHN. Prinsloo himself. Bastard didn't even stand up when I walked in. And by the way . . . I had to sign. *Ja!* I had to sign a form to say that I had been officially told of the result of my appeal . . . that I had three months to go. *Ja.* I signed!

WINSTON [*without the slightest doubt*]. It's three months, John.

JOHN [*relaxing and living with the reality for the first time*]. Hell, Winston, at the end of those three months, it will be three years together in this cell. Three years ago I stood in front of that magistrate at Kirkwood—bastard didn't even look at me: 'Ten years!' I watched ten years of my life drift away like smoke from a cigarette while he fidgeted and scratched his arse. That same night back in the prison van to the cells at Rooihel. First time we met!

WINSTON. *Ja.* We had just got back from our trial in Cradock.

JOHN. You, Temba, ...

WINSTON. Sipho....

JOHN. Hell, man!

WINSTON. First time we got close to each other was the next morning in the yard, when they lined us up for the vans....

JOHN. And married us!

[*They lock left and right hands together to suggest handcuffs.*]

WINSTON. Who was that old man ... remember him? ... in the corner handcuffed to Sipho?

JOHN. Sipho?

WINSTON. *Ja*, the one who started the singing.

JOHN [*remembering*]. Peter. Tatu Peter.

WINSTON. That's him!

JOHN. Hell, it comes back now, man! Pulling through the big gates, wives and mothers running next to the vans, trying to say goodbye ... all of us inside fighting for a last look through the window.

WINSTON [*shaking his head*]. Shit!

JOHN. Bet you've forgotten the song the old man started?

[*Winston tries to remember. John starts singing softly. It is one of the Defiance Campaign songs.* Winston joins in.]

WINSTON [*shaking his head ruefully*]. By the time we reach Humansdorp though, nobody was singing.

JOHN. Fuck singing. I wanted to piss. Hey! I had my one free hand on my balls, holding on. I'd made a mistake when we left the Rooihel. Drank a gallon of water thinking of those five hundred miles ahead. Jesus! There was the bucket in the corner! But we were packed in so tight, remember, we couldn't move. I tried to pull you but it was no bloody good. So I held on—Humansdorp, Storms River, Blaaukrantz ... held on. But at Knysna, to hell with it, I let go!

[*Gesture to indicate the release of his bladder. Winston finds this enormously funny. John joins in.*]

You were also wet by then!

WINSTON. Never!

JOHN. Okay, let's say that by George nobody was dry. Remember the stop there?

WINSTON. *Ja.* I thought they were going to let us walk around a bit.

JOHN. Not a damn! Fill up with petrol and then on. Hey, but what about those locals, the Coloured prisoners, when we pulled away. Remember? Coming to their cell windows and shouting ... 'Courage, Brothers! Courage!' After that ... ! Jesus, I was tired. Didn't we fall asleep? Standing like that?

WINSTON. What do you mean standing? It was impossible to fall.

JOHN. Then the docks, the boat. ... It was my first time on one. I had nothing to vomit up, but my God I tried.

WINSTON. What about me?

JOHN. Then we saw this place for the first time. It almost looked pretty, hey, with all the mist around it.

WINSTON. I was too sick to see anything, *broer.*

JOHN. Remember your words when we jumped off onto the jetty?

[*Pause. The two men look at each other.*]

Heavy words, Winston. You looked back at the mountains ... 'Farewell Africa!' I've never forgotten them. That was three years ago.

WINSTON. And now, for you, it's three months to go.

[*Pause. The mood of innocent celebration has passed. John realizes what his good news means to the other man.*]

JOHN. To hell with everything. Let's go to bed.

[*Winston doesn't move. John finds Antigone's wig.*]

We'll talk about Antigone tomorrow.

[*John prepares for bed.*]

Hey, Winston! I just realized. My family! Princess and the children. Do you think they've been told? Jesus, man, maybe they're also saying ... three months! Those three months are going to feel as long as the three years. Time passes slowly when you've got something ... to wait for. ...

[*Pause. Winston still hasn't moved. John changes his tone.*]
Look, in this cell we're going to forget those three months. The whole bloody thing is most probably a trick anyway. So let's just forget about it. We run to the quarry tomorrow. Together. So let's sleep.

SCENE THREE

The cell, later the same night. Both men are in bed. Winston is apparently asleep. John, however, is awake, rolling restlessly from side to side. He eventually gets up and goes quietly to the bucket for a drink of water, then back to his bed. He doesn't lie down, however. Pulling the blanket around his shoulders, he starts to think about the three months. He starts counting the days on the fingers of one hand. Behind him Winston sits up and watches him in silence for a few moments.

WINSTON [*with a strange smile*]. You're counting!

JOHN [*with a start*]. What! Hey, Winston, you gave me a fright, man. I thought you were asleep. What's the matter? Can't you sleep?

WINSTON [*ignoring the question, still smiling*]. You've started counting the days now.

JOHN [*unable to resist the temptation to talk, moving over to Winston's bed*]. *Ja*.

WINSTON. How many?

JOHN. Ninety-two.

WINSTON. You see!

JOHN [*excited*]. Simple, man. Look . . . twenty days left in this month, thirty days in June, thirty-one in July, eleven days in August . . . ninety-two.

WINSTON [*still smiling, but watching John carefully*]. Tomorrow?

JOHN. Ninety-one.

WINSTON. And the next day?

JOHN. Ninety.

WINSTON. Then one day it will be eighty!

JOHN. *Ja!*

WINSTON. Then seventy.

JOHN. Hey, Winston, time doesn't pass so fast.

WINSTON. Then only sixty more days.

JOHN. That's just two months here on the Island.

WINSTON. Fifty . . . forty days in the quarry.

JOHN. Jesus, Winston!

WINSTON. Thirty.

JOHN. One month. Only one month to go.

WINSTON. Twenty... [*holding up his hands*] then ten...five, four, three, two...tomorrow!

[*The anticipation of that moment is too much for John.*]

JOHN. NO! Please, man, Winston. It hurts. Leave those three months alone. I'm going to sleep!

[*Back to his bed, where he curls up in a tight ball and tries determinedly to sleep. Winston lies down again and stares up at the ceiling. After a pause he speaks quietly.*]

WINSTON. They won't keep you here for the full three months. Only two months. Then down to the jetty, into a ferry-boat...you'll say goodbye to this place...and straight to Victor Verster Prison on the mainland.

[*Against his will, John starts to listen. He eventually sits upright and completely surrenders himself to Winston's description of the last few days of his confinement.*]

Life will change for you there. It will be much easier. Because you won't take Hodoshe with you. He'll stay here with me, on the Island. They'll put you to work in the vineyards at Victor Verster, John. There are no quarries there. Eating grapes, oranges...they'll change your diet...Diet C, and exercises so that you'll look good when they let you out finally. At night you'll play games...Ludo, draughts, snakes and ladders! Then one day they'll call you into the office, with a van waiting outside to take you back. The same five hundred miles. But this time they'll let you sit. You won't have to stand the whole way like you did coming here. And there won't be handcuffs. Maybe they'll even stop on the way so that you can have a pee. Yes, I'm sure they will. You might even sleep over somewhere. Then finally Port Elizabeth. Rooihel Prison again, John! That's very near home, man. New Brighton is next door! Through your cell window you'll see people moving up and down in the street, hear the buses roaring. Then one night you won't sleep again, because you'll be counting. Not days, as you are doing now, but hours. And the next morning, that beautiful morning,

John, they'll take you straight out of your cell to the Discharge Office where they'll give you a new khaki shirt, long khaki trousers, brown shoes. And your belongings! I almost forgot your belongings.

JOHN. Hey, by the way! I was wearing a white shirt, black tie, grey flannel trousers ... brown Crockett shoes ... socks? [*A little laugh.*] I can't remember my socks! A check jacket ... and my watch! I was wearing my watch!

WINSTON. They'll wrap them up in a parcel. You'll have it under your arm when they lead you to the gate. And outside, John, outside that gate, New Brighton will be waiting for you. Your mother, your father, Princess and the children ... and when they open it. ...

[*Once again, but more violently this time, John breaks the mood as the anticipation of the moment of freedom becomes too much for him.*]

JOHN. Stop it, Winston! Leave those three months alone for Christ's sake. I want to sleep.

[*He tries to get away from Winston, but the latter goes after him. Winston has now also abandoned his false smile.*]

WINSTON [*stopping John as he tries to crawl away*]. But it's not finished, John!

JOHN. Leave me alone!

WINSTON. It doesn't end there. Your people will take you home. Thirty-eight, Gratten Street, John! Remember it? Everybody will be waiting for you ... aunts, uncles, friends, neighbours. They'll put you in a chair, John, like a king, give you anything you want ... cakes, sweets, cooldrinks ... and then you'll start to talk. You'll tell them about this place, John, about Hodoshe, about the quarry, and about your good friend Winston who you left behind. But you still won't be happy, hey. Because you'll need a fuck. A really wild one!

JOHN. Stop it, Winston!

WINSTON [*relentless*]. And that is why at ten o'clock that night you'll slip out through the back door and make your way to Sky's place. Imagine it, man! All the boys waiting for you ... Georgie, Mangi, Vusumzi. They'll fill you up with booze. They'll look after you. They know what it's like inside. They'll fix you up with a woman. . . .

JOHN. NO!

WINSTON. Set you up with her in a comfortable joint, and then leave you alone. You'll watch her, watch her take her clothes off, you'll take your pants off, get near her, feel her, feel it. . . . Ja, you'll feel it. It will be wet. . . .

JOHN. WINSTON!

WINSTON. Wet *poes*, John! And you'll fuck it wild!

[*John turns finally to face Winston. A long silence as the two men confront each other. John is appalled at what he sees.*]

JOHN. Winston? What's happening? Why are you punishing me?

WINSTON [*quietly*]. You stink, John. You stink of beer, of company, of *poes*, of freedom. . . . Your freedom stinks, John, and it's driving me mad.

JOHN. No, Winston!

WINSTON. Yes! Don't deny it. Three months time, at this hour, you'll be wiping beer off your face, your hands on your balls, and *poes* waiting for you. You will laugh, you will drink, you will fuck and forget.

[*John's denials have no effect on Winston.*]

Stop bullshitting me! We've got no time left for that. There's only two months left between us. [*Pause.*] You know where I ended up this morning, John? In the quarry. Next to old Harry. Do you know old Harry, John?

JOHN. Yes.

WINSTON. Yes what? Speak, man!

JOHN. Old Harry, Cell Twenty-three, seventy years, serving Life!

WINSTON. That's not what I'm talking about. When you go to the quarry tomorrow, take a good look at old Harry. Look into his eyes, John. Look at his hands. They've changed him. They've turned him into stone. Watch him work with that chisel and hammer. Twenty perfect blocks of stone every day. Nobody else can do it like him. He loves stone. That's why they're nice to him. He's forgotten himself. He's forgotten everything ... why he's here, where he comes from.

That's happening to me, John. I've forgotten why I'm here.

JOHN. No.

WINSTON. Why am I here?

JOHN. You put your head on the block for others.

WINSTON. Fuck the others.

JOHN. Don't say that! Remember our ideals. . . .

WINSTON. Fuck our ideals. . . .

JOHN. No, Winston ... our slogans, our children's freedom. . . .

WINSTON. Fuck slogans, fuck politics ... fuck everything, John. Why am I here? I'm jealous of your freedom, John. I also want to count. God also gave me ten fingers, but what do I count? My life? How do I count it, John? One ... one ... another day comes ... one. . . . Help me, John! . . . Another day ... one ... one. . . . Help me, brother! . . . one. . . .

[*John has sunk to the floor, helpless in the face of the other man's torment and pain. Winston almost seems to bend under the weight of the life stretching ahead of him on the Island. For a few seconds he lives in silence with his reality, then slowly straightens up. He turns and looks at John. When he speaks again, it is the voice of a man who has come to terms with his fate, massively compassionate.*]

Nyana we Sizwe!

[*John looks up at him.*]

Nyana we Sizwe ... it's all over now. All over. [*He moves over to John.*] Forget me. . . .

[*John attempts a last, limp denial.*]

No, John! Forget me ... because I'm going to forget you. Yes, I will forget you. Others will come in here, John, count, go, and I'll forget them. Still more will come, count like you, go like you, and I will forget them. And then one day, it will all be over.

[*A lighting change suggests the passage of time. Winston collects their props together for Antigone.*]

Come. They're waiting.

JOHN. Do you know your words?

WINSTON. Yes. Come, we'll be late for the concert.

SCENE FOUR

The two men convert their cell-area into a stage for the prison concert. Their blankets are hung to provide a makeshift backdrop behind which Winston disappears with their props. John comes forward and addresses the audience. He is not yet in his Creon costume.

JOHN. Captain Prinsloo, Hodoshe, Warders, . . . and Gentlemen! Two brothers of the House of Labdacus found themselves on opposite sides in battle, the one defending the State, the other attacking it. They both died on the battlefield. King Creon, Head of the State, decided that the one who had defended the State would be buried with all religious rites due to the noble dead. But the other one, the traitor Polynices, who had come back from exile intending to burn and destroy his fatherland, to drink the blood of his masters, was to have no grave, no mourning. He was to lie on the open fields to rot, or at most be food for the jackals. It was a law. But Antigone, their sister, defied the law and buried the body of her brother Polynices. She was caught and arrested. That is why tonight the Hodoshe Span, Cell Forty-two, presents for your entertainment: 'The Trial and Punishment of Antigone'.

[*He disappears behind the blankets. They simulate a fanfare of trumpets. At its height the blankets open and he steps out as Creon. In addition to his pendant, there is some sort of crown, and a blanket draped over his shoulders as a robe.*]

My People! Creon stands before his palace and greets you! Stop! Stop! What's that I hear? You, good man, speak up. Did I hear 'Hail the King'? My good people, I am your *servant* . . . a happy one, but still your servant. How many times must I ask you, implore you to see in these symbols of office nothing more, or less, than you would in the uniform of the humblest menial in your house. Creon's crown is as simple, and I hope as clean, as the apron Nanny wears. And even as Nanny smiles and is your happy servant because she sees her charge . . . your child! . . . waxing fat in that little cradle, so too does Creon— your obedient servant!—stand here and smile. For what does he see? Fatness and happiness! How else does one measure the success of a state? By the sumptuousness of the palaces built for its king and princes? The magnificence of the temples erected to its gods? The achievements of its scientists and technicians who can now send rockets to the moon? No! These count for nothing beside the fatness and happiness of its people.

But have you ever paused to ask yourself whose responsibility it is to maintain that fatness and happiness? The answer is simple, is it not? . . . your servant the king! But have you then gone on to ask yourself what does the king need to maintain this happy state of affairs? What, other than his silly crown, are the tools with which a king fashions the happiness of his people? The answer is equally simple, my good people. The law! Yes. The law. A three-lettered word, and how many times haven't you glibly used it, never bothering to ask yourselves, 'What, then, is the law?' Or if you have, then making recourse to such clichés as 'the law states this' . . . or 'the law states that'. The law states or maintains nothing, good people. The law defends! The law is no more or less than a shield in your faithful servant's hand to protect YOU! But even as a shield would be useless in one hand, to defend, without a sword in the other, to strike . . . so too the law has its edge. The penalty! We have come through difficult times. I am sure it is needless for me to remind you of the constant troubles on our borders . . . those despicable rats who would gnaw away at our fatness and happiness. We have been diligent in dealing with them. But unfortunately there are still at large subversive elements . . . there are still amongst us a few rats that are not satisfied, and to them I must show this face of Creon . . . so different to the one that hails my happy people! It is with a heavy heart, and you shall see why soon enough, that I must tell you that we have caught another one. That is why I have assembled you here. Let what follows be a living lesson for those among you misguided enough still to harbour sympathy for rats! The shield has defended. Now the sword must strike! Bring in the accused.

[*Winston, dressed as Antigone, enters. He wears the wig, the necklace of nails, and a blanket around his waist as a skirt.*]

Your name!

WINSTON. Antigone, daughter of Oedipus, sister of Eteocles and Polynices.

JOHN. You are accused that, in defiance of the law, you buried the body of the traitor Polynices.

WINSTON. I buried the body of my brother Polynices.

JOHN. Did you know there was a law forbidding that?

WINSTON. Yes.

JOHN. Yet you defied it.

WINSTON. Yes.

JOHN. Did you know the consequences of such defiance?

WINSTON. Yes.

JOHN. What did you plead to the charges laid against you? Guilty or Not Guilty?

WINSTON. Guilty.

JOHN. Antigone, you have pleaded guilty. Is there anything you wish to say in mitigation? This is your last chance. Speak.

WINSTON. Who made the law forbidding the burial of my brother?

JOHN. The State.

WINSTON. Who is the State?

JOHN. As King I am its manifest symbol.

WINSTON. So you made the law.

JOHN. Yes, for the State.

WINSTON. Are you God?

JOHN. Watch your words, little girl!

WINSTON. You said it was my chance to speak.

JOHN. But not to ridicule.

WINSTON. I've got no time to waste on that. Your sentence on my life hangs waiting on your lips.

JOHN. Then speak on.

WINSTON. When Polynices died in battle, all that remained was the empty husk of his body. He could neither harm nor help

225

any man again. What lay on the battlefield waiting for
Hodoshe to turn rotten, belonged to God. You are only a man,
Creon. Even as there are laws made by men, so too there are
others that come from God. He watches my soul for a
transgression even as your spies hide in the bush at night to see
who is transgressing your laws. Guilty against God I will not
be for any man on this earth. Even without your law, Creon,
and the threat of death to whoever defied it, I know I must die.
Because of your law and my defiance, that fate is now very
near. So much the better. Your threat is nothing to me, Creon.
But if I had let my mother's son, a Son of the Land, lie there as
food for the carrion fly, Hodoshe, my soul would never have
known peace. Do you understand anything of what I am
saying, Creon?

JOHN. Your words reveal only that obstinacy of spirit which has
brought nothing but tragedy to your people. First you break
the law. Now you insult the State.

WINSTON. Just because I ask you to remember that you are
only a man?

JOHN. And to add insult to injury you gloat over your deeds!
No, Antigone, you will not escape with impunity. Were you my
own child, you would not escape full punishment.

WINSTON. Full punishment? Would you like to do more than
just kill me?

JOHN. That is all I wish.

WINSTON. Then let us not waste any time. Stop talking. I
buried my brother. That is an honourable thing, Creon. All
these people in your state would say so too, if fear of you and
another law did not force them into silence.

JOHN. You are wrong. None of my people think the way you do.

WINSTON. Yes they do, but no one dares tell you so. You will
not sleep peacefully, Creon.

JOHN. You add shamelessness to your crimes, Antigone.

WINSTON. I do not feel any shame at having honoured my
brother.

JOHN. Was he that died with him not also your brother?

WINSTON. He was.

JOHN. And so you honour the one and insult the other.

WINSTON. I shared my love, not my hate.

JOHN. Go then and share your love among the dead. I will have no rats' law here while yet I live.

WINSTON. We are wasting time, Creon. Stop talking. Your words defeat your purpose. They are prolonging my life.

JOHN [*again addressing the audience*]. You have heard all the relevant facts. Needless now to call the state witnesses who would testify beyond reasonable doubt that the accused is guilty. Nor, for that matter, is it in the best interests of the State to disclose their identity. There was a law. The law was broken. The law stipulated its penalty. My hands are tied.

Take her from where she stands, straight to the Island! There wall her up in a cell for life, with enough food to acquit ourselves of the taint of her blood.

WINSTON [*to the audience*]. Brothers and Sisters of the Land! I go now on my last journey. I must leave the light of day forever, for the Island, strange and cold, to be lost between life and death. So, to my grave, my everlasting prison, condemned alive to solitary death.

[*Tearing off his wig and confronting the audience as Winston, not Antigone.*]

Gods of our Fathers! My Land! My Home!

Time waits no longer. I go now to my living death, because I honoured those things to which honour belongs.

[*The two men take off their costumes and then strike their 'set'. They then come together and, as in the beginning, their hands come together to suggest handcuffs, and their right and left legs to suggest ankle-chains. They start running . . . John mumbling a prayer, and Winston a rhythm for their three-legged run.*

The siren wails.

Fade to blackout.]

NOTES

No-Good Friday

p. 5 *A backyard in Sophiatown* ... : one of the few urban areas where blacks could own property, named after the wife of a certain Mr Tobiansky who bought a plot of land some four and a half miles west of the centre of Johannesburg in the early years of the century, and whose dreams of turning it into a posh white suburb were shattered by the Town Council's decision to place its sewage disposal facilities nearby, with the result that Tobiansky sold much of it to Africans coming in to work in the rapidly growing city between the wars. According to Father Trevor Huddleston (on whom Father Higgins was based), who arrived as priest-in-charge of the Anglican Mission there in 1943, it was a slum in the sense that its population of 70,000 was twice what it should have been, and there was squalor, violence, and alcoholism (illegal for blacks, hence the shebeens). But Sophiatown was also a vibrant, living community, the 'close-packed, red-roofed little houses' seen against a skyline of distant blue gums, the Church of Christ the King rising above the smoky haze from braziers and chimneys, reminiscent of 'an Italian village somewhere in Umbria'. This was Huddleston's description in *Naught For Your Comfort*, published in 1956 on his recall to England. He had long been considered a thorn in the flesh of the authorities; to Africans he was 'Makhilipele', an undaunted leader. He had been involved in everything from the formation of a Jazz Club (including Zakes Mokae and Hugh Masekela), to superintending St Peter's School (the 'Black Eton'), to helping to set in motion one of the largest and most well-known voluntary social services in the country, the *African Children's Feeding Scheme* (see p. 10). But above all Huddleston protested against the Native Resettlement Act of 1954 (an extension of the Group Areas Act of 1950), which enforced the removal of African residents of all the western districts of Johannesburg, including Sophiatown, Martindale, and Newclare (see p. 5), to a new, ethnically zoned wasteland called Meadowlands, twelve miles from the city. Other white liberals spoke up, Congress organized passive resistance, but all in vain against a massive force of armed police.

p. 50 *a resolution at the next Congress*: the Congress Alliance, first proposed as a Congress of the People by Professor Z. K. Matthews, president of the Cape branch of the African National Congress, in response to the Nationalists' re-election in 1953. Three thousand representatives of the ANC, the Indian Congress, the Coloured People's Organizations, the radical white Congress of Democrats, as well as the trade union movement and other organizations, met at Kliptown near Johannesburg in 1955 to ratify a Freedom Charter, which still stands as the basic document of the freedom movement in the country: affirming that South Africa belongs to everyone in it, demanding a non-racial, democratic system of government and equality before the law, and so on. Its adoption was followed by a wave of repression, including the notorious Treason Trial, which weakened protest during the late 1950s. By then, too, many Africans were choosing, for example, homes in the new townships such as Meadowlands, rather than no homes at all. This may help explain the scepticism towards political activists implied by the character of Watson; although he is a parody of real black resisters in the townships of the time.

Nongogo

p. 57 *Queeny's shebeen in one of the townships around Johannesburg . . .* : despite the end of prohibition on hard liquor for Africans in 1962, and the appearance of Government-sanctioned, regimented drinking halls, and (after 1981) the licensing of shebeens as 'taverns', urban blacks continue to use unlicensed and illegal, but friendly and casual, local shebeens in township rooms or backyards. Brewing beer was a traditional skill of African women, but this is not the only reason so many shebeens have been run by black women, called 'queens' or 'aunties'. As the actress Thoko Ntshinga and the director Lucille Gillwald observed at the time of the 1981 revival of *Nongogo* at the Market Theatre, shebeen queens achieve some personal and financial independence, while most black women remain caught midway between a tribal culture of family values for which they often yearn, and an urban one from which they have been largely excluded by the effects of the migrant labour system. Soliciting at bus stops or outside the mineworkers' compounds has been for many the only alternative for women left alone with their families. Many shebeen queens (unlike their male counterparts, the shebeen kings) have earned the respect of township people by providing food, loans, small jobs, or even housing. (See 'Shedding a New Light on Shebeen Queens', *The Star*, Johannesburg, 24 Nov. 1981.)

The Coat

pp. 124, 144 *Cradock has become a part of New Brighton*: because the trials which resulted from the purge of the area in 1963–5 took place in this small Karroo town, far from the homes and families of those involved, so as to minimize disturbances and protest. Fugard took Serpent Player Norman Ntshinga's wife Mabel Magada with him for Ntshinga's trial there, where the playwright testified as a 'witness in mitigation'—in vain: Ntshinga was sentenced to five years on Robben Island for belonging to the ANC and distributing leaflets. It was May Magada who brought back from Cradock the coat which became the focus of the Players' first exercises in improvising upon their own everyday experiences. For details, see Mary Benson (ed.), *Athol Fugard: Notebooks 1960–1977* (Faber, 1983), *passim*; and Benson's autobiography, *A Far Cry* (Penguin, 1990), 194–205.

Sizwe Bansi is Dead

p. 153 *Armstrong on the moon!*: on 21 July 1969 Neil Armstrong became the first man to land on the moon; implying an ironic parallel between the advance of American technology and the situation of the black workers at the American-owned Ford plant, who lack even minimal protection from their machinery.

p. 163 *He fought in France so that this country and all the others could stay free*: war service helped develop the political consciousness of blacks in South Africa (as elsewhere in colonial Africa): some 45,000 'Coloureds' and 80,000 black South Africans served as non-combatants, but returned to find even their simplest freedoms being eroded.

p. 174 *Dig gold for the white man*: the reason the Mines Recruiting Office used to worry less about Influx Control was the difficulty they had in persuading black South Africans to take on the poorly paid and dangerous work. Further, the Africans (many from neighbouring countries or the 'reserves') who were offered work there used to have to accept conditions making it a criminal offence to strike, and live in vast, primitive barracks.

p. 178 *Ciskeian Independence is shit*: these derogatory remarks, expanded and applied to the Transkei in their production of the play there in October 1976 (shortly before 'independence' was granted by South Africa), led to the detention of John Kani and Winston Ntshona in the 'capital', Umtata. During the performance in the small rural town of Butterworth, to an audience largely consisting of security men, the actors had predicted bloodshed in the Transkei on 'independence day'. After strong protests around the world, they were released and deported from the 'homeland', having spent a fortnight in solitary confinement.

The Island

p. 195 *a cell on Robben Island*: the majority of convicted political prisoners were, until recently, held on this small island about seven miles off the Atlantic coast at Cape Town. The Island, as it is commonly known, has been a place of banishment or imprisonment since the beginning of white settlement: a leper colony for much of the nineteenth century, it was also used to imprison African chiefs who resisted the whites, and as a mental asylum. The island has greater extremes of climate than the nearby mainland, the summer heat intensified by the salt air, sparse vegetation, and lack of shade; in winter it is very damp, and subject to frequent fog and sea storms. In 1959 a maximum security prison was built, at first housing convicted criminal offenders as well as 'politicals'. The prisoners were black, the warders white. The prison had a capacity of 650 prisoners. It used to be divided into three sections, one with single cells, the others containing larger communal cells; a fourth section was created after the Soweto rising of June 1976, to cope with the large influx of new prisoners. High walls and fences keep the sections separate, in particular the isolation section, which contained the 'old men' (p. 200), who none the less established their authority over the others—Mandela, Mbeki, Sisulu, and Kathrada, all sentenced to life in 1963. Most prisoners were allowed to receive only two letters a year, and two visits (though most received none, because of the island's inaccessibility). No radio sets or newspapers were permitted, and any reading matter strictly censored. The prisoners organized 'shows' for each other, including songs, poems, and, of course, the memorable two-man version of *Antigone*; although they were, strictly speaking, illegal, and they were forbidden to applaud—so they would 'brush' or rub their hands silently together instead. During the mid and late 1960s, frequent acts of brutality against prisoners took place. Stone-breaking, collecting seaweed, and work in the lime quarry were the main occupations. Several prisoners developed tuberculosis; some died as a result of inadequate or no treatment for their ailments. International pressure led to some improvement in these conditions until, finally, a decision was taken to close a place which had become a symbol of white South African tyranny, and indeed a theme in modern South African literature (e.g. in the poetry of Dennis Brutus, D. M. Zwelonke's *Robben Island,* 1977, and Naidoo/Sachs, *Island in Chains,* 1982). Prisoners such as Nelson Mandela were moved to lesser-known and more 'modern' environments inland. The letters and reminiscences of imprisoned Serpent Players such as (mainly) Norman Ntshinga provided Fugard, Kani, and Ntshona with their inspiration, and the detail for most scenes (see Mary Benson (ed.), *Athol Fugard: Notebooks 1960–1977* (Faber, 1983), *passim*).

p. 195 *The prison uniform of khaki shirt and short trousers*: These 'short trousers' were designed by the authorities to be baggy and over-long, thereby adding to the humiliation of the men who wear them.

p. 198 *Antigone's necklace*: John's explanation of the 'plot', and then the opening of Scene Four, provide the audience with all they need to know of Sophocles' original Greek classical drama, which, in this version, focuses upon the conflict between Creon and Antigone.

p. 200 *That's another play*: Sophocles' *Oedipus Rex*, in which the mother of Polynices (Jocasta, not Antigone) has a major role.

p. 202 *June 1965*: recalling the performances of *Antigone* which went ahead without the arrested Haemon, Norman Ntshinga. Serpent Players' production, with Nomhle Nkonyeni and George Mnci, took place in St Stephen's Hall, New Brighton, as a police round-up in the area was in full force. 'Mulligan' was another Player in the production, Mulligan Mbikwane. Other names (Sipho, Simon) refer, again, to members of the group.

p. 214 *It is one of the Defiance Campaign songs*: i.e. from the 1952 mass Campaign of passive resistance and defiance against apartheid, when more than 8,000 people were arrested.

232

GLOSSARY

African (predominantly Xhosa in origin here) and Afrikaans words and phrases are printed in bold, other South African expressions or names in bold italic.

administration office: see ***Influx Control***

Advisory Board: i.e. to 'advise' the running of the 'bantustans'; see ***Ciskei***

Ag: 'oh', exclamation (pronounced like German 'ach')

Ag, kak: 'oh, shit'

Ag sies tog: expression of dismay, roughly equiv. to 'oh no' ('g' as in 'ach'; see also **sies**)

Ag, voetsek!: offensive command, originally to a dog: as in 'oh, fuck/bugger off!'

Ai!: exclamation of surprise (see **Haai!**)

Alex: i.e. Alexandra township, Johannesburg, occupied by family units until the 1960s, when it was converted into a vast hostel for unmarried domestic servants

baas: 'boss/master'

betaal, jong!: 'pay, you!' ('jong', colloq. Afrikaans for young fellow)

biltong: air-dried strip of meat, usually game

bioscope: 'cinema'

blanket-boy: rural migrant, originally from the reserves (q.v.), typically wearing a long blanket

boet, boetie: literally 'brother', 'little brother'; colloq, address to a friend, as in 'pal'

book of life: identity document, pass (q.v.)

boss-boy: 'headman' (q.v.)

broer: 'brother'

Ciskei: a so-called *homeland* or *bantustan*: area of the country set aside under policy of 'separate development' initiated by Dr Verwoerd for a particular tribal or ethnic group of black people, in some cases regarded as 'self-governing' (e.g. Ciskei, Transkei, for the Xhosa), although supported by, and under the control of, the white authorities (see Notes)

compound: workers' barracks or living quarters

Congress: Congress Alliance (see Notes)

Cradock: small Karroo town (see Notes)

dagga: (pron. dacha, 'ch' as in German 'ach') marijuana, hashish

Dankie, my baas!: 'Thank you, boss!'

domboek (or **dompas**): colloquial African term (from

Afrikaans, literally, 'stupid-book') for passbook (q.v.)

ewe: 'yes'

Goli (or **eGoli**): the Golden City, (colloquial black name for) Johannesburg

Gqokra Izi Khuselo Zamehlo Kule Ndawo: 'Put On Safety Glasses Here'

Haai!: exclamation of surprise or alarm (from Xhosa 'hayi' = no)

Headman: tribal head of a village or group of people, petty chief (see **induna**); white-appointed head officer e.g. in township administration

Hier is ek, my baas!: 'Here I am, boss!'

Hodoshe: 'carrion fly'; also nickname for chief warder on Robben Island; used in original title of *The Island, Die Hodoshe Span*, 'Hodoshe's work-team'

Houghton: wealthy white Johannesburg suburb

impi: armed band of men (formerly regiment, part of an army)

induna: originally headman appointed by a chief, also used of black foreman of a band of farm labourers

Influx Control: government control of movement of black people, begun centuries ago (as was the pass system) but massively reinforced under apartheid, with the introduction of a huge and cumbersome administrative organization involving white-run but increasingly black-staffed offices in the townships, 'Native Affairs Commissioners' (later 'Bantu Affairs Commissioners'), and a Labour Bureau. Opposition was ceaseless. Scrapped in 1986

Iscor: i.e. I.S.C.O.R., state-owned Iron and Steel Corporation of South Africa

Ja: 'yes', frequently used affirmative

Junior Certificate: see *Standard Six Certificate*

Kaffir, **kaffer**: term of abuse for black or African people

kieries: name for fighting-clubs or sticks (also 'knobkierie')

King William's Town: 'capital' town of the so-called Ciskei 'bantustan' or 'homeland' (q.v.), and Winston Ntshona's birthplace

lap, lappie: 'cloth', 'cleaning-rag'

location: segregated area for blacks outside town or city (now more commonly 'township')

Machadodorp: small country town in the eastern Transvaal

Makulu baas: 'big boss', literally, 'grandmother boss'

Matric: matriculation; see *Standard Six Certificate*

moeg: 'tired'

Moer!/*to* **moer** *you*: abusive expletive, equivalent to 'Fucker!'; 'to thrash/beat you up'

Native Affairs Commissioner: see *Influx Control*

New Brighton: black township on northern outskirts of Port Elizabeth, established during the late 1950s as one of the 'new', segregated urban areas under the Group Areas Act for a single ethnic group, the Xhosa

nongogo: township slang meaning a woman for two-and-six, term formerly used of prostitutes soliciting among lines of gold-mine workers queuing for their pay

Nyana we Sizwe!: Xhosa rallying cry, used in English in last scene of *The Island*, as 'Son of the Land!'; also a praise-term for heroes, as used by the great nineteenth-century Xhosa poet, Ntsikana

off-sales: retail shop attached to or owned by a hotel, in which bottled liquor sold for drinking off the premises

ons was gemoer vandag: 'we were fucked/buggered today' (see **moer**)

outa: 'old man', also mode of address to elderly black man, often respectfully by children, but now often taken as demeaning (see also **Tatu**)

pass, passbook: (or *reference book*, *book of life*, also **domboek**, **dompas**): identity document required of all Africans, and the keystone of white control over their lives; which all Africans over 16 had to carry; providing proof of permission (or otherwise) to live and/or work in a specific area; inability to produce on demand invariably meant arrest and automatic penalties, including imprisonment. In the year 1972–3, on average nearly 1,500 trials for pass law offences took place daily. Abolished 1986

Poes!: obscene slang, 'Cunt!'

pondok, pondokkies: 'shack', 'little shacks'

punkies: 'tarts', 'loose women'

reference book: name given to identity document required of all Africans under the mis-named Natives Abolition of Passes Act (1952), which in fact extended the pass laws to black women as well

reserve: area of land set aside exclusively for African occupation, in terms of the Native Land Act of 1913, some 13 per cent of the surface area of South Africa; later, during the 1950s, redesignated *homelands* or *Bantustans* (see **Ciskei**)

Rooihel: literally 'red hell', Port Elizabeth prison, familiar to New Brighton inhabitants arrested in mid-1960s

St George's Strand: beach near Port Elizabeth

samp: staple food among black people, cereal made from coarsely crushed maize kernels

shebeen: unlicensed establishment

for the sale of illicit liquor to black people, usually run by black women known as shebeen queens; home-brewed concoctions to the poor in a backyard, 'white' hard liquor acquired from bootleggers to the middle-class in a living-room. Prohibition for blacks ended in 1962. (See also Notes.)

Sibonda: colloquial name for black official in township administration office (q.v.)

sies (also **sis**): exclamation of disgust

Single Men's Quarters: primitive barrack-like living quarters for male black workers (who may have wives and families in the 'reserves'), set up on the outskirts of the white urban areas

sis, **sissy**: black urban colloquial abbreviation of 'sister', to address a woman of the same community, and often with a name, e.g. Sis Joyce (*The Coat*); see also **sies**

site and service: self-built shanty scheme, a temporary measure by the authorities, offering a plot with water points and sanitation while they built township housing for blacks; the shanties often remained, since the housing proved inadequate

Sky's place: famous New Brighton shebeen, after the owner's name

Speedy Gonzales!: hero of a well-known series of lewd jokes

spook: 'haunt' or 'frighten'

Standard Six Certificate: in white schools (until recently segregated and massively subsidized compared to black schools) the normal achievement of a 12-year-old. 'Junior Certificate' similarly, for a 15-year-old. 'Matric', i.e. school-leaving certificate for a 17-year-old white

Tatu: 'father', respectful mode of address to older man

Tshotsholoza ... Vyabaleka ...: Work steady, the train is coming ...: a work-song, also used as a song of defiance

tsotsis: flashily-dressed urban black thugs, speaking 'tsotsitaal', their own argot, literally 'gangsterspeak'

tula: exclamation, 'be quiet'

Victor Verster prison: prison for 'politicals' *en route* to release, in Paarl, near Cape Town

vyf bob: 'five bob', five shillings ('tsotsitaal' (see above))

yessus: Jesus

yo!: 'whew!', exclamation of surprise

American Literature

British and Irish Literature

Children's Literature

Classics and Ancient Literature

Colonial Literature

Eastern Literature

European Literature

History

Medieval Literature

Oxford English Drama

Poetry

Philosophy

Politics

Religion

The Oxford Shakespeare

A complete list of Oxford Paperbacks, including Oxford World's Classics, OPUS, Past Masters, Oxford Authors, Oxford Shakespeare, Oxford Drama, and Oxford Paperback Reference, is available in the UK from the Academic Division Publicity Department, Oxford University Press, Great Clarendon Street, Oxford OX2 6DP.

In the USA, complete lists are available from the Paperbacks Marketing Manager, Oxford University Press, 198 Madison Avenue, New York, NY 10016.

Oxford Paperbacks are available from all good bookshops. In case of difficulty, customers in the UK can order direct from Oxford University Press Bookshop, Freepost, 116 High Street, Oxford OX1 4BR, enclosing full payment. Please add 10 per cent of published price for postage and packing.

Expand your collection of

VERY SHORT INTRODUCTIONS

Available now

1. Classics
2. Music
3. Buddhism
4. Literary Theory
5. Hinduism
6. Psychology
7. Islam
8. Politics
9. Theology
10. Archaeology
11. Judaism
12. Sociology
13. The Koran
14. The Bible
15. Social and
    Cultural Anthropology
16. History

Available soon

Ancient Philosophy
Animal Rights
Art Theory
Bioethics
Chaos
Continental Philosophy
Economics
Emotion
Ethics
The European Union
The First World War
Free Will
Indian Philosophy
Intelligence
Logic
Mathematics
Opera
Philosophy of Religion

A complete list of Oxford Paperbacks, including Oxford World's Classics, Oxford History of Art, Past Masters, and Oxford Paperback Reference, is available in the UK from the Trade and Reference Publicity Department, Oxford University Press, Great Clarendon Street, Oxford OX2 6DP.

In the USA, complete lists are available from the Paperbacks Marketing Manager, Oxford University Press, 198 Madison Avenue, New York, NY 10016.

Oxford Paperbacks are available from all good bookshops. In case of difficulty, customers in the UK can order direct from Oxford University Press bookshop, Freepost, 116 High Street, Oxford OX1 4BR, enclosing full payment. Please add 10% of published price for postage and packing.